AFRO-DOG

AFRO-DOG

BLACKNESS AND THE ANIMAL QUESTION

BÉNÉDICTE BOISSERON

Columbia University Press   *New York*

Columbia University Press
Publishers Since 1893
New York   Chichester, West Sussex
cup.columbia.edu
Copyright © 2018 Columbia University Press

Library of Congress Cataloging-in-Publication Data
Names: Boisseron, Bénédicte, author.
Title: Afro-dog : blackness and the animal question / Benedicte Boisseron.
Description: New York : Columbia University Press, [2018] |
Includes bibliographical references and index.
Identifiers: LCCN 2018000865 | ISBN 9780231186643 (cloth) |
ISBN 9780231186650 (pbk.) | ISBN 9780231546744 (e-book) Subjects: LCSH:
Animal rights. | Animal welfare. | Human-animal relationships. | Race
relations. | Speciesism.
Classification: LCC HV4708 .B654 2018 | DDC 179/.3—dc23
LC record available at https://lccn.loc.gov/2018000865

Cover design: Julia Kushnirsky
Cover image: © Afro Newspaper/Gado/Getty Images

To Frieda

CONTENTS

INTRODUCTION

Blackness Without Analog

I grew up biracial in a racially homogeneous white town near Paris. *Négresse* and *noiraude*, the usual racial slurs, were nothing next to the exaggerated, so-called African accent that boys enjoyed emulating when addressing me. This mimetic trend was initiated by Michel Leeb, a French stand-up comedian from the 1980s famous for his impression of a grotesque gorilla-like African man. Today, the in-your-face conjoined racism in Leeb's skit would not make the French laugh the way it did so shamelessly and painfully then. Its censorship, however, would only camouflage lingering traces of intersectional fantasies of racialization and animalization that have sporadically come back to the surface, such as when a politician in 2013 compared black Christiane Taubira, French minister of justice, with a monkey,[1] echoing the depiction of Barack Obama as Curious George the monkey during the 2008 presidential campaign.[2] The black-animal subtext is deeply ingrained in the cultural genetics of the global north, an inherited condition informed by a shared history of slavery and colonization. The long and twisting arms of the gorilla stretch from the French empire to the New World, as King Kong's roar on top of the Empire State Building still resounds.

The idea for this book was partially prompted by author
Marjorie Spiegel's recent dispute over her 1988 book, *The Dreaded
Comparison: Human and Animal Slavery*.[3] In the book, the author
compares modern animal cruelty with black slavery, a type of
comparison that the animal rights organization People for the
Ethical Treatment of Animals (PETA) would also use in its
2005 fund-raising exhibit "Are Animals the New Slaves?"
Though Spiegel's book was highly praised by scholars and writers upon its release, the general public and civil rights activists
widely contested PETA's exhibit. Very soon after the exhibit was
launched, Spiegel and her organization, Institute for the Development of Earth Awareness (IDEA), filed a complaint against
PETA for copyright infringement, arguing that the exhibit would
negatively taint the perception of her own book. Undoubtedly,
both the book and the exhibit had used a similar approach aimed
at associating the predicament of blacks in the past with the mistreatment of animals in the present, but the book had been
spared the criticisms that the exhibit received. In 2011, the court
ruled in favor of PETA, stating that the idea of comparing slavery to the treatment of animals, "regardless of its validity"
(direct quote from Judge Castel in *IDEA v. PETA*), was neither
entitled to copyright protection nor unprecedented.[4] The well-
known Australian philosopher Peter Singer had already made a
similar comparison with his use of the word "speciesism" (first
coined by Richard D. Ryder in 1970), a neologism referring to
the prejudice against animals similar to racism and sexism.[5] In
his ruling, Judge Castel conceded to having no say in the validity of the comparison, a validity that still remains to be addressed
outside of a court of law. And indeed, under which—if any—
circumstances is the comparison between blacks and animals
valid and acceptable?

In the last decade, the academic field of critical animal studies
has grown exponentially, in both French- and English-speaking

contexts. Concomitantly, political concerns over animal rights have forced the passage of new animal protection laws in various Western countries (e.g., the 2002 German Animal Welfare Act, 2005 Treaty of Lisbon, 2014 French Civil Code). In animal rights discourse, slaves and animal victims have repeatedly been perceived as sharing a common battle, so much so that abolitionism, once restricted to slavery, is now a word applied to animal welfare. Well-known legal scholar Gary Francione contests the property status of animals in a theory identified as the Abolitionist Approach, in reference to the movement to end black slavery.[6] The comparison between slavery and animals has so far mainly been used as a tool to serve animal rights, regardless of its impact on African Americans and the Afro-Caribbean community. The race-animal comparison is a rarely addressed topic in black diasporic studies. One reason for this neglect, as Philip Armstrong argues in "The Postcolonial Animal,"[7] is that comparing human and animal suffering carries the risk of trivializing the human condition. Another reason, as the NAACP has argued about PETA's exhibit, is that comparing animals to blacks demonstrates racial insensitivity. Valid or not, however, the slave-animal comparison cannot be ignored, if only because it reveals a long-standing trend in American and transatlantic consciousness to associate blackness with animality.

As author Claire Jean Kim admits in *Dangerous Crossings*, after initially feeling that PETA's "We Are All Animals" and "The Animal Is the New Slave" campaigns were important reminders of "the arbitrariness of the animal-human divide," she has come to realize that the analogy is unsound because the message "attempts to ground the argument for the moral considerability and grievability of animals upon the elision of race."[8] While questioning the animal-human divide is essential to animal rights activism, contesting the divide with a racial paradigm indeed carries the potential effect of reinscribing a discriminative approach that one had sought to reject in the first place. On the other hand, there is no denying that there are important parallels to be drawn between the rationale behind opposing animal oppression and that behind condemning discrimination against minorities. In both cases, it is a question of arbitrary divides. Kari Weil points out in *Thinking Animals* that animal studies follows after women's studies and ethnic studies, two fields that have sought to establish their voices and reject the white patriarchal hegemonic lenses through which minorities have been represented.[9] Like the animal rights discourse today, the primary goal of (broadly defined) subaltern studies was to denounce the arbitrariness of the ethnically—or racially—based divide that fueled the "us" versus "them" colonial rhetoric. The work of Edward Said is one example. In *Orientalism*, Said uses the concept of "Orientalism" to underscore the fabrication of the "Other" by a Western "Us." Said exposes the fallacy of a nongeographical dividing line that separates the West from a so-called Orient as an object of European fantasy: "In short, from its earliest modern history to the present, Orientalism as a form of thought for dealing with the foreign has typically shown the altogether regrettable tendency of any knowledge based on such hard-and-fast distinctions as 'East' and 'West' to channel thought into a West or an East compartment."[10] Said's idea of "a West or an East compartment" itself descends from Frantz Fanon's representation, in *Les Damnés de la terre* (*The Wretched of the Earth*),[11] of the colonial superstructure in French-owned Algeria as what he calls a "compartmentalized society." Likewise, V. Y. Mudimbe in *The Idea of Africa* presents Africa as a Western creation essentially based on the notion of difference. As he explains, with the Enlightenment came "the science of difference: anthropology," which "'invents' an idea of Africa."[12] In other words, be it Orientalist, Africanist, or colonial, those representations are based on a putative divide between "us" and "them," or as Stuart Hall calls it, "the West and the rest."[13]

Exposing the arbitrariness of divides—whether based on race, gender, or species—is the root of any resistance against discrimination and oppression. The compartmentalization of sentient beings in terms of human hegemony and animal subordination is undoubtedly caused by our global economy and politics of animal exploitation. Yet replacing the human-animal divide with a debate about a race-animal divide that frames animal subjugation as analogous to black slavery is a perverted form of recompartmentalization where the black is once again removed from the human species. The main argument here is that, though one should not ignore entangled forms of oppression, analogizing can be harmful when it is meant to serve one cause over the other; when its sole function is, for example, to serve the animal cause by instrumentalizing the black cause. But as Kim also argues, the same holds true when the analogy is put in the service of the black cause. The author uses the example of those who pitted the rescue of pets by the Humane Society against the failed rescue of black residents in the aftermath of Hurricane Katrina in August 2005. The conclusion drawn was that America cares more about animals than blacks. This kind of rhetoric, Kim posits, rests upon the elision of species, as it "reduces nonhuman animals to instruments for measuring degrees of anti-Blackness."[14] Kim's ultimate argument is that one should not have to resubordinate the animal in order to defend blackness, and vice versa. The analogy's inherent vice lies in its propensity to give the upper hand to one entity over the other, bringing us back to the common ethical conundrum of whether to rescue the (good) dog or the (bad) man on a quickly sinking ship, except that, in this case, the two to be rescued are innocent victims.

The animal cause and subaltern studies differ in that animals cannot gain agency through their voice, or "at least not in the languages we recognize," as Weil puts it.[15] Women's and ethnic studies, as Weil also explains, were built upon the pressing need to bring "women's and minorities' voices into the academy to write and represent themselves,"[16] a claim to agency that the animal obviously cannot achieve within the field of animal studies. Because there is no possibility for self-representation, as we know it, the animal remains the silent one, bound to be represented by "us" humans. Through the human prism, the animal is tied irrevocably to what Jacques Derrida describes as the *animot*[17]—a human word and a human representation. The fact that animals cannot, semantically, "talk back with a vengeance" to their oppressors makes the work of counterbalancing the elision of race in the animal discourse all the more challenging since the animal discourse is just that, a discourse, a *mot*, an *animot* in the midst of resounding animal silence.[18] Because our perception of the animal is saturated with words, adding more words to the black-animal question may, instead of counterbalancing a skewed analogy, only make the absence of animal repartee even more salient. *Afro-Dog* is a book that engages in a corrective tactic, as it seeks to counterbalance a recent discourse that has served the animal cause by utilizing race as a leverage point. The challenge, however, is to be mindful of not over-correcting this imbalance by emphasizing black suffering to the detriment of animal suffering, and thus re-inscribing the contention.

The "America-likes-pets-more-than-blacks" attitude that Kim deplores is symptomatic of a system that convulsively pits blackness against animality, forcing blacks themselves to engage in a battle over spared likability. The answer is not to try to change this attitude but rather to bring attention to the system that created it in the first place. The preference of pets over blacks needs to be understood in the context of rapper Kanye West's comment that "Bush doesn't care about black people," made at an NBC charity telethon for Hurricane Katrina's victims, a visionary comment that preceded the Black Lives Matter movement by almost a decade. Images on television covering not only the direct impact of the disaster but also the living conditions of blacks in New Orleans before the hurricane brutally exposed the systemic precarity of black life in the American South.[19] West's impromptu comment on live television added words to the images on the screen that flaunted the triviality of black existence, a condition reminiscent of that of the slave deemed to be chattel/cattle—fungible and disposable, unlike a pet. "America cares more about pets than blacks" adds an animal dimension to Kanye West's "black life does not matter" message, recalling the slavery era measurement of subordinate existence in an equation of life where the black and the animal have to battle in order not to be last. The black-animal analogy inherently and inevitably reenacts this interspecies battle, as it perpetuates a rivalry that traps the contenders in a paradigm that precludes any chance for the escape of either from this hierarchical measuring system. Within this context, the Black Lives Matter phrase is based on an elliptically suppressed yet recurrently present comparison between blacks and animals. When talking about the value of black existence, the animal comparison is intrinsically part of our culture, so much so that there is no longer a need to mention it. Thus, when the "America likes pets more than blacks" phrase is spoken, it feels like an overstatement, something that should not be said.

Since Singer and Spiegel, the animal rights discourse has shown even more interest in the dreaded analogy, as it is manifested with the frequent use of the buzzword "speciesism" (analogous to racism) in Francione's Abolitionist Approach and PETA's exhibits. This interest coincides, but also clashes with, an equally fast-growing school of thought in black studies that insists that the black condition cannot be analogized. This movement, referred to as Afro-Pessimism, argues that the Middle Passage created the unprecedented phenomenon known as "Blackness," which is a condition like no other in our modern history. The pessimistic nature of this movement is due to the essential idea that the black condition created by the slave trade is permanent and irreversible. "I, too, live in the time of slavery, by which I mean I am living in the future created by it,"[20] Saidiya Hartman wrote in her memoir. Some young influential writers may not self-identify as Afro-Pessimists, but they contribute to this ever-more-visible school currently mapping the durability of the black slavery superstructure in our modern culture. Michelle Alexander is one obvious example,[21] but Ta-Nehisi Coates and Teju Cole—both inspired by Africa American novelist and essayist James Baldwin, who paved the way for the enduring inquiry into the immutable black condition in America—are strong black voices that bring attention to the fact that "this fantasy about the disposability of black life is a constant in American history. It takes a while to understand that this disposability continues."[22] This school also aligns with the Francophone tradition—Frantz Fanon, Achille Mbembé—that addresses the endurance in our modern era of the 1685 Code Noir (in the French context), the slavery-era legal document that regarded the black as a thing (*meuble*). "I found that I was an object in the midst of other objects,"[23] Fanon famously says in his 1952 *Peau noire, masques blancs* (*Black Skin, White Masks*).

The reification of the black is unique in our modern history. As Mbembé writes in *Critique de la raison nègre* (*Critique of Black Reason*), "the Negro [Nègre] is, in terms of modernity, the only human being whose flesh was made to be a thing and his mind a merchandise."[24] What is interesting in *Critique of Black Reason* is that the author sees the fungibility of the black as a condition which, instead of disappearing, has now exceeded race to apply more generally to our neoliberal Euro-American culture, a culture that substituted humanity with marketability. We have all become "man-thing, man-machine, man-code, man-flux,"[25] hence what Mbembé calls the *devenir-nègre du monde*, "the becoming black of the world." Mbembé's view, however, might not fit completely with that of the Afro-Pessimist Frank B. Wilderson, who sees in black fungibility a unique condition, exclusively born out of the violence of slavery. Wilderson argues that black positionality is uncommunicable because it has no referent and no analog: "The violence that turns the African into a thing is without analog. . . . This is why it makes little sense to attempt analogy."[26] The idea of blackness as nonanalogizable is recurrent in Wilderson's work. The important idea in Afro-Pessimism is that the black, though sentient, is the only human being in modern times defined as a disposable thing.[27]

For Wilderson, all positionalities, no matter how extreme the degree of suffering, are part of our archaeology of humanity—except black positionality. Wilderson even argues that the Holocaust is different from slavery in that this tragedy was a historical perversion that brought about a hiatus in the otherwise historical humanity of the Jew. "The Muselmann, then, can be seen as a provisional moment within existential Whiteness, when Jews were subjected to Blackness and Redness—and the explanatory power of the Muselmann can find its way back to sociology, history, or political science, where it more rightfully belongs."[28] For Wilderson, even Native Americans are not "off the map," the way blacks are.[29] As he says, "even Native Americans provide categories for the record when one thinks of how the Iroquois constitution, for example, becomes the U.S. constitution."[30] Wilderson goes to great length to single out the black condition from other modern tragedies. His main point is that analogizing the black condition with other ones is a trompe l'œil and a "ruse" that disavows the incommensurability of black (non-)existence.

Staying clear of analogizing the black condition is something that Wilderson successfully accomplishes—except when it comes to the animal. "But still we must ask, what about the cows?,"[31] Wilderson ponders. The author uses the example of the emergence of Taylorism in Chicago's meatpacking industry during the turn of the century to show the difference between the worker's exploitation and the black's fungibility. The worker from the slaughterhouse—though exploited—is still part of civil society, while the black is associated with the cow to be slaughtered for consumption. The author writes, "the cows are not being exploited, they are being accumulated and, if need be, killed,"[32] a phenomenon similar to what black bodies endured during slavery and endure today in America's industrial prison systems. As Wilderson argues, "the chief difference today, compared to several hundred years ago, is that today our bodies are desired, accumulated, and warehoused—like the cows."[33] Ironically, *The Jungle*, Upton Sinclair's 1906 novel depicting the same labor conditions of immigrants in the meatpacking industry in Chicago's Packingtown,[34] is famous for having drawn parallels between the exploited workers and the slaughtered animals. Following in Sinclair's footsteps, Wilderson reclaims the analogy for the exclusive use of the black condition. In so doing, Wilderson recalls the elliptical nature of the animal presence in the black narrative: The black condition is without analog, *except* for the animal. "Black Lives Matter," "Bush doesn't care about black people," "America likes pets more than blacks," it seems that the black condition, even when said to be nonanalogizable, implicitly and ineluctably brings us back to the animal comparison.

Looking at connections between racism and speciesism reveals the inextricable entanglement of the black and the animal. But, even though the two may mutually—or alternately—elide each other, they can empower each other as well by turning this intersectional bond into defiance. In *Citizen*, a lyrical meditation on race and racism in American everyday life, poet and essayist Claudia Rankine writes, "they achieve themselves to death by trying to dodge the buildup of erasure,"[35] hereby suggesting the counterproductivity of fighting against erasure. Since preventing racial or species elision by overdetermining race or animality may ultimately lead to the erasure of both, the alternative is to reclaim their addressable condition instead. Why should the black become so blatantly visible against the animal rights discourse backdrop? And why should a monkey have to take part in a racist language that targets black politicians (Taubira and Obama)? Judith Butler was once asked what makes language hurtful. It is the exposure, the fact of being addressable, that is hurtful, she answered. Rankine says in *Citizen* that she always thought that racist language erases you, but, through Butler, she now understands that it makes you exposed and hypervisible. The racist language takes the measure of your addressability. Likewise, the animal-black analogy is not only a question of racial or species elision, but also one of (hyper-) visibility and addressability. The addressability of both in a malapropos context makes them as visible as an uninvited guest at an intimate dinner party. One may then argue that this uninvited guest should not shy away from her hypervisibility and should not let the other guests give her the cold shoulder, but rather, she should disrupt the dinner party by making the others feel ill at ease in her inopportune presence. If the analogy makes you awkwardly addressable, then you should be addressed, fully, and in plain sight. Instead of ignoring the monkey standing awkwardly next to the black politicians or the black slave yanked to the table of animal rights activists, the goal is precisely to bring attention to their mutual addressability and expose a system that compulsively conjures up blackness and animality together to measure the value of existence.

To not shy away, to talk back, is what this book intends to do by looking at various instances, in the cross-Atlantic history of the black diaspora, of intersectional encounters, analogies, and battles, that reveal the inextricability of the animal and the black. Looking at the black Atlantic (mainly colonial France, the Caribbean, and North America), *Afro-Dog* examines understandings of race in a way that brings together animal and black studies, while rejecting the instrumentalization of the comparison between racialized human beings and animals. I intend, in this book, to offer an alternative to the self-serving comparative approach through a focus on interspecies connectedness, the main goal being to determine how the history of the animal and the black in the black Atlantic is *connected*, rather than simply comparable, in order to reorient the discussion on black-animal relations toward an empowering frame of reference. To do so, I address instances in which blacks and animals—in real or imagined contexts—have fought alongside, against, or with each other as they assert their dignity. With its focus on defiance, this book seeks to defy the construction of blacks and animals as *exclusively* connected through their comparable state of subjection and humiliation, and instead focus on interspecies alliances.

With the exception of Derrida's pussycat in the last chapter, the image of the dog is the running metaphor tying the book together. The neologistic term "Afro-Dog" adds a layer to W. E. B. Du Bois's double-consciousness: "It is a peculiar sensation, this double-consciousness. . . . One never feels his two-ness,—an American, a Negro; two souls, two thoughts, two unreconciled strivings."[36] The hyphen in "Afro-Dog" refers to this double-consciousness, "an American, a Negro," the modern African American, while the animal component of the hyphenated word conveys the as-of-yet-unaccounted-for animal analog intrinsic to the black identity.

The opening chapter of *Afro-Dog*, "Is the Animal the New Black?," addresses the intersections between animal studies and black studies and their limitations. The chapter identifies the recent animal turn in academia as—chronologically and ideologically—a follow-up to the postcolonial turn initiated in the 1980s. By relying on the legacy of movements that traditionally fought against black oppression and de-personhood, including the abolitionist and civil rights movements, animal rights advocacy has sought to emphasize the overlap between forms of domination. Through this lens, animal rights advocacy has been able to look at chattel slavery and lynching as essentially tied to industrialized farming. But the risk of this approach is to think of the animal as "the new black," as Che Gossett puts it,[37] which presupposes that we are past blackness in our considerations of de-personhood. This type of animal rights discourse forces us to think about and reassess the question of the permanence of black subordination in our society, a question that is central to this chapter, particularly in its critique of the sequential nature (first race, then the animal) of the new—animal rights–related— abolitionist discourse. There is no doubt that relying on intersectionality, as a theoretical tool, is instrumental in exposing embedded patterns of oppression, but the challenge of this tool lies in, as this chapter shows, the risk of addressing the entanglement of all forms of oppression by obstructing the idiosyncrasies of each.

The second chapter of the book traces back the genesis of the (canine) animalization of the black concomitant with the racialization of the dog in the Americas. This chapter, entitled "Blacks and Dogs in the Americas," is motivated by the oft-overlooked historical fact that not only humans but also animals were transplanted into the New World during the slave trade. In plantation societies, dogs were brought over from Europe or Cuba to be used as watchdogs, tracking and terrorizing fugitive slaves. The chapter investigates the lingering effects, postslavery, of the association between race and dogs in America. Harriet Beecher Stowe's novel *Uncle Tom's Cabin* greatly contributed to making the image of the "mean dog" running after the "bad," disobedient slave iconic.[38] Since then, specific instances in media, literature, and the arts have compulsively recreated, and continually reignited, the association of the vicious dog with the bad black. Central to this argument is the historical attack of black protesters by police dogs during the 1963 civil rights riots in Birmingham, Alabama. More recently, police dogs have also been used against rioters in Ferguson, Missouri, which further prompts us to revisit the ever-present association between black civil disobedience and canine repression in America.

As a result of the slave trade, the transplanted peoples initially from Africa and Europe acclimated to the new location, gradually becoming what one refers to as "Creole." After having been brought to the Americas, animals followed a comparable Creolization process. So far, only the human Creole population has attracted scholarly attention; scholars have yet to address the ramifications of the animal diaspora. Chapter 3 focuses on the Creole dog, the ancestor of the master's watchdog shipped to the Americas to chase and attack slaves. This chapter, titled

"The Commensal Dog in a Creole Context," looks at the Creole dog as a prototype of a third category of animals, one that does not fit in the "domesticated" or "wild" categories. In *Zoopolis*,[39] Sue Donaldson and Will Kymlicka call "liminal" those animals that are neither domesticated nor feral, such as urban deer, rats, and squirrels. As we know, however, in the Western world liminal animals are commonly considered to be pests and thus excluded from the house, backyard, and even front yard, while what I call the "commensal" animal does not abide by a dichotomy of private-public space. In ecological terminology, commensalism refers to a class of relationship in which two organisms mutually benefit without adversely affecting each other. This chapter analyzes instances in the Caribbean, as portrayed in Truman Capote's "Music for Chameleons," where commensal animals live openly with human beings in a windowless, doorless, nonexclusive space, typical of the Creole house and garden.[40] Following Michel Serres's *The Parasite*,[41] the chapter ultimately argues that commensalism is a poetics of postcolonial resistance that, though modeled after the Creole dog, also applies to the human Creole culture.

Afro-Dog seeks to bring attention to how much the dog has been atavistically conditioned, throughout history, to engage with the black as a racialized being. The animal has watched the black negotiate the historical spectrum, ranging from property status to full legal personhood. The dog has undergone some status variations as well, as a watchdog, pet, and Creole stray dog. The question of ownership, or the lack thereof, has been an important factor in the relationship between the dog and the black, and it continues to be so. Chapter 4, "Dog Ownership in the Diaspora," uses the recent controversy over the 1685 French Slave Code in the French Caribbean as a platform to address the question of ownership in a racial and animal context. French historian Jean-François Niort controversially argues in his 2015 book, *Le Code Noir*, that the Slave Code is not about the dehumanization of the slave but rather, and only, *de-personhood*.[42] Though legally defined as personal property like a chair or an animal, the chattel slave would, according to Niort, still be viewed as human. The question remains, however, to what extent is dehumanization precisely, and inextricably, tied to the question of ownership—not only being owned as an animal but also owning an animal? This chapter examines the relationship between dehumanization and property in historical contexts that have challenged minorities' right to pet ownership, including the 1942 decree banning Jewish ownership of pets, the ban on dog ownership for slaves, and the modern breed-specific legislation banning the ownership of pit bulls—dogs that have been predominantly viewed as urban and black. As this chapter argues, the right to own is as much part of the question of personhood as the right not to be owned.

The last chapter takes a different angle, as it focuses on—animal and black—silences. This chapter, entitled "The Naked Truth About Cats and Blacks," revisits French philosopher Jacques Derrida's seminal work, "The Animal That Therefore I Am," within a slavery and racial context. Derrida famously describes the existential shame at the sudden awareness of being seen naked by the house pet (a cat), the invisible and silent observer. This chapter compares this ontological experience with the master's shame of becoming aware, through slave narratives, of having been observed and judged all along by the seemingly invisible and silent slave. The same is true for Négritude, a pan-African movement from the 1930s that suddenly made the French colonizer aware, as French philosopher Jean-Paul Sartre argues in "Black Orpheus,"[43] of the shame of being regarded by the Other. This chapter examines the extent to which the moment when the black, in an abolitionist, anticolonial, or postcolonial context, starts talking back, is similar to what the emerging field of animal studies currently attempts to do by speaking vicariously on behalf of the animal. Does animal studies contribute to another eye-opening moment in the history of the oppression and exploitation of sentient beings, or is it just another form of speaking for the animal? This chapter does not seek to offer a race-animal comparison that serves and hence instrumentalizes one cause over the other. Its goal is, rather, to show how those two subjectivities, the animal and the black, and those two fields, animal studies and black studies, can defiantly come together to form an interspecies alliance against the hegemonic (white, human, patriarchal), dominating voice.

I wrote this book in the midst of the 2015 Ferguson and 2016 Standing Rock demonstrations. The demonstrations against the Dakota Access Pipeline project in North Dakota turned violent in September 2016, as bulldozers were brought in to start construction. Security officers (contracted by the construction company) were filmed using dogs against the demonstrators guarding the Standing Rock Sioux tribe's sacred land.[44] Native American activist Winona LaDuke told a journalist on location, "This is not Alabama. You know? This is 2016." The images of security dogs attacking Native American protesters prompted a déjà vu experience arching back to the 1963 civil rights riots in Birmingham, Alabama, where German shepherd police dogs, under the command of Commissioner of Public Safety Bull Connor, were photographed attacking black rioters. Since the 2015 report about the investigation of the Ferguson Police Department that uncovered a blatant correlation between race and the use of attack dogs by the police in the city of Ferguson, it has become evident that old habits die hard. The habit of launching dogs on the racialized Other started, however, much before Bull Connor, even before the slavery era. Spanish conquistadors were the first to use attack dogs in the island of Hispaniola, as they launched canines on natives as a retaliative and offensive technique to control the land. In his 1552 *Short Account of the Destruction of the Indies*, Spanish friar and historian Bartolomé de Las Casas documents at length the extremely cruel and inhumane use of dogs against the so-called Indians in the West Indies.[45] French writer Guillaume Raynal would draw a similar conclusion in his 1798 monumental account of the history of the Indies, positing that Indians at the time were worth less than the dogs launched against them.[46] Raynal depicts a dreadful scene involving native rebels devoured by dogs and conquistadors vowing to kill twelve Indians a day in honor of the twelve Apostles. As canine attacks against Native Americans have abruptly resurfaced in Standing Rock, it spurs a need to understand how history has come full circle. Why the recent use of dogs against specific groups of "rebels" but not against those who occupied Wall Street or against the armed militia that took over a federal building in Oregon? French historian Phillipe Girard posits that the idea of using dogs against slave rebels during the famous 1803 slave rebellion in Saint-Domingue may have originated in the books, among them those by Casas and Raynal, that General Leclerc brought along with him during his cross-Atlantic expedition to Saint-Domingue.[47] Leclerc would have picked up the idea of using canine attacks against black leader Toussaint Louverture's army in historical books. But when it comes to Ferguson and North Dakota, how did the police and security officers come to the idea of using canine weaponry against, respectively, African Americans and Native Americans? The security guards and the Ferguson police have probably never come across Bartolomé de Las Casas's account. To what extent, therefore, is the intersection of racialization and animalization atavistically ingrained in our collective memory, and to what extent is it simply an idea picked up somewhere, randomly, like Leclerc on his boat?

AUTHOR'S NOTE

All English translations are mine unless otherwise noted. In many cases I have provided the original French text in the notes.

AFRO-DOG

1

IS THE ANIMAL
THE NEW BLACK?

The recent "animal turn" across the humanities and social sciences, which demonstrates a fast-growing interest in animal studies, has often been presented as a follow-up to the "post-colonial" turn initiated,[1] as Achille Mbembé puts it, "a quarter of a century ago."[2] This new field of studies is supported by a commonly known comparative strategy consisting of bringing together the historical discrimination against blacks and that against animals today. Animal studies scholars and animal rights advocates have used the legacy of the abolitionist and civil rights movements to contextualize their discourse, emphasizing the importance of intersectionality in any system of oppression, regardless of the victim's human or nonhuman nature. Animal rights activist Marjorie Spiegel, for example, has addressed this legacy in her 1988 illustrated essay *The Dreaded Comparison: Human and Animal Slavery*, which places side by side pictures of auctioned slaves and cows at the market. As the author says, our modern society knows that it is and was wrong to treat blacks like animals. So why, she wonders, do we not come to the same conclusion about animals, instead of treating them, "as they say, 'like animals?'"[3] Because of a cross-continental history impacted by colonialism and thus notoriously inclined to see blackness as less than human, there has been, inversely, a need today to include the question of blackness in our reflections on the meaning of animality. The risk in the race-animal combination, however, is to see race only as a platform to set the scene of animal studies rather than viewing it as a permanent presence inextricably part of the animal question. The race-animal question begs to be addressed as a true combination rather than as a succession of thoughts that, as in academia, look at race first and then move on to the animal question. The animal turn, and subsequently the wealth of scholarship presently available on the animal question, offers a unique chance to take an in-depth look at the modern impact of a historically grounded system of mutual racialization and animalization. For this to happen, however, blackness cannot simply be used as a means to serve the next cause, or as Carol J. Adams would say about the commodification of animals, "as a means to others' ends."[4] In other words, blackness cannot be treated "as they say, 'like animals.'"

Animal rights activist Aymeric Caron, also a French journalist and television personality, has recently sought to popularize the concept of "speciesism" in his country, introducing it to a mainstream audience incognizant of *Cahiers antispécistes*, a more than two-decades-old French journal mainly on the radar of animal rights advocates. By bringing the Anglophone tradition of animal ethics to a French audience, Caron's 2016 best seller, entitled *Antispéciste*,[5] attempts to make Richard D. Ryder (who coined the term "speciesism" in 1970) and utilitarian philosophers Jeremy Bentham and Peter Singer household names. Antispeciesism, as Caron explains in the foreword to his book, aligns with antiracism, antisexism, and antihomophobia in its fight to end discrimination against groups unfairly viewed as "inferior." The main difference, however, between the exploitation of humans and animals, as the author points out, is that humans can speak for themselves while animals do not have access to human language or human actions to fight for their cause. Slaves are known to have led successful rebellions against their oppressors in the Americas, a type of achievement that animals will obviously never be able to accomplish. The most famous and successful slave rebellion in the history of the Americas allowed slaves in Saint-Domingue (now Haiti) to snatch their own emancipation from the hands of the French Napoleonic troop in 1804, an ideal of rebellion that factory farm animals will never reach. But even more interesting than the slave rebellion in Saint-Domingue is the *Amistad* case, as Caron argues. This case best shows the importance of not only human action but also the human language in successful acts of liberation. In 1839, slaves captured in Sierra Leone aboard the *Amistad* slave ship managed to free themselves and to kill most of the crew in an attempt to sail back to Africa. Yet, the rebels were soon recaptured off the coast of Long Island and sentenced in an America court of law for piracy and murder. Once under American jurisdiction, the slaves were in need of a legal defense, which would be provided by abolitionists and translators. Former slaves who spoke Mende were able to assist the slaves by translating their testimonies into English, and in 1841, in *United States v. The Amistad*, the U.S. Supreme Court ruled in favor of the Mende slaves, declaring them legally free. As Caron posits, those translators fulfilled the same role as what animal advocates are doing today, namely speaking on behalf of the incapacitated victims. "The animals that we raise do not speak our language and we make sure not to hear what they have to say."[6] In other words, Caron's *Antispéciste* reiterates what Spiegel argued in *The Dreaded*

Comparison, namely that, like slaves then, exploited and slaughtered animals now need abolitionists to voice their rights. Abolitionism is a continuum starting with slavery and pursuing its battle for justice with animal advocacy. "Anti-speciesists are the translators of *The Amistad*,"[7] Caron concludes.

The intersection between black slavery and animal exploitation is not new. English philosopher Jeremy Bentham famously drew attention to the connection that one should make between the movement to end slavery and the need to extend moral considerations to animals in his 1789 (first privately published in 1780) *Introduction to the Principles of Morals and Legislation*.[8] Likewise, politician William Wilberforce, who in England led the abolitionist movement to end the slave trade, was also one of the founders of the world's first Society for the Prevention of Cruelty to Animals (SPCA) in 1824. The so-called abolitionist approach to animal rights today, spearheaded by legal scholar Gary L. Francione and philosopher Tom Regan,[9] is tightly (and semantically so) related to the initial abolitionist movement to end black slavery, a relation that cannot be ignored in modern animal rights advocacy. The core value of abolitionism is that all systems of oppression, be they against humans or nonhumans, are interrelated; but as history shows, animal and black oppression, more than other oppressed groups, have had a particularly tight connection throughout history.

Caron acknowledges this historical connection using the *Amistad* case, and yet the author misses a chance to see how this connection plays out in our modern society.[10] In one of the opening chapters of *Antispéciste*, Caron addresses the 2015 killing of Cecil the lion in South Africa by a modern-day safarist and American dentist and argues that the international outrage over the incident is a sign of the world's growing empathy for the animal cause. Yet, because the author has, in the preceding

pages, drawn a connection between racism (that has led some—
as he argues—to be viewed as "savages"[11]) and speciesism, the
Cecil the lion case seems incomplete without addressing the racio-
historical significance of the continent in which Cecil was
killed. After all, Cecil has been used as a prize, the same way
that the *Amistad* slaves captured in Africa were considered to be
"property" by the Spanish claimants in the *United States v. The
Amistad* case. By not mentioning the geohistorical importance
of Africa in the story, Caron somehow dismisses the fact that
the black continent, as the birthplace of an epistemology of
racial power and domination, does matter in the slaughter of
Cecil the lion. Caron's oversight reenacts the colonial inclination, as V. Y. Mudimbe posits in *The Invention of Africa*,[12] to see
the black continent as the epistemological Other, namely that
which essentially does not concern us. Let us keep in mind that
the word "Africa," which is potentially etymologically related to
Afer, Abraham's son, is also evocative of the English "afar,"
namely, "far away" from us. Africa is, literally and semantically
speaking, that which is far from us. As Caron represents it, the
African crime scene in the Cecil case is a blank slate untainted
by colonial vestiges of Western imperialism. The irony is that,
as Mbembé says, "discourse on Africa is almost always deployed
in the framework (or on the fringes) of a meta-text about the
animal—to be exact, about the *beast*."[13] But while Africa is
hardly human "in the discourse of our times,"[14] when, paradoxically, the African animal enters our discourse, the black continent seems to have no voice in the story. Granted, as Caron
argues, one of the conclusions that one has to draw from the
reaction to the killing of Cecil is that the romanticized Hem-
ingwayesque fantasy of the safari has become outdated. But
more importantly, Caron's handling of the Cecil case also
exemplifies how an antispeciesist discourse can supersede racial

concerns even though their inextricability is incidentally what begs to be addressed. In his chapter on the *Amistad* case, Caron follows a trend in animal discourse initiated by Bentham's aforementioned book that looks at the animal as what should be the next concern in a long history of oppressed minorities. But the editorial choice to disconnect the early chapter addressing the Cecil the lion from the chapter on the *Amistad* case (featured much later in the book) separates what is, precisely so, enmeshed.

THE NONPERSON

In *Just Mercy*, Bryan Stevenson shares his experiences in court as a social justice activist and lawyer fighting against the false convictions of racial minorities in America. The book covers the case of African American Walter McMillian, who spent six years on death row for a murder he had not committed. In the chapter "I'm Here," Stevenson focuses on McMillian's hearing in the Alabama Court of Criminal Appeals, a hearing that provided a chance for attorney Stevenson to prove his client's innocence and get the conviction overturned. On the first day of the hearing, McMillian's supporters are in attendance, their positive whispers filling the room as Stevenson brings witnesses to the stand who successively recant their prior testimonies against his client. Stevenson initially gains ground in the hearing, but on the morning of the second day, he finds McMillian's supporters outside the courtroom, prevented from entering by a large metal detector and a German shepherd. After meeting with the judge, Stevenson is granted permission to let the supporters fill the last few seats in the room. An older black lady, Mrs. Williams, is happy to be one of the chosen few allowed to show support inside the courtroom. As this proud and well-dressed lady makes her way into the room, she stops dead in her tracks at the sight of the police German shepherd nearby. Mrs. Williams never made it into the room that day. At the end of the day, Stevenson comes to talk to her, and the old lady explains, "When I saw that dog, I thought about 1965, when we gathered at the Edmund Pettus Bridge in Selma and tried to march for our voting rights. They beat us and put those dogs on us."[15] Yet, not willing to accept defeat, Mrs. William tries again the following day. In a manner reminiscent of six-year-old Ruby Bridges in 1960 mumbling prayers as she crossed the line of white protesters in front of the newly integrated elementary school in Louisiana, Mrs. Williams whispers repeatedly to herself, "Lord, I can't be scared of no dog. I can't be scared of no dog,"[16] while she bravely walks past the German shepherd and into the courtroom. Once inside the room and after the judge sits down and the audience follows soon after, the old lady continues to stand demonstratively. People look at her quizzically, and, with tears in her eyes, the black lady shouts in the silent room, "I'm here!," before taking her seat.

The story of Mrs. Williams is a parable of intersectionality, an example of how social injustice intersects with the personal, the racial, the historical, and the animal. The German shepherd in the courtroom is a reminder of German shepherd police dogs attacking blacks in Birmingham, Alabama, during the civil rights riots. The enmeshed narratives of oppression come together at one point, in a single event, as a mnemic symbol of things once thought to be irrevocably past. In "Necropolitics," Mbembé argues that the brutality of colonization springs from the "racial denial of any common bond between the conqueror and the native."[17] "In the eyes of the conqueror," he writes, "*savage life* is just another form of animal life."[18] The judicial system is one example of an arena where the specter of the animal still influences the fate of racial difference and where the racial denial of a common human bond haunts personal stories of conviction. The dog barring access to the courtroom is a reminder of the fragile—not to say incomplete—person status of the black. No longer a chattel slave, no longer legally perceived as property, the black has not yet been fully granted civil rights. When deprived of the freedom to represent herself (to be "present" in the courtroom), the old lady sees herself as less of a person, as the animal reminds her of her imperfect personhood.

The dispossession of minorities' rights is a complex and insidious practice. Feminist and vegetarian Brigid Brophy wrote in her piece "Women: Invisible Cages" that women are like animals in a modern zoo: "There are no bars. It appears that cages have been abolished. Yet in practice women are still kept in their place as firmly as the animals are kept in their enclosures."[19] Brophy wrote this piece in 1963, the same year that black rioters in Birmingham, Alabama, attempted to break the visible legal fences enclosing them while police dogs prevented them from doing so. Today, the police dogs that were used in Birmingham (1963) or in Selma (1965) may not be as visible as in Mrs. Williams's case, but the animal remains, depriving blacks access to civil rights. Mrs. Williams was not barred from the courtroom by an actual court order but by the presence of a dog working as a trauma trigger for the type of oppression that plagued the civil rights era. Dogs in Birmingham and Selma prevented blacks from entering a space of legal representation, just as Mrs. Williams saw the dog as preventing her from being present in the legal space of the courtroom. The presence of police dogs during the 2014 riots in Ferguson, Missouri, shows that, even in the post–civil rights era, police dogs can still fulfill the function of keeping blacks from claiming their rights.[20] In response, Bryan Stevenson, as a lawyer and the director of the Equal Justice Initiative in Montgomery, Alabama, escorts blacks past the invisible dog of a racially biased system into the courtroom to fight against their wrongful or excessive sentencing. Even when invisible, the dog is still (an unwilling) participant in the history of social injustice.

The mass incarceration of black males in America concomitant with the massive felony disenfranchisement of the black population are together, according to legal scholar Michelle Alexander,[21] what has created in modern America a new kind of Jim Crow. This new Jim Crow is a mix of a modern and an old zoo: though the prison bars are visible, this mass incarceration is not often seen as a racially invested denial of personhood. Similarly, Colin Dayan's *The Law Is a White Dog* examines the legal history of depersonification as a continuum where the "medieval fiction of civil death" persists today in different forms. As she says, "The felon rendered dead in law is no anachronism but a continuing effect of dehumanizing practices of punishment."[22] While Guantánamo provides extreme cases of humans dead in law, the black felon is nonetheless, unarguably, also on the spectrum of systematic legal dispossession, another form of legal death. Mass incarceration, Alexander explains, is essentially what sustains the continuum of dispossession in America. As Afro-Pessimist scholar Frank Wilderson provocatively writes, "We are meant to be warehoused and die."[23] The racial discrimination of the legal system, or as Mumia Abu-Jamal would call it, "the criminal system of injustice, suffused with the toxin of racism,"[24] has put a large portion of the black male population into prison. In Alabama, incidentally the state where police dogs infamously attacked civil rights rioters, reportedly one third or so of the black male population has permanently lost their right to vote due to their ex-felon status.

The current rate of black disenfranchisement is gradually bringing us back to a state prior to the Voting Rights Act of 1965.[25] The school-to-prison pipeline, mass incarceration, and legalized discrimination (blacks losing privileges as ex-felons) have been as effective, Alexander provocatively argues, "as Jim Crow laws once did at locking people of color into a permanent second-class citizenship."[26] Our modern society maintains a lack of black freedom of movement but has ceased to show its legal enclosures. "What is completely missed in the rare public debates today about the plight of African Americans is that a huge percentage of them are not free to move up at all. It is not just that they lack opportunity, attend poor schools, or are plagued by poverty. They are barred by law from doing so,"[27] Alexander writes. Blacks are therefore still partially tied to their chattel property status, in the sense that their movability —"chattel" being in the strict legal sense a question of movability and immovability—is controlled by a legal and repressive system that always already owns them, like captive animals in a zoo.

As Alexander explains, three-strikes laws ("Three Strikes and You're Out") and the war on drugs initiated by the Clinton administration in the 1990s did not specifically target racial minorities and yet those "tough-on-crime" policies brought a spike in imprisonment that has mainly impacted minorities. "Ninety percent of those administered to prison for drug offenses in many states were black or Latino,"[28] the author explains. The racially tainted tough-on-crime policies uncannily resemble, in their discriminative and punitive impact, legislative measures taken against pit bulls starting in the same period. In her book in defense of pit bulls, author Bronwen Dickey argues that "like their owners, the dogs [pit bulls] tend to be stereotyped as 'criminals,'"[29] a categorization that has necessitated a special kind of legislation prohibiting the ownership of pit bulls in various cities and housing facilities in America. New York City mayor Ed Koch was the first to impose a pit bull ban in his city in 1989. Denver followed soon after. As Dickey explains, between 1992 and 2009, 5,300 dogs belonging to the so-called and loosely defined pit bull breed were impounded, and 3,497 of them were killed in the country. "Being tough on pit bulls," Dickey writes, "was an essential part of being tough on crime,"[30] which explains why, since the 1990s, pit bulls have been banned from public housing in various cities, the same way and at the same time as President Clinton took his "One Strike, You're Out" initiative to the literal level, by legislatively facilitating the eviction of ex-felons from public housing. While the New York City Housing Authority passed a number of regulations that made it impossible to keep pit bulls in public housing, Clinton also made sure that (many black) ex-felons would not have access to public housing. "From now on, the rule for residents who commit crime and peddle drugs should be one strike and you're out" [from public housing],[31] Alexander quotes Clinton. Since the 1990s, both the breed-specific legislation and tough-on-crime policies have cleaned up American cities, putting away or putting down the "dangerous" breed/race. Just like discriminative policies, as Dayan simply puts it, "in breed-specific legislation, the taint and incapacity of the disenfranchised live on."[32]

RACIAL IRRELEVANCE AND THE ANIMAL QUESTION

The fact that the massive loss of rights for blacks has gone unnoticed is partially due to the color blindness of the so-called postracial America of the Obama era. The common belief that the 2008 election of the first black president in America would pave the way for an era of color blindness has proven not only to be wrong,[33] but, on the contrary, as Black Lives Matter (2012)

and the series of events that precipitated the creation of this movement show, racial relevance is more than ever a pressing matter in
our modern era.[34] Racial consciousness has been, paradoxically,
proportionate to the perception of America as color-blind. In
other words, as the fantasy of color blindness has increased, so
has racial consciousness. This exponential phenomenon can be
explained by comparing it with the example of France, where
color blindness has been an intrinsic value of French republican-
ism since 1946, after the World War II debacle. The French
constitution sees its people as "one and indivisible," regardless
of racial, religious, or cultural backgrounds. France's ideal of
indivisibility, along with its anticommunitarianism, has made it
unrepublican to formally collect statistical data on racial differences and quotas. Though a noble cause in theory, racial invisibility in the French Republic has, in practice, created a situation
in which racial discrimination cannot be addressed since race
does not officially exist.[35] Instead of ending racial discrimination, the fallacy of color blindness in France has reinforced it.
As Mbembé puts it in "Provincializing France?," "the perverse
effect of this indifference to difference is thus a relative indifference to discrimination."[36] Jean-François Lyotard calls this kind
of conundrum a *différend*, which occurs when a wrong cannot
be redressed because the wrong is "not a matter of litigation
under the . . . law,"[37] for the very reason that the said law is
responsible for the wrong. How is one to address under French
law the refusal to acknowledge the existence of racialized
French citizens if one's racial invisibility is precisely due to one's
legal status as French citizens?

Institutionalized color blindness results in making not just
race but also racial discrimination a nonproblem. Racial irrelevance is a slippery slope: When one's blackness can no longer
figure in the question, it creates a *différend* that gags racialized victims, preventing them from voicing their feeling of

inadequacy due to their race. Racial *différends* often begin with good intentions since they are supposed to positively highlight the progress made on behalf of the victim, so much so that the subject no longer needs to be perceived as a victim. But the flip side is that racial irrelevance ushers activists onto the next battle, leaving the preceding one behind instead of looking at both, together, as one ongoing battle. Che Gosset's online essay "Blackness, Animality, and the Unsovereign" is an important contribution to the investigation of intersectionality because of the way Gosset exposes the sequential nature of racial and non-human animal activism. As Gosset writes, for "many in animal liberation and animal studies, abolition is imagined as teleological; first slavery was abolished and now forms of animal captivity must be, too. It is as though animal is the new black even though blackness has already been racialized through animalization."[38] This logic of subsequence, in which the clairvoyance that once benefited the chattel slave should now apply to animals, leads to a dangerous kind of racial blindness. It presupposes that we have progressed beyond blackness in our considerations of (de-) personhood, when blackness should constitute the primary matrix in which we think about animal rights: "Blackness remains the absent presence of much animal studies and animal liberation discourse."[39] Making the presence of blackness relevant in animal studies requires an understanding that the racial question is not a stepping-stone to a main point but rather the platform on which the animal should be addressed. But instead, blackness has often been brought up in animal discourse only to be brushed aside with a rhetoric that, as Gosset so poignantly puts it, introduces the animal as the new black, thus presenting the racial question as *passé*.

We can trace back the "animal as the new black" rhetoric to the (aforementioned) English utilitarian philosopher Jeremy Bentham, one of the forefathers of the modern animal rights movement. Inspired by the universalist values of the French Revolution, Bentham made a plea in *An Introduction to the Principles of Morals and Legislation* for universal compassion for all sentient beings, a plea that led him to compare the fate of blacks with that of animals in the eyes of the law.

> The day has come, I grieve to say in many places it is not yet past, in which the greater part of the species, under the denomination of slaves, have been treated by the law exactly upon the same footing as, in England for example, the inferior races of animals are still. The day *may* come, when the rest of the animal creation may acquire those rights which never could have been withholden from them but by the hand of tyranny. The French have already discovered that the blackness of the skin is no reason why a human being should be abandoned without redress to the caprice of a tormentor. It may come one day to be recognized, that the number of the legs, the villosity of the skin, or the termination of the *os sacrum*, are reasons equally insufficient for abandoning a sensitive being to the same fate.[40]

Bentham's animals-slaves comparison precedes his famous anti-Cartesian comment on interspecies suffering: "What else is it that should trace the insuperable line? Is it the faculty of reason, or, perhaps, the faculty of discourse? . . . The question is not, Can they *reason*? nor, Can they *talk* but, Can they *suffer*?"[41] Bentham wants to believe in a better world for all sentient beings and sees French Universalist thought as a model to follow. Having printed the book in 1789, the year of the French Revolution and of the Declaration of the Rights of Man and of the Citizen, the British philosopher saw a giant step forward in the French disregard for the color of the skin in their pursuit of human rights. That said, because in 1789 slavery had not yet been abolished in the French colonies,[42] Bentham's comment about the French perception of blackness addresses a momentum rather than a completion. Yet, while Bentham thought in terms of momentum, his followers in the twentieth and twenty-first centuries tend to put emphasis on the question of completion, which explains the modern logic of sequences such as "after the black comes the animal." In his groundbreaking *Animal Liberation*, Utilitarian philosopher and forefather of the modern animal rights movement Peter Singer famously uses Bentham's comparison between black rights and animal rights to stage his theory. Singer popularized Richard D. Ryder's term, "speciesism," which the former defines as, "by analogy with racism . . .[43] a prejudice or attitude of bias toward the interests of members of one's own species and against those of members of other species."[44] Singer situates Bentham's passage at a time when, Singer writes, "black slaves had been freed by the French but in the British dominions were still being treated in the way we now treat animals."[45] But again, in 1789 the blacks in the colonies had not yet been freed: in 1790, the French National Assembly had indeed granted political rights to free blacks and mulattoes in Saint-Domingue, but the number of free blacks amounted to a very small portion of the black population, the majority of which was still enslaved and living under the 1685 Code Noir (Slave Code), an edict that codified the cruel and unjust treatment of slaves by masters throughout the French colonies until 1848 (except for Saint-Domingue, where a slave rebellion broke out in 1791, leading to independence in 1801). Bentham's comment most likely did not imply that French slaves had been freed, but only that the French, and particularly the Société des amis des noirs (Society of the Friends of the Blacks), had been able to see past skin color in their pursuit of human rights and their public opposition to the Code Noir. For

Singer to imply completion is symptomatic of the modern trajectory of animal liberation and animal studies that looks at
black and animal intersectionality with a conditional logic—"if
freedom happened once with blacks, it should happen again
with animals"—even though Bentham then, and Alexander,
Wilderson, Stevenson, and Dayan now, would argue that rights
for blacks are still in a state of momentum and are yet to be
brought to completion. As Claire Jean Kim says, this kind of
analogizing "den[ies] the continuing derogation of Blacks as
subhumans, and conceal[s] the unfinished status of the Black
struggle (as well as the reasons why it will always remain unfinished)"[46]—reasons that the Afro-Pessimist movement exposes
in detail.[47] Blackness and de-personhood are not yet a thing of
the past. As Saidiya Hartman writes, "if slavery persists as an
issue in the political life of black America, it is not because of an
antiquarian obsession with bygone days or the burden of a too-
long memory, but because black lives are still imperiled and
devalued by a racial calculus and a political arithmetic that were
entrenched centuries ago."[48]

BLACKNESS

In *The Animal Rights Debate*, legal scholar Gary L. Francione
explains the difference between the abolitionist and the welfarist position in the animal rights debate. Welfarists advocate
for the protection of animal interests and more humane treatment of animals but, unlike animal abolitionists, do not ask
for the radical abolition of all animal use by humans. Francione
deplores the fact that Bentham, who follows the utilitarian
principle of consequentialism, which consists of weighing the
consequences of each action in terms of pleasure and pain for all
sentient beings involved, spoke on behalf of animal interests but

failed to advocate abolitionism for all beings, regardless of their human or no-human species.[49] Bentham is an abolitionist when it comes to black slaves, because, according to him, the pain inflicted on slaves outweighs the pleasure that masters can derive from slavery. But Bentham's opposition to the use of animals as chattel is not as categorical as his opposition to black slavery, given that, in the case of animals, the morality of their use depends on the balance between man's pleasure and animal suffering. Bentham is therefore not, as we now call it, "an abolitionist" when it comes to animal rights, even though Francione asks whether there is "a good reason not to accord the right not to be treated as property to non-humans?"[50] Like Caron, Francione chooses to use the word "abolitionism" to address animal rights, examining blackness as a logical justification for taking the next step—abolitionist veganism. However, like Caron as well, in the rest of Francione's book he ignores this initial black presence. Quoting Bentham is almost a sine qua non in animal rights rhetoric, but blackness, the purpose of Bentham's quote, lingers as a ghastly presence after its introduction. Blackness is, to paraphrase Gosset, the "absent presence";[51] that which supports the argument but has no life beyond its rhetorical purpose. Concerned with this phenomenon, Toni Morrison, in *Playing in the Dark*, examines the perception of blackness in the white Western canon because, as she says, she is interested "in the way black people ignite critical moments of discovery or emphasis or change in literature not written by them."[52] The way blackness is articulated in animal studies tends to show that the black presence is indeed the ignition of the critical moment of discovery even though some scholars seem oblivious to its essential role in their text. And yet, as Morrison says, "the contemplation of this black presence is central to [any] understanding."[53]

Take for example, Michael Vick's treatment in the press, where race plays a more prominent role than initially apparent.

Francione argues that quarterback Vick, convicted for his illegal dog-fighting ring, was anathemized for a type of animal cruelty in which meat eaters and users of animal products partake on a daily basis. By titling his piece "We're all Michael Vick,"[54] Francione seeks to ignite guilt in nonvegans by provoking their identification with Vick. What is absent from the equation, however, is Vick's blackness, which makes us all *not* Michael Vick. The perception of blackness alongside the animal presence complicates the Vick case in that, as Claire Jean Kim explains,[55] Vick's demonization is inseparable from his race; because blackness, according to Gosset's axiom, has always been "racialized through animalization," the dog and Vick are enmeshed in a praxis of racialization and animalization. In *The Nation*, scholar and television personality Melissa Harris-Perry attempts to explain the complexity surrounding the Vick case, arguing that, "for many observers, the decision to demonize Vick seems motivated by something more pernicious than concern for animal welfare. It seems to be about race."[56] When sportswriter Jim Gorant, as we see in more detail in chapter 2, depicts in *The Lost Dogs* Vick's physical appearance as "almost canine" with his "thick and compact" build, his "small wide nose," and his "strong jaw,"[57] Vick is clearly being depicted as a pit bull, an identification that has far-reaching implications given that, as previously shown, pit bulls have been historically used in America as a weapon of stigmatization against blacks. In her book *Pit Bull*, Dickey quotes actor Michael B. Jordan addressing this identification: "Black males, we are America's pit bull. . . . We're labeled vicious, inhumane and left to die on the street."[58] Going back to the comparison between Vick's cruelty against animals and that of nonvegans, there is no doubt that provocation is useful in animal advocacy as a way to raise awareness and to gather interest in the fight against animal

exploitation. But as Maneesha Deckha explains,[59] those strate-
gies should not be used at the expense of other exploited (human)
groups. About PETA's "I'd rather go naked than wear fur" campaign, where sexualized female bodies speak on behalf of animal victims, Deckha says that the commodification and sexual
exploitation of women in this campaign is a disservice to cross-
species exploitation awareness. By ignoring the entangled nature
of animal and sexist forms of oppression, advocates run the risk
of perpetuating one form of oppressive discourse in their effort
to end another.[60] But as Deckha also argues in another essay on
posthumanist feminism, which focuses on two axes of difference, animality and gender, it is not sufficient to unveil the mul-
tifaceted mechanism at work in exploitation of marginalized
groups. An awareness of, as Deckha says, "the postcolonial and
racialized manifestations of animal practices" is an essential part
of both ecofeminism and antispeciesism.[61] Because our society is
fallibly racialized in its systems of oppression, there is no ignoring race in a discussion of that oppression.

That said, looking at the animal debate though the exclusive
lens of race and black slavery also raises objections. In *The
Dreaded Comparison*, Spiegel takes Bentham's analogy to a new
level by making black slavery the main subject of her book on
animal rights. In the book, the author compares modern animal
cruelty with black slavery, showing that "when both blacks and
animals are viewed as being 'oppressible,' the cruelties perpe-
trated upon them take similar forms."[62] Spiegel juxtaposes pictures of black slaves and dogs wearing similar obedience collars
and muzzles, masters branding blacks and farmers branding
cows, hens stacked against each other in a silo egg factory and
slaves stacked on a slave boat, finishing with a print of *The
Liberator*, an abolitionist newspaper founded by famed abolitionist William Lloyd Garrison in 1831 next to a print of *The*

Abolitionist, a British antivivisection magazine first published in 1898. As the title of her book suggests, Spiegel is aware that she is entering dangerous territory with her comparative approach since the analogy between animal and black slavery is a sensitive and, as she says, "dreaded" issue. But, as she argues, "comparing the suffering of animals to that of blacks (or any other oppressed group) is offensive only to the speciesist: one who has embraced the false notions of what animals are like."[63] Spiegel follows her antispeciesist comment by saying, "to deny our similarities to animals is to deny and undermine our power."[64] The possessive pronoun "our" here no longer refers to blacks but to the human species. However, her book does not deal with a comparison between animals and the human species more generally, but between animals and *blacks*; and as we know, the "dreaded" nature of the comparison is not its interspecies quality but rather its racial and animal component, reminiscent of the racist discourse that supported the slave trade. Spiegel's antispeciesist comment creates a syntactic slip, meant to obliterate the racial component of the comparison, making it sound as if the book were about—the less historically charged—human versus animal comparison. The consequence of this slip is to turn blackness into the absent presence in spite of its blatant presence. Spiegel's euphemistic twist of substituting black slavery for the "human slavery" of her subtitle avoids a real and direct confrontation with the truly "dreaded" analogy; blackness is, again, dismissed.[65]

The intersectionality of racialized minorities and animals is not exclusive to the question of blackness. Charles Patterson's *Eternal Treblinka: Our Treatment of Animals and the Holocaust* examines "how the enslavement of animals served as the model and inspiration for the enslavement of humans,"[66] focusing on Nazi Holocaust victims. PETA's Animal Liberation Project

(ALP), the umbrella project for "Are Animals the New Slaves?," was launched with a 2004 campaign entitled "Holocaust on Your Plate," which compared animal mistreatment with Holocaust victims. The exhibit used Jewish Isaac Bashevis Singer's quote, "To Animals, All People are Nazis" as the main message of the campaign. In 2009, Germany's high court banned the "Holocaust on Your Plate" traveling display due to the concern that the exhibit made "the fate of the victims of the Holocaust appear trivial and banal," a ban that Peter Singer later criticized on behalf of freedom of speech.[67] The fear of trivializing human tragedy is what, Philip Armstrong explains in "The Postcolonial Animal," has kept many postcolonialists from approaching the human-animal question, aware as they are of the risk of "trivializing the suffering of human beings under colonialism."[68] Jewish philosopher Emmanuel Lévinas, who was a prisoner of war in a camp in Germany during the Second World War, uses the image of a stray dog greeting concentration camp prisoners behind a fence as an allegory of humanity in oppression: Lévinas's dog was the only one able to see the real human being behind the dehumanized prisoner, just as Ulysses's dog, in Homer's *Odyssey*, was the only one capable of recognizing the identity of his master upon his return.[69] Lévinas's rhetorical use of the animal in the context of the Holocaust is meant to humanize the victim, but this use can be equally depersonalizing when the animal is confined to a liminal role, located behind the fence of the historical tragedy, viewed exclusively as an allegorical tool of comparison, identification, or differentiation.

How can one avoid trivializing and essentializing the victim when addressing human and animal oppression? How can one avoid not only color blindness but also other marginalized groups blindness and individual blindness when speaking about the animal and racial question together? These questions should not be restricted to human victims alone. Jacques Derrida insists that the animal in question in his essay "The Animal That Therefore I Am"[70]—incidentally his own cat—is not a metaphor, an image, or just a word, an *animot* (*mot* meaning "word" in French), but a *real* cat. His plea for realness is inspired by the fact that many philosophers, from Descartes to Kant and Heidegger, have too often talked about animals as a generic group, with no regard for their specificities as species or individual beings. Essentializing the silent subject or the victim has a tendency to desensitize the situation, thereby negating the real (sentient) individual, whether animal or human. Animals, women, blacks, and Jews become merely ideas and concepts, caught in a rhetoric of similes, analogies, and metaphors. In that regard, by saying that "even though we may think of the experiences of black people in this country as being unique,"[71] their tragedy is similar to that of animals, Spiegel, in her book, dismisses the unique pain of being discriminated against as a black individual as much as she dismisses the unique experience of being slaughtered as a cow—an avoidable dismissal in any investigation of intersectionality.

In *Animal Happiness*, animal trainer Vicki Hearne deplores the fact that *suffering* is often the only focus of animal lovers, many of whom are inspired by Bentham. As she writes, "the constant citation of Bentham, along with many other details, makes it as plain as anything can be that what interests some people is not the joy and intelligence and difficulty and difference of animals, but only their pain."[72] Likewise for the black, reducing the slave exclusively to a state of suffering risks equating blackness with a generic feeling, a capacity for sentience, which obliterates the complexity and uniqueness of the individual who should not be defined by her pain alone. Analogizing the black experience with the animal experience in an exclusive state of suffering results in essentializing both and desensitizing us to the actual being.

INTERSECTIONALITY

The word "intersectionality" was first coined by legal scholar Kimberlé Crenshaw in her 1989 essay, "Demarginalizing the Intersection of Race and Sex," a crucial theoretical contribution to the black feminist movement.[73] In the essay Crenshaw argues that gender discrimination cannot single-handedly account for the wrong done to black women since these women are potentially victimized not only as women but also as black. And, likewise, racism cannot address the full extent of the discrimination against black women since racism does not take into consideration their gender minority status. For that reason, white women and black men, both partially (and chiasmus-like) part of the dominant structure as white and men, respectively, fail to represent black women, who are in the unique position of being minoritized in several ways and thereby stand at the very bottom of the structure. Crenshaw advocates an approach where black women would be treated as a "multiply-disadvantaged class" and where "the complexities of compoundedness" would be fully appreciated;[74] as she posits, "because the intersectional experience is greater than the sum of racism and sexism, any analysis that does not take intersectionality into account cannot sufficiently address the particular manner in which Black women are subordinated."[75] While in the early 1990s intersectionality was a response to the perception of insufficient black representation in feminism, a movement seen then as racially homogeneous (white), the same semantics has recently resurfaced in animal studies to indicate a kind of interconnectedness between the treatment of gender and that of animals. The post-human turn in feminist theory has gradually paved the way for a broader perspective of the concept of intersectionality. Ecofeminism has drawn attention to the overlapping oppression between the treatment of nature and of women. Carol J. Adams, in *The Sexual Politics of Meat*,[76] famously describes eating meat as an expression of patriarchal domination, what Derrida would later refer to as "carno-phallogocentrism."[77] But more importantly, ecofeminism and vegan ecofeminism have not limited their scope to gender since the very purpose of intersectionality is to open the question of entangled oppressions to all vulnerable groups—human and nonhuman.[78] The anthropocene, speciesism, sexism, racism, ageism, ableism, classicism, and homophobia have all been shown to overlap in systems of exploitation and discrimination.

As Carol J. Adams and Lori Gruen point out in their edited volume *Ecofeminism*, the term "intersectionality" has now become a "buzz word" in animal studies.[79] The word refers to the idea that speciesism intersects with sexism and other forms of -isms in their shared models of oppression. In the modern use of intersectionality, the animal, and no longer race, has become the focal point alongside gender. The semantic appropriation signals an important paradigmatic shift. The new use of intersectionality treats the question of race as, not racial *passé*, but racial *passing*, in a fashion redolent of Nella Larsen's 1929 Harlem Renaissance novel *Passing*, in which the fair-skinned protagonist is married to a white man unaware of her racial background as she seeks to pass for white. But her eyes, "Ah! Surely! They were Negro eyes!,"[80] betray her enduring blackness. Like racial passing, the animal question leaves an unavoidable trail of disavowed blackness behind it.

Jennifer C. Nash defines intersectionality in black feminism as a "buzzword" as well.[81] But the shortcoming of this concept, as she explains, is its essentializing effect on a category referred to as "black women." In addition to gender and race, Nash argues that the lived experiences and particularities of each black woman need to be added to intersectional considerations, which include class, privilege, education, time and place, and other categories. Or else, as the author says, "black women's race and gender are treated as trans-historical constants that mark *all* black women in similar ways."[82] In other words, intersectionality holds the risk of *always already* reproducing what it means to reject by making those multiply faceted subjects uniformly indistinct through the scope of their combined race and gender.

Intersectionality, as a theoretical tool, is instrumental in dealing with entangled systems of oppression, in spite of the fact that it is also a tool that tends to privilege general categories over particularities: the very tendency that, paradoxically enough, intersectionality seeks to denounce. This embedded contradiction shows the challenges, and potential shortcomings, of any intersectional endeavor, including mine. As Nash argues in her critique of Crenshaw, "Intersectional projects often replicate precisely the approaches that they critique."[83] Derrida's own efforts to individualize the life of his cat in *The Animal That Therefore I Am* partially failed because his cat is somehow essentialized in her embodiment of the broader animal question. My work is up against this very contradiction, as it grapples with essentialism and is fully aware of the risk of privileging a generic group (race, species) over the individual subject (black or animal), not to mention one group (blacks) over another (animals).

There are no easy answers to address the challenges of the intersectional approach. One cannot address the entangled oppression of humans, minorities, and animals while doing justice to all groups and individuals equally. Particularities being infinitesimal, the goal of intersectionality should simply be to open our minds to the exponentiality of intersections but with no ambition to address them all. Jakob von Uexküll's *Umwelt* theory is, in that respect, essential to the intersectional approach. From *um* (surrounding) and *welt* (world), *Umwelt* refers to the infinitude and particularities of all human and nonhuman animal perceptions. The German biologist has argued that, like Derrida's *animot*, the generic concept of "the animal" is an inadequate and anthropocentric perception of the animal world. There exists a multitude of unique and idiosyncratic animal *Umwelten*, and the human perceptional environment is only one *Umwelt* among this multitude. In "A Stroll Through the Worlds of Animals and Men," Uexküll shows that all animal (human and nonhuman) worlds are both autonomous and interconnected. Further, Giorgio Agamben, who wrote a piece on Uexküll in his book *The Open*, says about the *Umwelt*:

> Where classical science saw a single world that comprised within it all living species hierarchically ordered from the most elementary forms up to the higher organisms, Uexküll instead supposes an infinite variety of perceptual worlds that, though they are uncommunicating and reciprocally exclusive, are all equally perfect and linked together as if in a gigantic musical score.[84]

Uexküll's example of tiny organisms, such as the sea urchin or the tick, which are often perceived as insignificant to man, best shows man's inability to relate to the diversity and yet interconnectedness of human and nonhuman animal worlds. The tick, which, as Uexküll explains, patiently waits on a bush's branch for a warm-blooded victim to walk by so that it can drop onto it and suck its blood, lives in a world utterly different from that of man. And yet, if a human being happens to walk underneath this branch, the life of the tick and the human will intersect in a symbiotic relationship, their *Umwelten* will connect in the most substantial way until the parasite is extracted.[85] This accidental and fleeting moment of intersection between the animal and man demonstrates that man and the tick, this insignificant animal, or as Uexküll says, "an unpleasant guest of mammals,"[86] relate to each other in an organic way. The singular experience of this tick and its human prey, the elusive interplay of their distinct *Umwelten*, is what intersectionality tries to address. The *Umwelt* of black women is fundamentally unique, but within this *Umwelt*, and in connection with other *Umwelten*, each black woman is also unique, like Uexküll's tick.

Interestingly enough, Uexküll uses the example of a black man, a "Negro," along with other animals, to further clarify his theory of distinct perceptional worlds. As he explains, the manner in which one perceives an image will adjust to the function ascribed to this image. For example, a crab will use a sea anemone either as protection or as food, depending on its needs. Likewise, a dog trained to the command "chair" may use a basket or a table as a chair, if the chair is no longer available. Uexküll's conclusion is that the "tone" of an object may vary according to the species and the animal's mood or needs. Man would never conceive of a table or basket as a seating accommodation, but a dog may very well do so. A similar variance applies to man, as Uexküll also explains. Here, the biologist uses the example of "a very intelligent and agile Negro . . . from the heart of Africa,"[87] brought to Dar-es-Salaam. The "Negro" has no knowledge of European tools. When Uexküll asks him to climb on a ladder, the man retorts, "How am I to do that, I see nothing but rods and holes?"[88] Then another "Negro" shows him how to use the ladder, and the man from the "heart of Africa" is able to complete the task.[89] As Uexküll concludes, "the *receptor image* of rods and holes had been supplemented by the *effector image* of his own action; through this it had acquired a new meaning."[90]

Uexküll's "Negro" is meant to signal a difference of cultural perception. The man from the heart of Africa represents what is the farthest from European traditions. But Uexküll's example is not only culturally but also racially invested, as it indirectly underlines the fundamental difference between white and black perceptions of the world, while approximating the black with the animal. The dog learns from man the function of a chair just as the black man from the bush learns the function of a ladder in the presence of the white man. Seeing a deeper racial meaning in Uexküll's trivial example could admittedly be said to be part of a "hermeneutics of suspicion," a term coined by Paul Ricoeur,[91] or even "paranoid reading," as Eve Sedgwick calls it.[92] There is a probability that race is, as a young vegan activist told black vegan A. Breeze Harper, a "feeble matter" in Uexküll's example.[93] But Mel Y. Chen in *Animacies* convincingly argues that seemingly random enunciations are never completely innocent, mostly when it comes to approximating minority groups with animals. For example, as Chen explains, in *How to Do Things with Words*, linguist J. L. Austin uses the marriage between a man and a monkey as an example of what would be a "nonauthorized official speech." Austin calls this kind of union a "mockery, like a marriage with a monkey."[94] But, as Chen explains, Austin's choice of example is not trivial,[95] rather, it is inscribed in the historical context of Austin's enunciation: "a time of intensive societal and legal flux in which both heterosexuality and racial purity actively shored up."[96] It is no coincidence, as Chen continues, that Austin's book was published in 1961, the year of the passage of the Commonwealth Immigrants Act following an unwelcome wave of immigration from the West Indies. The monkey is a personification of the Other and represents that which is like a human but not quite so. As for Uexküll, the Negro from the heart of Africa is the vector of perceptual difference. The Negro perceives and is consequently perceived differently, just like the crab and the dog perceive and are perceived differently from (the white) man. Even though Uexküll's Negro example is meant to compare Europe with what is far from Europe (Africa, *Afer*, afar), the omnipresence of the black in the animal question, her or his proximity to the animal, is pregnant with meaning, especially with regard to the *Umwelt*.

The application of the term "intersectionality," first to black women and now to animals, ties the two groups together in a special kind of gender, race, and animal interconnectedness. Black women and animals become those who, to quote Chen, "occupy proximal category membership."[97] The trajectory of the theoretical concept of intersectionality suggests that black women's *Umwelten* are the closest to the animal's *Umwelt*, and both, equally, grapple with the difficulties of communicating their unique state of oppression. But while ecofeminism carries a strong tradition of exploring the intersection between sexism and speciesism with the work of Josephine Donovan, Carol J. Adams, Marti Kheel, and Lori Gruen, to name a few, black intersectional feminism seems to carry less of an inclination to do so. While Harper's edited volume, *Sistah Vegan*, focuses on the importance of black participation in veganism, most of the contributions in the book look at veganism as a primary concern for the welfare of the black community. The contributors advocate the end of soul food and adopting a healthier diet with less saturated fat, sugar, and meat; a diet more adjusted to African Americans who are prone to lactose intolerance, diabetes, cardio-vascular diseases, and other debilitating illnesses. Veganism as decolonization is an answer to what contributor Pattrice Jones names "dietary racism," "dietary colonialism," and "dietary imperialism,"[98] which specifically target the black community. In the face of, as contributor Adama Maweja puts it, "the staggering statistics of the disproportionate percentages and the rates at which we African-Americans [are] sick, diseased, imprisoned, dysfunctional, obese, and dying,"[99] veganism is seen as a political call to action, a sort of "health activism," as Harper says, "that resists institutionalized racism and neocolonialism."[100] In the midst of other authors addressing health concerns, Tashee Meadows is one of the only contributors in the book to explicitly connect black suffering with animal exploitation. In her piece entitled "Because They Matter," she writes, "I thought of my ancestry as a Black woman: the rapes, unwanted pregnancies, captivity, stolen babies, grieving mothers, horrific transports, and the physical, mental, and spiritual pain of chattel slavery."[101] Animal lives matter, and Meadows claims to have become more acutely aware of that fact through racial and female solidarity with the animal victims. Meadows follows in the footsteps of Alice Walker, who was one of the first, as a black feminist ("womanist") in the 1980s, to speak on behalf of animal rights by comparing black slavery with our treatment of animals.[102] But aside from Meadows's contribution, the intersection between racism and speciesism, which may have been expected to be a recurrent theme in *Sistah Vegan*, is deemphasized, possibly due to the still-prevalent preconception that the animal rights movement, as both the introduction and the afterword mention, is some sort of a white privilege. In her "Afterword," Jones talks about her hope that the edited volume will provide "an antidote to the erasure of Black vegans implicit in the dismissal of veganism as 'a white thing.'"[103] Likewise, Harper admits that in college, she reductively saw veganism as something for "bored overprivileged rich white kids."[104] By emphasizing health activism against dietary racism over the question of animal rights, the contributors to Harper's volume show the enduring unease, even among black vegan women, to connect blackness with animal oppression. Veganism is showcased in the book only minimally as a call for animal liberation, and more prominently as a call for black decolonization through a diet-oriented liberation of the black body.

If Harper first saw vegan activism as a "white thing," it is mainly due to the fact that, as she explains, her "vegan classmates weren't trained or well read enough in antiracist and antipoverty praxis to deliver their message to [her] in a way that connected to [her] social justice work as a Black working-class female trying to deal with sexism, classism, and racism at Dartmouth."[105] Harper ascribes the failures of PETA's "Are Animals the New Slaves?" campaign to a similar lack of racial sensitivity: "Perhaps PETA's exhibit, and the ensuing controversy, were handled insensitively. The lack of sociohistorical context by PETA is perhaps what is upsetting to many racial minorities, for whom such images and textual references trigger trauma and deep emotional pain."[106] Harper does not experience Spiegel's *Dreaded Comparison*, on the other hand, as offensive because, for her, Spiegel's comparison is, in contrast to PETA's campaign, historically grounded and offers "sensitive and scholarly explorations of these topics."[107] Nonetheless, Harper herself avoids the dreaded comparison and instead examines veganism though the lens of ethical black health activism, as her most recent project, "The Sistah Vegan Project: A Critical Race Feminist's Journey Through the 'Post-Racial' Ethical Foodscape . . . and Beyond," attests.[108]

It seems difficult, even for those who identify as "black vegans"—although this term is based on the nexus of race and animal—to bring the animal and the black together with equal consideration for both parties. In a blog post entitled "Samuel Dubose, Cecil the Lion, and the Ethics of Avowal,"[109] philosopher Lori Gruen addresses the outrage that some have felt over the fact that the public generally reacted more vocally to the killing of Cecil than to the loss of black lives at police hands.

Gruen finds this outrage counterproductive since, as she argues, engaging in one cause over another does not equate privileging one cause over the other. Seeing the public reaction to Cecil the lion as a sign that "white people care more about lions than black people" is, for Gruen, not the answer to ending all forms of oppression, whether the victim is racialized, gendered, or perceived as an animal. Of upmost importance for Gruen is rather seeing the intersection between cases of injustice by bringing attention to the thread of oppression tying, for example, the July 1, 2015, slaughter of Cecil the lion to the July 19, 2015, execution of unarmed African American civilian Samuel DuBose by a University of Cincinnati policeman. "Very little attention has been focused on the commonalities between the murders of DuBose and Cecil and the racist, humanist, colonialist structures that support white men killing black men, women and animals," Gruen writes. There is indeed no reason to believe that the outpouring of empathy over the death of an animal comes at the expense of empathy for black lives. But the fear of racial concerns being overshadowed by the animal reaches back to the founding of modern America and is symptomatic of a historical malaise surrounding the question of the value of life in our society. The outpouring of concern for Cecil, which some may perceive as surpassing interest in DuBose's fate, is evocative of a plantation era where some masters, like Frederick Douglass's, were said to care more about the well-being of their horses than that of their slaves.[110] Any situation that brings the black and the animal together, even slightly hinting that the animal carries more weight in the public opinion than the black, holds a historical resonance. The same is true for the May 28, 2016, killing of Harambe, a gorilla from the Cincinnati Zoo. Fearing for the life of a three-year-old African American boy, a zoo worker shot and killed the gorilla after the boy climbed into the gorillas' enclosure. Public outrage soared over the killing of the innocent gorilla. The outrage exhibited, in some instances, a subtle analogy between black life and animal life. For example, a memorial vigil in front of the Cincinnati Zoo included an "All Animal Lives Matter—Justice for Harambe" sign—a visible reference to the Black Lives Matter movement—a phrase that has since gone viral. Ironically, both Harambe and Samuel DuBose were killed in Cincinnati; both could be said to have been captive, one in an old-fashioned zoo, the other in a modern zoo.[111] More ironically, the Harambe case implied the predicament of having to weigh the life of a gorilla with that of a black (boy) from Cincinnati. Gruen's appeal to look at the commonalities between the fate of the animal and that of the black could not be more pertinent than in the Harambe case. Yasmin Nair, in an online article entitled "Racism and the American Pit Bull," addresses the Harambe case, arguing that our perception of apes has evolved over time and that apes are no longer the signifier for blackness while blacks remain so. As she writes:

[Apes] are treated with compassion and dignity, recognized for their intelligence and sophistication. Yet no such transformation has occurred in the treatment of race for humans. Black bodies are still shot at will and caged by hundreds of thousands. . . . Animals have finally transcended race. It is only black humans who must continue to bear its burden.[112]

By pitting animals against blacks, Nair's argument presupposes that animals now have access to some rights (namely, the right to be treated outside of the stigma of blackness) to which blacks have not. In this kind of rhetoric, the Black Lives Matter movement is indirectly caught in a tug of war with animal rights movements (for example, the Great Ape Project), somehow putting racial concerns and animal concerns in competition with each other. It should not be a question of who in our modern society, between the black and the animal, is better off, but rather, as Gruen has argued, how one becomes attuned to the interconnectedness in all forms of oppression.

"Ethics of avowal" is an expression, used by Gruen from Kim's *Dangerous Crossings*, highlighting the need to think about the entanglement of oppression of minorities and animals. Kim defines it as a "multi-optic vision" that recognizes "the connectedness of multiple forms of domination and [acts] against them in concert."[113] This ethics of avowal also requires an awareness that the treatment of blacks is, like no other human race in human history, connected to that of the animal. Douglass says in his autobiography, "we were all ranked together at the valuation. Men and women, old and young, married and single, were ranked with horses, sheep, and swine. There were horses and men, cattle and women, pigs and children, all holding the same rank in the scale of being, and were all subjected to the same narrow examination."[114] Such a state of affairs is bound to eventually create a counterreaction where blacks no longer want to be "ranked together" with the animal and might even want to, in "the scale of being," *matter more* than the animal, what one may see as overcorrection or simply a preemptive defense against the weight of history.

Cecil's sympathizers have also been accused of caring more about the fate of the exotic lion than about the pigs, cows, and chickens slaughtered everyday for human consumption. This is a type of rhetoric reminiscent of Francione's abolitionist views. Why should a lion matter more than a pig, and Dubose more than Cecil? How valid is the human grid of perception when it comes to the hierarchization of nonhuman and human animal lives? In *The Sexual Politics of Meat*, Carol J. Adams posits, "a

feminist-vegetarian critical theory begins . . . with the perception that women and animals are similarly positioned in a patriarchal world, as objects rather than subjects."[115] At stake in the
Cecil case is not the valuing of the exotic animal over the pig,
but rather the fetishizing and feminization of the lion as an
object meant for, not dietary, but visual consumption. To recall
Brophy's words, both animals and women inhabit a zoo, whether
the zoo is old or modern. The common appeal for the exotic
animal in the Western world targets the woman, and even more
so, in a system of intertwined racism, sexism, and speciesism,
the black woman. Think of the Hottentot Saartjie Baartman,
nicknamed "Vénus Noire" and "Black Venus," a black woman
with extremely large buttocks, who was brought from South
Africa to Europe in the early nineteenth century by exotic animal trainer S. Réaux to be exhibited in salons. Baartman epitomizes the interrelatedness of gender, race, and animality on
display like a lion, straight out of Africa. Likewise, African
American performer Josephine Baker, who in the 1920s in the
"La Revue Nègre" stage show in Paris, capitalized on Europe's
fascination with race and animality; she was well known for
impersonating the exotic bird, panther, serpent, and gorilla in
her dance moves in order to entertain her white audience. As
Terri J. Gordon explains, Baker "was described in the press as 'a
beautiful savage animal,' a 'gracious, small, exotic animal,' and
a 'strange and splendid savage beast.'"[116] The black woman,
when exoticized, instigates both pleasure and awe, just like
Cecil, or like any other "object" deemed exotic and unfamiliar.

Since Crenshaw, intersectional theory has made the connection between race, gender, and animality more visible, putting
the animal and the black woman on the same spectrum. Intersectionality today looks at the points of intersection between racism,
sexism, and speciesism within the human white patriarchal

system of oppression. This spectrum, however, can carry opposite effects if it is addressed in the reductive scope of a simple
comparison between the mistreatment of slaves and that of animals. The comparative approach is an archaic way of ranking the
racialized subject and the animal in, to quote Douglass again,
"the scale of being." In contrast to this approach, one needs to
look at human-animal encounters through the prism of black
and animal defiance. Examining defiance rejects the construction of blacks and animals as exclusively connected through their
comparable state of subjection and humiliation, and instead
focuses on interspecies alliances. In other words, to what extent
are Josephine Baker's animal impersonations not only a white-
crowd-pleasing performance but also a means to reclaim her
voice in a sort of auto-interpellation, as Louis Althusser calls
it?[117] Like the *nigga* or *dawg* (for "dog") appellation used in the
urban African American community, Baker's animal impersonations turn a racial slur into gold, or social currency, by making
it a sign of racial empowerment. As rapper Tupac Shakur says,
"niggers was the ones on the rope, hanging off the thing. Niggas
is the ones with gold ropes, hanging out at clubs."[118]

2

BLACKS AND DOGS IN
THE AMERICAS

M alcolm X once said:

> If a dog is biting a black man, the black man should kill the dog,
> whether the dog is a police dog or a hound dog or any kind of
> dog. If a dog is fixed on a black man when that black man is doing
> nothing but trying to take advantage of what the government
> says is supposed to be his, then that black man should kill that
> dog or any two-legged dog who sicks the dog on him.[1]

Should the black man kill the dog launched upon him by the
two-legged dog?

By killing the dog, the black man focuses on the suffering
caused by the dog—canicide being a sort of cauterization in an
attempt to mitigate his bleeding and pain. Also, by killing the
dog, the black man reacts as a sentient being, driven first by his
capacity to feel pain. If the black man does not kill the dog, however, killing the two-legged dog is also an option. By killing the

white man, the black man reacts like a reasonable animal, taking the white man's responsibility and agency into consideration. The crux of the conundrum lies in the duality between sentience (the ability to feel) and *scienter* (to know). Should the black man focus on stopping the immediate pain or on getting even with the one who purposely launched the dog at him? Colin Dayan uses the legal term *scienter* in the context of dog ownership,[2] referring to prior knowledge of a dog's vicious temperament. Under the law, if the dog owner has prior knowledge of the dog's propensity to attack, the dog owner is deemed responsible for the injury.[3] As for sentience, it denotes the capacity to feel, and—within the context of animal rights advocacy—to feel pain. In Malcolm X's example, the white man knowingly inflicts pain (*scienter*), while the black man feels the pain (sentience), and the dog acts as the go-between. The black man is made to feel pain like an animal but also to question his condition like a reasonable human. Which overrules the other: immediate or deferred pain, sentience or *scienter*? Akin to W. E. B. Du Bois's double-consciousness (being American and black),[4] this situation raises the question of the black man's triple-consciousness: sentient like the animal, reasonable like man, and black, like no other.

The Department of Justice's 2015 investigation of the Ferguson Police Department uncovered a correlation between race and the repressive use of police dogs in the city of Ferguson, Missouri. As the report stated:

> The department's own records demonstrate that, as with other types of force, canine officers use dogs out of proportion to the threat posed by the people they encounter, leaving serious puncture wounds to nonviolent offenders, some of them children. Furthermore, in every canine bite incident for which racial information is available, the subject was African American.[5]

Dogs, though supposedly color-blind, work on cues, and, in the case of the Ferguson police, seem to have been trained to direct their aggression toward the black population. While police dogs were also present during the 2014 protests that followed the death of African American teen Michael Brown in Ferguson, politician Hyland "Buddy" Fowler Jr. noted their absence during the 2015 Baltimore riots, suggesting (via social network) that attack dogs should be launched against those who took to the streets after the death of African American Freddie Gray.[6] Fowler Jr.'s comment has prompted me to examine the extent to which the association between canine aggression and black civil disobedience is still very much ingrained in the fabric of our society. The post-Ferguson era has brought back to consciousness a racial prism that many wished had died in "post-racial America" after Obama's first inauguration in 2009; viewed through this prism, race and dogs insidiously intersect in tales of violence.

Donna Haraway opens *Companion Species Manifesto* with the following tribute to her Australian sheepdog named Ms. Cayenne Pepper:

> Ms. Cayenne Pepper continues to colonize all my cells—a sure case of what the biologist Lynn Margulis calls symbiogenesis. I bet if you checked our DNA, you'd find some potent transfections between us. Her saliva must have the viral vectors. Surely, her darter-tongue kisses have been irresistible.[7]

In close physical contact with the human being, the pet dog is an infectious agent in the most hospitable way. Haraway's depiction borrows semantically from the field of zoonosis, particularly from rabies, a disease transmitted from animals to humans through saliva. As Bill Wasik and Monica Murphy explain in *Rabid*, "the special role of dogs in spreading rabies is . . . due to the way the virus is perfectly matched to the dog as host, expressing itself in canine saliva at levels rarely achieved in other four-footed wildlife."[8] Haraway relies on a human-companion-animal ecosystem that conjures up popular images of rabies-inspired vampire folklore. But what she names an "irresistible" infection is not contracted through the common lycanthropic "virus with teeth,"[9] but through a nonthreatening licking tongue. Referring to species and taxonomy, Gilles Deleuze and Félix Guattari argue that "natural history can only think in terms of relationships (between A and B), not in terms of production (from A to *x*)."[10] Yet, for Deleuze and Guattari, human-animal becoming (*from* human *to* animal, or vice versa) exists within the realm of conceptual possibility.[11] Becoming animal is not a metaphor or mimesis but truly a metamorphosis. Haraway gives substance to Deleuze and Guattari's concept, as her relationship to her dog is not simply a *relationship* but a *production* or, as she names it, "transfection": "Co-constitutive companion species and co-evolution are the rule, not the exception."[12] Ms. Cayenne Pepper, *Canis familiaris*, a pet and companion animal, offers a model of mutual "human-animal becoming" that is highly desirable, a type of becoming expected from a "good" dog.

In agreement with Haraway, Harlan Weaver offers his personal account of human-animal becoming in his article "'Becoming in Kind.'" Weaver focuses on both the sociological and biological aspects of becoming, be it via gender or species. The author depicts how his pit bull, Haley, contributed to shaping his identity and to bringing him a sense of safety during his vulnerable time transitioning from female to male. While Haley was an instrumental support in Weaver's gender identity transformation, Weaver argues that his vulnerable state as a person in transition (no longer identifying as a woman, though not wholly manifested as a man), his race, and social class were equally important to Haley. While pit bulls are often incorrectly perceived as inherently dangerous, Weaver explains that Haley appeared to others as a less dangerous dog next to his white, middle-class, transitioning person. Weaver names this type of mutual becoming "becoming in kind," a phrase that emphasizes the importance of the reliance on others in any type of identity transformation, including transitioning: "Becoming in kind speaks to the joint building of a sense of togetherness, a we, and the kind of beings we become."[13] "Kind," by Weaver's definition, ontologically refers to the type of being that one becomes in contact with another species. But in Weaver's article, "kind" could also allude to the adjectival aspect of the word, namely the kindness of man's best friend. Lori Gruen uses the dog as an example of an animal capable of showing emotional empathy for humans, in that they feel sad or happy in response to their human companion's sadness and happiness. This basic form of empathy, which she calls "emotional contagion,"[14] reveals that human-dog becoming is essentially filled with kindness. The capacity for interspecies empathy also explains why human-dog companionship, from the German *Einfühlung*, feels *into* the other, eventually colonizes the companion's cells. In most Western cultures, and particularly in a white, middle-class, normative context, man and dog are presented as kind and beneficial to each other in a therapeutic bonding that involves a good amount of physical affection.

Those who are "becoming in kind" undoubtedly play nice, but it needs to be stressed, as Haraway and Weaver do, that Ms. Cayenne Pepper's and Haley's kindnesses are inscribed in a specific becoming that is meant for a special "kind" of people. Haraway and Weaver address the intersectionality of race, class, and gender in their pieces, and both situate their conjoining within a white, female, middle-class, and academic context. Haraway says, "One of us, product of a vast genetic mixture, is called 'pure-bred.' One of us, equally product of a vast mixture, is called 'white.' . . . We are both the freedom-hungry offspring of conquest, product of white settler colonies."[15] Haraway's pet is racially and socially determined through an infectious human-animal relationship, just as Weaver's dog is meant to contract the socio-racial status of her human companion. In other words, contact with a specific human race and gender will determine whether the dog is perceived as a threat or as a loving companion to humans. As Wasik and Murphy explain, in the European nineteenth century, the goodness or badness of the dog was very much determined in relation to the presence of rabies and the fear that this contagious disease provoked in the masses.[16] Canicide has been committed in waves over the last centuries, motivated either by a popular fear of rabies or by a panic over a specific breed. In nineteenth-century Paris, for example, the overblown fear of rabies led to dog massacres. More recently, in May 2005, the hysteria around pit bulls in Denver resulted in a pit bull ordinance that initiated a mass killing of dogs.[17] Cynophobia has shifted from the human fear of a zoonotic disease transmitted through dog bites to the fear of a specific dog breed. In *With Dogs at the Edge of Life*, Dayan speaks against "canine profiling,"[18] as the author examines legal cases in which "the breed alone would count as evidence that an individual animal is violent."[19] In the last few years, pit bulls in particular, as Dayan shows, have often been perceived as "bad dogs" in need of eradication the way that rabid dogs once were. Also, Vicki Hearne in *Bandit: Dossier of a Dangerous Dog*, a book in defense of pit bulls, draws an important connection between the role of the Royal Society for the Prevention of Cruelty to Animals in the 1880s rabies epidemics in England and the role that the

Humane Society of the United States played in the 1980s "pit bull epidemics." Hearne argues that, in both cases, the organizations' efforts to bring the "unexpected crisis" to the public's attention were part of a wider plan to collect funds or to seek legislative support.[20] Zoonotic contamination and dog breeds alike are biological concepts that can be turned into ideological weapons. But while the fear of rabies is based on a real disease, fear of pit bulls is predicated on more nebulous factors. As Susan McHugh argues in *Dog*, because the breed of a dog is mostly determined by visual or behavioral characteristics, categorization based on breeds is an imprecise taxonomical system. Defining a purebred is about determining "what breed a dog resembles."[21] But in the case of the pit bull, its biological or genetic reality is even more questionable since what is commonly known as "pit bull" is not an official breed but an umbrella term that can refer to various breeds, including the Staffordshire bull terrier, the pit bull terrier, and many kinds of bulldogs. Like the issue of race in humans, the pit bull exemplifies how much more "dog" and "breed" have to do with human perception and social construction than with science.

Dogs were once perceived as dangerous due to rabies, but today the black man is the one responsible for making the big dog look "un-kind." In America, the perception of canine aggressiveness has metonymically shifted from a zoonotic to a racial context. In the presence of a white—preferably female—subject, the pit bull is allegedly rehabilitated and therefore appears to be safe to humans, only because the black male is the one who carries the (sublimated) rabies vector. The function of the white, middle-class, and, preferably, female subject is to rehabilitate the dog from its association with black men, not because black men have historically had a bad influence on the dog; rather because, over the centuries, white collective consciousness in the Americas has been imposing images of ferocious dogs on black men.

As Claire Jean Kim points out in "The Wonderful, Horrible Life of Michael Vick," what is perceived as a "pit bull" today has been "racialized as urban/black/dangerous."[22] Its bad reputation is a remnant of a long-standing rabid imaginary that has mutated into a racial and social stigma.[23] Just as, in a rabid imaginary, Ms. Cayenne Pepper's darter-tongue kisses subvert a historiography of the dog seen over the centuries as predisposed to hydrophobia (foaming mouth, inclination to bite), in a racial context, Weaver's companionship challenges the racially and socially oriented bad rap of the pit bull. The shift from a zoonotic to a racially charged rabidity is also supported by the (scientifically unsound) theory, prevalent in eighteenth- and nineteenth-century Europe, which asserted that rabies led to hypersexuality. Wasik and Murphy name two sources that were, in part, responsible for the connection between sexual appetite and the disease. The first source is an eighteenth-century doctor named Albrecht von Haller who claimed that a man under the influence of rabies "ejaculated thirty times in one day";[24] the second is nineteenth-century scientist Henry William Dewurst, who, in an address to the London Veterinary Medical Society, claimed that rabies was contracted through a lack of sexual activity, a correlation first reported in dogs. As Wasik and Murphy explain, "medical opinion had coalesced around a new, rather lurid theory: namely, that many if not most cases of dog rabies were caused by a lack of sexual satisfaction."[25] From the rabid dog, the sexual paradigm moved to humans through contamination, and has eventually targeted the black man alone. The sexually charged representation of the disease has resurfaced in the stereotypical image of the black man's putative hypersexuality and predation toward white women from the slavery era on.

The 2007 Michael Vick case is the latest installment in a long history of cyno-racial (dog-black) representations. After a raid at Michael Vick's Virginia mansion in 2007, the federal government indicted the star quarterback from the Atlanta Falcons football team on charges related to an illegal dogfighting ring. Vick pleaded guilty to the charges after compelling evidence incriminated him. The investigation showed that Vick had taken an active role not only in financing the operation but also in attending the fights and, more disturbing yet, in drowning, bludgeoning, or electrocuting the dogs deemed not aggressive enough for combat. The media coverage quickly evolved racialized undertones, as if Vick's being black had to be an essential part of the story. Kim details the reactions of Vick defenders and proponents. The defenders argued that the prosecution treated Vick unfairly because of his race, while animal rights advocates focused on the predicament of the dogs, vehemently denying that race had anything to do with the case. Kim cites one caller on NPR's *Talk of the Nation* saying: "I don't care if Michael Vick was black, white, green, purple. To me, this is not a story about color."[26] Yet, as Kim argues, color takes part in everything: "No one in this country has ever been enslaved, auctioned off, or lynched for being green, purple, or orange."[27] The Vick case epitomizes our modern era of micro-aggression, where the existence of racism, when disavowed, penetrates even deeper into the community. The manner in which the country reacted to the Vick case highlights the importance of the intersectionality of race and animal species in America. By animalizing Vick (asking for Vick to be neutered) and anthropomorphizing his dogs (suggesting that on a human-animal spectrum Vick is more of an animal than his dogs), the media engaged in a three-centuries-long habit of equating black men with animals. The public reaction to the case brought to the surface a deeply rooted tradition of conjoined racialization and animalization—from eighteenth-century taxonomical discourses locating blacks closer to the ape in their phylogenetic development to the 2008 presidential campaign, where images of presidential candidate Barack Obama as Curious George surfaced.

In addition to the intersection of race and species, the Michael Vick case ultimately leads us to a better understanding of "kindness" as a social and racial construct. In his *New York Times* bestseller on Michael Vick's dogs, Jim Gorant depicts how volunteers and professionals rescued Vick's pit bulls after their owner was incarcerated. The rescue efforts were geared toward saving the dogs from both euthanasia and repairing their bad reputation. Gorant's book is itself an attempt at salvaging the pit bull's public image. In it, Gorant includes pictures illustrating the rescue efforts. Those pictures show white workers and volunteers (many women and children) in close physical contact with endearing looking pit bulls. In one of the pictures, a group of unidentifiable blacks are walking in the direction of the camera, alongside Vick's emptied kennels. The kennels look like a canine death row at the end of which a fenced door, the door closest to the camera lens, has been left wide open. The open door, certainly evocative of the very recent release of the dogs, also brings to mind the escape of a dangerous convict (or "con-Vick," as Gorant names Vick). Gorant's photographs attest to the inclination in America to perceive canine badness within a racial paradigm since the only blacks featured in Gorant's series of photos are associated with the pre-rehabilitation phase and the cement urban landscape of incarceration. The animalization of the racial paradigm is all the more salient in Gorant's description of Vick at the beginning of the book:

> Vick was now twenty and fully grown. At two hundred pounds
> and slightly less than six feet tall, he was thick yet compact. His

large brown eyes and small wide nose were offset by a strong jaw
that made it look as if he had an underbite. Topped off with a
goatee, the total effect of these traits was to give Vick an appearance that, while handsome, could fairly be described as almost
canine.[28]

In lieu of seeking to eradicate the rampant demonization of the
pit bull in America, as the book promised, Gorant shifts the
vicious pit bull stigma onto the black man. With his "strong
jaw" and "small wide nose," Vick literally embodies the vicious
pit bull, thereby reasserting the conjoined animalization and
racialization of the black man and the dog.

This also brings to mind the 2001 Diane Whipple case, in
which a young blonde woman was the victim of a fatal dog
attack, and, as a result, the guardians of the killer dogs were
indicted for second-degree murder and involuntary manslaugh-
ter. Diane Whipple was killed by two massive Perro de Presa
Canarios in the hallway of her apartment building. At the time
of the attack, the dogs were under the care of a couple living in
the same building as Whipple. The black male dog, named
Bane, was euthanized right after the attack since it allegedly
was the one responsible for the attack. The tan female dog,
Hera, whose role in the murder was uncertain, was euthanized
a year later. As Carla Freccero points out, the media coverage of
the Whipple case indicates that the interracial story superseded
the interspecies dimension in this tragedy. The media fed on, as
Freccero explains, "the 'myth of the black rapist,' at the scene of
the murder, uncannily accented by the ultra-whiteness of
Whipple in photographs and the ultra-blackness of Bane that
circulated in the press."[29] Race is vicariously guilty of the animal misdeed in a slavery-old logic in which the violence inflicted
on a white woman by a black subject (in this case, a dog) is

compelled to be read within a sexual paradigm the same way that the rabid dog once was the "black beast," being then both human and animal.

Identifying the attack dog with the race of the owner (Vick) or seeing physiological connections between a black murderous dog and a black rapist (Bane) is symptomatic of some unresolved issues in America, undoubtedly dating back to slavery. During slavery, bloodhounds imported from Cuba or Germany were trained to pursue escaping slaves in both the Caribbean and the American South. The white slaveholder trained the dogs to become ferocious only when in contact with blacks. Although not much is known about the early presence of dogs in the Americas, in *A History of Dogs in the Early Americas*, Marion Schwartz explains that Columbus found small, nonbarking dogs that he used as company and, occasionally, as food, during his trip to the Antilles. The indigenous Tainos called them *Aons*.[30] Pre-Conquest *Aons* are an extinct species today, but intra- and post-Conquest dogs are still very much part of the Americas. Large mastiffs were first imported to the Americas in order to track recalcitrant Indians and later on, during slavery, to chase runaway slaves. This type of canine importation was prevalent in the history of the Spanish, French, and English colonies in the Americas, from the Conquest to the plantation era. Based on what we know now, it is safe to say that large dogs were imported to the Americas as "mean dogs," and their role was to discipline the "bad," disobedient black.

The phenomenon of the dog trained to threaten the putative reprobate slave is what I call interspecies "becoming against." "Becoming against" adapts Weaver's "becoming in kind" to a black diasporic context. The preposition "against" polysemously takes into account the extreme closeness and the belligerent nature of the antagonistic physical contact, while "becoming" suggests that the dog and the slave are mutually shaped by the construction of themselves as inherently violent beings. In his novel *L'esclave vieil homme et le molosse* (*The Old Slave Man and the Mastiff*),[31] Martinican author Patrick Chamoiseau depicts an old slave being chased by the master's dog in a way that resonates with Jacques Derrida's "The Animal That Therefore I Am (More to Follow)." By *following after* the slave, as Chamoiseau shows, the dog has initiated a mutual slave-dog becoming in which the two species *take after* each other. Derrida highlights two paths of interspecies *becoming* inherent to the polysemous genre, "Being-after-it in the sense of the hunt, training, or taming, or being-after-it in the sense of a succession or inheritance?"[32] In this mutual "becoming against," one can no longer determine which—the dog or the slave—seems bad in reaction to the other's perceived badness. Without the old slave's disobedience, the dog would not have needed to enact his "bad dog" persona and chase him, just as without the presence of the dog on the plantation, the old slave—as Chamoiseau tells us—may not have felt the need to run away.

Moreover, it is important to note that the slave and the dog are legally bound in the history of the Americas in a way that can also explain their putative conjoined "viciousness." While, for centuries, American and British laws have been unable to determine whether the dog should be deemed "ownable," the status of the slave as personal property has been subject to little legal doubt in the Americas. In the 1685 Code Noir (French Black Code) and in the various southern slave codes, the slave is understood to be *meuble*, or chattel, a movable property like a piece of furniture. Chattel is etymologically related to cattle, both suggesting the idea of capital (from the Latin *capitalis*). As Dayan explains,[33] there have been various legal attempts since the sixteenth century to determine the ownability of the dog, due to the widely shared assumption that the canine species is a hybrid entity, neither completely domesticated, like cattle, nor fully wild, like wolves. Dayan shows that the uncategorizable status of the dog is based on the perceived tension between the dog's trainable nature and its propensity toward viciousness. In light of this, laws asserting that slaves were fully ownable stand in jarring contrast to the slave's equally imperfect ownable pre-disposition: "property," yet human. But as much as law has put the dog's potential relapse into ferociousness at the heart of the debate over its property status, the slave's property status law has only been viable provided that the slave's untamable predis-position be ignored. Like a symptom of the rabid imaginary, however, this disavowal of tamability was bound to resurface in what we may call the "Cudjoe Effect."

Cujo, the title of Lewis Teague's 1983 horror film, is the name of the St. Bernard protagonist who, after having been bitten by a vampire bat, develops rabies, eats its owner alive, and turns against everybody in hydrophobic madness. But Cudjoe, as Paul Youngquist, the author of "The Cujo Effect,"[34] is quick to remind us, is also the name of one of the most celebrated Maroon leaders in the history of Jamaica, a fearless rebel boast-ing numerous bloody victories against the British. Cudjoe's attacks were so successful that the British rulers of the island resigned themselves to signing a Peace Treaty in 1739, granting freedom to Cudjoe and his men in return for the guarantee that the Maroons would no longer attack them or harbor new run-away slaves. The "Cudjoe" and "Cujo" amalgam hints at a retal-iative or "ferocious" propensity in the slave and the dog alike, the former being motivated by a claim to humanity and the latter by a wolfish instinct. But it seems as though the Ameri-can collective consciousness retrospectively carries the burden of having ignored the slave's natural right for retaliation in its belated, modern assumption of kinship between dogs and blacks. The cyno-racial assimilation is a trend that did not end with the abolition of slavery. Ironically enough, American civil rights rioters in the 1960s were subject to terrorization and attack by police dogs, just as during slavery blacks were hunted by dogs. As Youngquist so eloquently puts it, "bloodhounds are biological weapons deployed against an enemy whose animal ferocity justifies a response in kind."[35] What brings the dog, the slave, and the civil rights protestor together under the same "ferocious" stigma is their common claim to freedom, perceived ultimately as a feral claim.

Cognizant of the controversial nature of the cyno-racial comparison, Dayan points out that it is the "language [that] makes possible such a compulsion for analogy."[36] The author's tour de force is putting side by side two legal cases in *The Law Is a White Dog* that bring out a striking resonance between laws as applied to blacks and laws as applied to dogs. Both are related to the question of (restricted) movement in America. The well-known 1896 racial case *Plessy v. Ferguson* and the 1897 dog case *Sentell v. New Orleans and Carrollton Railroad Company* reached the Supreme Court one year apart, and, in both instances, Justice Henry Brown was left with the task of determining what kind of restrictions of movement should be imposed on blacks and on dogs. In *Sentell v. New Orleans*, Sentell sought compensation for the loss of property after an electric car negligently killed his pregnant dog that, standing on the tracks, could not move fast enough to avoid the approaching car. When the case reached the Supreme Court, Justice Brown ruled against Sentell, stating that in Louisiana, dogs are conditional property, meaning that the dog must be registered and wear a collar in order to be legally considered personal property (Sentell's dog was not registered). But, more importantly, Justice Brown argued that "property in dogs is of an imperfect or qualified nature and that they stand, as it were, between animals *ferae naturae*, in which, until killed or subdued, there is no property, and domestic animals, in which the right of property is perfect and complete."[37] Because they are "more or less subject to attacks of hydrophobic madness," Justice Brown posits, dogs are unreliable and must be monitored and restrained. For Justice Brown, there is no place for a dog on the loose since the dog is by nature a loose cannon.

As for *Plessy v. Ferguson*, Justice Brown's decision to withhold the constitutionality of racial segregation in public facilities under the "separate but equal" doctrine also guaranteed that no blacks be free to roam. The 2012 Quentin Tarantino movie, *Django Unchained*, can be seen as the enactment of Justice Brown's negative fantasy, though adjusted to the slavery era. The movie shows the extreme goriness resulting from a black unchained and on the loose. "It's a nigger on a horse," an astounded man tells a woman as Django enters the city on a horse alongside the German bounty hunter Dr. King Schultz, played by actor Christoph Waltz. The town freezes at the sight of a black man openly using the horse not for labor on the plantation but for his free mobility. "They ain't never seen no black man on a horse," Django explains to Schultz, who feigns surprise at having attracted so much attention. Through Frederick Douglass's memoir, one can observe that the horse and the slave were often treated in a comparable fashion on the plantation. In Douglass's case, however, his master Colonel Lloyd had a horse fetish and cared more about the welfare of his horses than his slaves. Stories of slaves mounting horses freely and galloping about are scarce, with the exception of Toussaint Louverture, former slave and the leader of the slave rebellion in Saint-Domingue, who was an exceptionally gifted horse rider. The sight of blacks on horseback brings to mind the hysterical fear of black freedom of movement, black horseback riders like Louverture being associated with dominance, rebellion, and disobedience. From slaves being on foot while masters are on horses to free men of color being required to dismount their horses when reaching the gates of cities to runaway slaves stealing horses,[38] the act of riding a horse has always been a symbol of freedom determined by race in America. Interestingly enough, in the post–Civil War era, the majority of jockeys and horse trainers were black, a racial landscape that would change again rapidly in the twentieth century, Jimmy Winkfield being the last black jockey to win a Kentucky Derby, in 1902.[39] Horses, like dogs (and dog fighting in the South), are important racial markers highlighting the fluctuating nature of the categorizations of race, humanness, and animality.

Django Unchained includes a scene in which a runaway slave is torn into pieces by a dog while Django is forced to watch. The scene is only a prelude to Django's own near fate. At the end of the movie, Django is hung upside down and barely escapes having his genitals cut off with a knife. Knives and dog fangs are both weapons used as punitive and preventive methods against the black's will to violate his or her restriction of movement. As punishment, it was not uncommon in the American South and the Caribbean to mutilate runaway slaves upon their capture. The Code Noir and Jamaican Black Code recommended cutting body parts—ears, sometimes a foot or a hand—to deter slaves from further escape attempts. Mutilation—performed by either a human or canine—was thought to remind the slave that she or he was, unlike the dog, a farm animal. But more importantly, like a farm animal, the slave is defined not only by his or her chattel status but also by his or her edibility. When the slave runs away, the master needs to symbolically reassert his domination through a ritualized act of flesh cutting. Derrida argues that, in contrast to women, men are predominantly carnivorous in order to assert their masculine domination, a claim that Carol J. Adams also makes in *The Sexual Politics of Meat*. Derrida names this patriarchal carnivorism "carnophallogocentrism," while Adams uses the expression "the male prerogative for meat."[40] Using dogs or mutilation to punish the slave also enacts a strategy of domination through a rhetoric of edibility, though here it is a racially invested kind of "carnophallogocentrism." Through the dog or the knife, the master enacts the symbolic act of eating the slave.

The Saint-Domingue slave rebellion brings the fantasy of edibility and blackness to its literal manifestation.[41] In 1801, First Consul of France Napoleon Bonaparte sent an expedition to the French colony of Saint-Domingue led by his brother-in-law Captain General Victoire Leclerc to crush Toussaint Louverture's control over the island. Louverture was a politician and military leader who had successfully led the 1791 slave rebellion that culminated in the abolition of slavery in 1794. In 1801, as the newly self-proclaimed leader for life of Saint-Domingue, Louverture drafted an autonomist constitution and conveyed it to Napoleon, which prompted the latter to send a military expedition to the colony with the intention of reinstating French authority. Napoleon secretly hoped to have Governor Louverture and his officers deported to France, but he wanted to reach that goal through negotiations and ruse rather than military violence. His plan failed, as Louverture and his officers refused to surrender to Leclerc and instead launched a counterattack against the French troops. By 1803, Leclerc had lost a large quantity of troops in combat; many were also decimated by the yellow fever that would eventually take Leclerc's life as well. Before dying, Leclerc had sent bloodhounds to

Cuba, intending to use them as live weapons against the black rebels. It was not a novel idea. As stated earlier, dogs had been deployed against the Tainos and were also being used to track runaway slaves in the colonies. Receiving inadequate—if any— troops from France, Leclerc was in desperate need of a new strategy. Leclerc hoped that the dogs would be better suited than soldiers to the type of guerilla resistance that Louverture and his acolyte Jean-Jacques Dessalines were using against French troops since the French Army was more accustomed to frontal and open conventional warfare. Leclerc, in a letter to Napoleon, complains about the guerilla resistance of the black troops. He writes, "This is a war of Arabs. We have hardly passed through when the blacks occupy the neighboring woods and cut our communication."[42] As nineteenth-century historian Antoine Métral puts it, "Everywhere this ground hid enemies, in a wood, behind a boulder; liberty gave birth to them."[43] Leclerc hoped that the dogs would be able to traverse difficult terrains, mountains, and tropical woods, ultimately flushing out the rebels into the open field for combat.

Leclerc died before his request materialized, but his successor General Donatien de Rochambeau persevered and had two hundred dogs from Cuba sent over to Saint-Domingue in three different ships.[44] When the first ship, *Napoléon,* reached Saint-Domingue with one hundred dogs onboard, the white French and some mulattoes greeted the dogs with much enthusiasm and acclaim as the animals were paraded through the streets. In his 1847 account of the event, Thomas Madiou describes the dogs as follows: "Those animals, who, by their height and size, looked like wolves, were covered with silk ribbons, their heads were adorned with feathers with extremely bright colors."[45] Even though the dogs were initially meant only to track black troops, Rochambeau eventually thought that they could also serve the purpose of eating them. Marcus Rainsford details the type of training that the dogs underwent in order to acquire a taste for black flesh. First, the dogs would be kept in kennels and introduced to a dummy resembling a black; blood and entrails would be inserted into the dummy. The next steps were as follows:

> This was exhibited before an upper part of the cage, and the food occasionally exposed as a temptation, which attracted the attention of the dogs to it as a source of the food they wanted. This was repeated often, so that the animals with redoubled ferocity struggled against their confinement while in proportion to their impatience the figure was brought nearer, though yet out of their reach, and their food decreased, till, at the last extremity of desperation, the keeper resigned the figure, well charged with the nauseous food before described, to their wishes. While they gorged themselves with the dreadful meat, he and his colleagues caressed and encouraged them.[46]

In March 1801, Rochambeau very publically and theatrically tested his plan on a black victim. A wooden arena was built for the occasion. The black victim was brought to the arena and attached to a pole while the dogs had been starved for days. Some historical accounts (they do not all concur) claim that the black victim was a loyal servant of General Pierre Boyer, Rochambeau's chief of staff. When the dogs were launched into the arena, with cheers from the spectators, the dogs did not immediately understand their carnivorous mission. Madiou depicts the scene:

> The executioners launch the dogs in the circus, with applause from the spectators. The animals sniff the wretched; but they

step back; the executioners incite them in vain. Then General Boyer, who was sitting next to Rochambeau, rushes to the arena, and pierces through the stomach of the wretched with his saber. At the sight of blood gushing out, he is seized by a ferocious excitement and drags one of the beasts against the victim. Suddenly, all the dogs run to the patient whose heart-wrenching screams double the applause; they devour the entrails, and do not give up their prey before feeling satiated with the quivering flesh.[47]

Once accustomed to craving human blood, the dogs' first battlefield would be the nearby Tortue Island (Tortuga), where a slave rebellion had been raging for weeks in spite of the French's tireless efforts to crush it. According to historian Philippe R. Girard, dogs were allegedly fed with black flesh during this mission. Girard mentions one French general who remembers that, "written orders asked that the dogs should each be fed half a Negro a day."[48] Girard also quotes Rochambeau informing the French commanding the mission that "no rations or expenses are budgeted for feeding the dogs; you should give them Blacks to eat."[49] Feeding the dogs with black human beings would have served the dual purpose of reducing the costs of dog maintenance while also using blacks as bait for attacks. Yet one had to make sure that the black-eating dogs would not be in contact with black allies, including the black troops who had remained loyal to the French, for fear of the dogs becoming accustomed to blacks as companions instead of as meals. But it proved impossible. Girard quotes a veteran of the expedition arguing that the dogs "did not have the intended effect in La Tortue, because they were used in front of black and mulatto detachments and had become familiarized with their odor,"[50] assuming that there is such a thing as a "black odor" to which dogs can grow accustomed. Indeed, historians hardly seem to question the axiom of a "black odor" in their accounts. Did the mission fail because dogs grew accustomed to the so-called black odor while in close proximity with the blacks who had remained loyal to Napoleon, or did the starving dogs simply fail their mission because they could not share the fallacious white fantasy of a distinct black odor? In fact, Girard mentions dogs turning against French troops and devouring the wounded in Tortue Island. Bell also depicts, on the island of Saint-Domingue, packs of dogs eating the corpses of the French troops that could not be retrieved from the field after black cultivators took "a large number of French and slew them with bayonets."[51] Despite the carnivorous plans of the French in Saint-Domingue, the human body became bait for indiscriminative hungry dogs.

During the Leclerc/Rochambeau expedition, dogs were intended to figure by proxy as an extension of the French body in combat with blacks. To compensate for French limitations, canines were supposed to go where the French could not, in more ways than one. In addition to infiltrating the dense, wild woods and tracking the rebels, dogs were also meant to devour blacks, an action taboo to the French, but deeply desired. Parading the dogs in the streets of The Cap and inviting a white audience to revel in the scene of dogs devouring a black attached to a pole have been described as scare tactics against blacks. As Sara E. Johnson explains in her article regarding the spectacle of dogs eating blacks in the Americas, "beyond being used to hunt down black rebels, dogs were employed to publicly consume them in a staged performance of white supremacy and domination. Much as with lynching, these public performances were designed as a stark warning, and the presence of community observers provided an air of legitimacy to the terror."[52] Scaring blacks was not the only justification for this public display of canine ferocity; the French had some stake in the brutality as well. The scene in the arena with the black victim attached to a pole carries all the elements of a totemic initiation ceremony. As Sigmund Freud explains in *Totem and Taboo*, sacrifice at the altar was always a public ceremony in primitive societies.[53] The execution by canine, reminiscent of Roman spectacles, contrasts with the so-called civilized culture of the eighteenth-century French Enlightenment. And yet, French reluctance to give blacks from the colonies the same *liberté* and *égalité* that they had just claimed for themselves during the French Revolution shows that the Enlightened superego—to pursue Freud's logic—was not viable in the Americas. The French were quick to unleash their primitive id once they felt trapped in this tortuous no-man's-land.

Paradoxically, the public nature of the sacrificial ceremony could have been a way to keep the breach of taboo from being exposed since all who participated willingly in the sacrifice would have to bear the responsibility for it. As in all initiations, the participants, together and united as brothers, shared the secrecy of the cannibalistic act. Sacrificing blacks to dogs reveals a need for whites to bond amongst themselves and to dissociate themselves from blacks as a distinct group. The canine presence led the white Napoleonic troops to physically separate themselves from black allies under the pretense of preventing dogs from getting familiarized with the black odor. Did the French fear the impact of creolization, a kind of racial contamination that the *grands blancs*, the white planters, were said to have experienced on the island?[54] Was turning blacks into edible flesh a way to assert, by contrast, their superior place in the food chain in an environment that decimated them and threatened their Napoleonic superiority? As Freud says, "the *killing of a sacrificial animal* originally belonged to those acts which were *forbidden to the individual and were only justified if the whole kin assumed the responsibility.*"[55] Rochambeau organized the sacrificial scene in the name of the collective French in order to assert their superiority and distinguish themselves as more human than food.

In "Le jeu le plus dangereux," Grégoire Chamayou recounts another side of the expedition. As a result of losing ground against the rebels, the French soldiers lost access to their food supply. The French troops resorted to eating the dogs that had been previously fed with the flesh of the blacks. Here, the simulation is no longer simulation; the French did eat their black counterparts, in the digested and assimilated form—dog meat. It is ironic that during the Middle Passage, Africans who were captured by slave merchants feared that the purpose of their deportation was to become a source of food for whites. As former slave and African-born (in a region now known as Nigeria) Olaudah Equiano says in his autobiography, once he was captured and on a slave ship, "I did not know what to think of these white people; I very much feared they would kill and eat me."[56] The same is true for white explorers in the New World; they also feared being eaten by the Other. On an exploratory trip to the islands, Christopher Columbus recounts speaking to local Indians (presumably through a translator) and misunderstanding the word "Carib" for "cannibal." Columbus had been told—with no existing proof—that the Carib tribe was cannibalistic. The semantic amalgam is pregnant with meaning, as it establishes the New World as a stage of primal encounters between blacks and whites and demonstrates the preexisting fear of cannibalism in the mind of the explorer and the captive alike. In *The Sexual Politics of Meat*, Adams explains that the Carib/cannibal semantic incident in the discovery of the New World was used as justification to colonize the Caribs since they were presumably man-eating savages: "derived from the Spaniards' mispronunciation of the name of the people of the Caribbean, it linked these people of color with the act."[57] Adams's phrasing, conveniently ambivalent, casts doubt as to what the "act" refers. Are "these people of color" linked to the "act" as eaters or eaten? If one looks at colonization as a sublimated form of cannibalism, it leads to the conclusion that colonizers have been cannibals from the moment they set foot in the New World. This theory also explains why colonizers misunderstood the word Carib for cannibal; they projected their own violation of the taboo upon those whom they intended to violate.[58] In *Powers of Horror*, Julia Kristeva writes, "How can I be without border? That elsewhere that I imagine beyond the present, or that I hallucinate so that I might, in a present time, speak to you, conceive of you—it is now here, jetted, abjected, into 'my' world."[59] The abjection of cannibalism has no borders, it is the Other becoming the "I," the feared and abject being born into "my" world. What I reject and spill out is already in me, the black is inside of me before I even attempt to reject him. Thus, by eating the Other, through a canine proxy, the French troops enacted their abjection for the black Other at the same time that they revealed their own compulsion for cannibalizing this Other, fearing that the Other was *always already* inside of them, a part of their own dreaded self.

What historiography tends to overlook about the Leclerc/ Rochambeau expedition is that the canine mission was bound to fail because dogs, unlike humans, are indiscriminate in their interaction with human races. Youngquist comments on the rationale behind the use of dogs in the Leclerc/Rochambeau expedition: "These ferocious bloodhounds scent, see, secure the difference that distinguishes their keepers from the animalized men they hunt. It's a difference of race."[60] Instead of visually distinguishing skin pigmentation, the dogs were believed to be able to scent racial difference in blood. The fallacy of race as a biologically traceable marker of difference, like the linguistic confusion of "cannibal" and "Carib," is a misunderstanding with far-reaching repercussions. The French expedition overlooked the fact that in using dogs to track slaves, the real cue had been the individual scent, and not blood; the dogs had to be given an object carrying the smell of the fugitive in order to track the slave down. As Rainsford explains, the dogs would get "a scent of the object" and "immediately hunt him down."[61] This explains why, in slave narratives, one sees that not all dogs react to all slaves the same way. For example, in *Twelve Years a Slave*, the author, (former slave) Solomon Northup, explains that a fellow slave named Celeste was not afraid of the master's dogs because, as he writes, "it is a fact, which I have never been able to explain, that there are those whose tracks the hounds will absolutely refuse to follow. Celeste was one of them."[62] Northup also explains in his narrative that he had a technique to make dogs fear him in order to prepare dogs for a potential future escape:

> The time might come, perhaps, when I should be running through the swamps again. I concluded, in that chase, to be prepared for Epps' dogs, should they pursue me. He possessed several, one of which was a notorious slave-hunter, and the most fierce and savage of his breed. While out hunting the coon or the opossum, I never allowed an opportunity to escape, when alone, of whipping them severely. In this manner I succeeded at length in subduing them completely. They feared me, obeying my voice at once when others had no control over them whatever. Had they followed and overtaken me, I doubt not they would have shrank from attacking me.[63]

This shows that, even if they were not masters to the dogs, slaves were fully aware that dogs were made to track and attack individuals rather than a whole race. At some point in history, the idea of the *scent* of a given slave must have metonymically slipped into the assumption of a generic "black odor." Not only were the French under the impression that dogs were able to scent a "black odor" but they also believed that canines could spot a "black form" since the dogs from the Saint-Domingue expedition were trained for aggression using "a figure roughly formed as a negro in wicker work."[64]

That dogs could be conditioned to independently detect black bodies, without any cues from their keepers, is the proposal that French writer Romain Gary undertook to explore in a creative form in his 1970 novel *Chien Blanc* (*White Dog*). The fictional story, set in 1968, is written in the form of a memoir. In the narrative, the "real" Gary adopts a lost German shepherd found on the steps of his Beverly Hills house. At first, the dog seems very good-natured. The animal is kind to Gary, his wife (the American actress Jean Seberg), their son, and their acquaintances. Gary calls him Batka. But soon enough, Gary realizes that, when in presence of black people, the nice German shepherd becomes a vicious animal. The animal is what is called in the South a "white dog," a dog trained by the police to attack black people. Gary seeks help from Jack Carruther, the owner of a zoo, in the hope that Jack could train the dog to become indiscriminately nice to people. Jack is convinced, however, that a "vitiated" older dog cannot change its ways and that euthanasia is the only other option.[65] Gary refuses to give up on the dog and agrees to leave Batka in the hands of Keys, a black employee at the zoo who has a vague resemblance to Malcolm X. Keys tells Gary, "In the old days, they trained them [the dogs] to track down runaway slaves. Things have changed. We don't run away any more. Now those dogs are used against us by scared cops."[66] Readers learn at the end of the book that Keys has secretly trained the dog to redirect his aggression toward whites. The story ends with Gary being viciously bitten by what used to be a "white dog." In this book, the French author envisions a place where animals are the last site of racial discrimination. The hypodescent rule in America, in which a white-looking man is still deemed black if one drop of black blood runs in his veins, is threatened by the growing impact of miscegenation. Gary's axiom allows us to envision the possibility of animals replacing humans in the process of racial discrimination. The axiom posits that, through atavism and by way of conditioning, dogs could one day respond to race as a biological phenomenon even though humans, by then, will no longer be able to track the racial difference.

Gary wrote this story as he was going through a divorce from American actress Jean Seberg. In addition to being an actress, Seberg was very involved in civil rights activism. Gary resented his wife's blind and naïve ways of being involved in this movement. The civil rights movement, Black Panthers activism, and the Detroit riots that followed the assassination of Martin Luther King Jr. are the backdrop of *White Dog*. In the book, Gary pits two fallacies against each other: on the one hand, the white, Hollywood, egocentric, guilty conscience about the condition of blacks in America, and on the other, black pseudo-activist racketeers using that guilty conscience for their personal gain. Gary concludes that it is the dishonesty on both sides that has overshadowed the work of genuine activists. Everybody in the story is a flat character meant to typify a group. Marlon Brando is the narcissistic demagogue who uses the black cause as a platform for self-promotion; Jean Seberg is the naïve actress financially and emotionally ruined by black con-men passing for activists; Keys is the enigmatic Malcolm X figure plotting retaliation against the whites; and Gary is the French cynic and disillusioned writer ready for his own revolution, the French social revolution of May 1968. Somehow, the dog alone must carry the responsibility of figuring out who is the real target in this smoke and mirrors group of impostors.

In 1982, American film director and master of low-budget movies Sam Fuller made a cinematic adaptation of Gary's book. Fuller's movie, also titled *White Dog*, features gory, B-move-style scenes of an immaculate white dog drenched in the blood of random blacks crossing his path. Due to the sensitive subject matter, Paramount Studios brought two consultants on the movie set, one of them the president of the Beverly Hills-Hollywood chapter of the NAACP. Upon its release, and after only a few screenings in France and the United States, Paramount Studios chose to shelve the movie, deemed too controversial for an American audience, although Criterion Collection released the movie again in 2008. The summer of 1982 was a sensitive time for *White Dog*, and its release reignited the still fresh collective trauma of the Atlanta murders (1979–81); during this two-year timeframe a serial killer slaughtered more than two dozen African Americans, mainly children, in Atlanta.[67] At the same time, people feared that the "white dog" would inspire the Ku Klux Klan, then very much alive, and the film also revived the recent, controversial, and very public use of police dogs against black protesters in Birmingham, Alabama, in 1963. In sum, *White Dog* was a graphic materialization of what American consciousness was not yet ready to face, namely a deeply ingrained history of violence—and even more troublesome "canine" violence—against its black population.

Due to the anagramic title and the canine topic, *White Dog* has been said to be the inspiration for *White God*, the 2014 drama by Hungarian director Kornél Mundruczó.[68] *White God*, set in Budapest, tells the story of a young girl who lost her mixed-breed dog, named Hagen, after her angry father abandoned him on a highway. A man captures Hagen on the street and trains him for dog fighting, training that requires extreme physical and emotional abuse. Hagen eventually escapes and leads a pack of 250 street dogs on a bloody revenge tour. Under Hagen's command, the canine army devours Hagen's abusers. In this film, Mundruczó intended the rejected mongrels to speak to the predicament of minorities in Hungary. But even though *White God* tackles the topic of minorities using a canine trope, the movie is very different from *White Dog*. In the Hungarian movie, the streets of Budapest are deserted, as humans fear for their lives and surrender to the ferocious power of the dogs. The intelligent animals take control of humans in a manner reminiscent of French author Pierre Boulle's 1968 *La planète des singes* (*The Planet of the Apes*).[69] In *White Dog*, on the other hand, the filmmaker purposely includes no sense of agency in the animal. The dog is a ticking bomb, a machine preprogrammed by humans. Mundruczó has said that *White God* is not inspired by Fuller's movie, but rather by South African J. M. Coetzee's novel *Disgrace*.[70] The kinship between the two movies is visible, mostly in *White God*'s mercy killing scene, when the female animal shelter employee euthanizes the canine protagonist while caressing him and reminding him that he will be better off far from harm. This pathos-laden moment mirrors one of the most poignant scenes in the novel *Disgrace*, where, during the last minute of the dog's life, the animal welfare employee Bev gives the dog her "fullest attention, stroking it, talking to it, easing its passage."[71] Both Mundruczó and Coetzee demonstrate how compassion for animals builds humanity. In both stories, the angry father who had fallen from professional grace redeems himself by learning to love, aided by the example of his daughter's relationship to dogs.

As it were, *Disgrace*, like *White Dog*, uses the canine trope as a catalyst to address stories about racism. The dogs in Coetzee's novel, who live with the daughter, Lucy, on a farm in Eastern Cape, embody the racial complexities of postapartheid South Africa; the animals are killed over a racially invested question of territories. In the movie *White Dog*, Fuller explains how the dog is conducive to stories about racism. Because they are reputedly color-blind, dogs see the world in black and white. As Keys explains in the film, "dogs live in a black-and-white world. Unlike ours, they live it visually and not racially." Keys exposing his bare hand in order to teach the dog how to dissociate black skin from the feeling of aggression demonstrates a literal form of racial discourse. The dog becomes the essentialist voice of racism in the film. The animal returns to basics, ultimately presenting race as a natural component rather than a social construct. As the camera zooms in on Keys's hand, the blackness of his skin is magnified on screen. Viewers hold their breath in anticipation of the white fangs tearing the flesh apart, the zooming camera already mutilating his body like a raw piece of meat. In keeping with the style of a low-budget pulp movie, many shots in Fuller's *White Dog* show the immaculate white fur exaggeratedly covered with the blood of black individuals. The blood is part of the animal as much as the animal is the source of the blood.

In his famous statement that animals are not only good to eat but also good to think with (*bon à penser*),[72] Claude Lévi-Strauss seeks to convey the idea that, more than a source of sustenance, animals have been instrumental in defining human essence. And, by turning the black into a fellow animal in various historical settings, the dog has been instrumental in defining human essence as white privilege. Granted, the animalization of the black is not the responsibility of the dog, the latter being only an accessory to racial discrimination. Yet, one may still question the liability of the dog in this bloody mess. As an accessory, should the dog share the burden of the crime? Haraway argues that dogs should not be scapegoats for other themes. Haraway writes, "dogs are not surrogates for theory; they are not here to think with. They are here to live with."[73] Haraway's comment about animals not being here "to think with" is a direct reference to Lévi-Strauss. Haraway follows a trend in animal studies, beginning with Derrida's "The Animal That Therefore I Am," which aims to distance abstraction and metaphors, in the hope of nearing the real and physical animal. As Derrida says to his audience at the Cerisy lecture series, "The cat I am talking about is a real cat, truly, believe me, *a little cat*. It is not the figure of a cat." [74] One of the most recent attempts to reach the nonfigurative animal comes from the field of performing arts, which Una Chaudhuri refers to as "interspecies performance" or "interspecies theatricality." Chaudhuri uses the expression "animal acts" to indicate that this form of performance is about the real animal. As the author explains, "animal acts" go beyond just talking about and addressing the idea of the animal. Like J. L. Austin's speech act theory, animal acts present animals who *do* things; they do not only *represent* things. Interspecies performance may be as close as one can get to the real animal when speaking about animals.[75] Emphasizing the real animal in animal discourses has strong repercussions. On the one hand, it protects the animal from its *animot* (Derrida) predicament, in which the animal is seen only as a word (in French, *mot*). It also helps account for animal sentience since it emphasizes the physicality of the animal. But on the other hand, it calls for animal responsibility. The animal can no longer be treated as a mere projection of the human mind. In that respect, the animal is not a signifier. The real animal is beyond abstraction and has a *real* impact on human life. The bite is real.

Treating the "white dog" as merely the result of a process of white transference would deny what Derrida, Haraway, and Chaudhuri have claimed for the animal: namely, individuality, physicality, and realness. In Gary's *White Dog*, the bite-inflicted pain is real, not a proxy. By incorporating the dog into his own flesh at the end of the story, Gary literally em-bodies the position of the victim and thus transcends the fixed image of the attack dog as only a symbolic tool used to address racism. French author Hélène Cixous achieved a similar effect in her autobiographical short story, entitled "Stigmates" (Stigmata). In it, Cixous connects the bite to a context of stigmatization (hence the title) and talks about a real bite, from a real dog. In her memoir, Cixous returns to Algeria, where she spent her Jewish *Pied-Noir* childhood. After the death of her father, a well-respected doctor, her family suddenly becomes exposed to the locals' wrath. On a daily basis, Arabs throw stones at her family, who live in a fenced house. Their dog, Fips, is the firsthand recipient of the abuse: he tirelessly jumps on the fence, barking, gnarling, and foaming at the mouth, in defense of himself and his human family members. The constant physical and emotional abuse inflicted by the neighbors makes Fips turn against Cixous:

> It seemed like from this bite I would die because it did not let me go, it went deeper and deeper, it was penetrating it planted all its teeth in my heart. The teeth lasted. As we cried we entered into mad eternity. The dog could not let me go. . . . We could not move, we were buckled down to the pain, frightened. The Earth was knocked over to the side.[76]

The description of the bite gives substance to Fips. By inflicting excruciating pain, the dog asserts his—extremely and painfully—real existence. The inflicted pain is a sort of counter-*Sprachlosigkeit* (counter-speechlessness of the animal), to paraphrase Heidegger.[77] The animal is not endowed with language but, instead, can convey his message through physical interpellation. The bite speaks to you, literally and figuratively. Basic physical pain cannot be ignored; it is universal and relatable. In the inflicted pain lies the animal's responsibility and agency. The bite is an expression of the animal's voice, no matter how conditioned the biting act itself has been. For his own good, the dog needs to take responsibility for the pain endured through the bite. As the bitten victim screams in agony, the sublimated voice of the dog (through the bite) speaks to externalize his own victimization. Inflicting pain may be the only way for the dog to testify to his own abuse through the scream of the victim proxy; his only way to claim his real existence and his own sentience, not just as an animal sensitive to physical pain but as a dog sensitive to moral and emotional abuse. As a victim of daily aggression, the dog transfers his abuse to Cixous, hence the religiously inspired title "Stigmata." Fips stands in the line of fire, gradually internalizing the inadequacy of being a Jewish *Pied-Noir* in colonial Algeria. "Am I Jewish?" the dog seems—according to Cixous—to question. The bite is, in that sense, the most primal way to make this Other literally part of oneself. Both the Jew and the dog become one in their painful condition of being reduced to a generic identity ("a Jew," "a dog"), a word (*mot*), and a stigma.

Even though, as Haraway argues, dogs "are not here to think with. They are here to live with," canines are enmeshed in a racialized human discourse by way of *living with* humans. What I call "afro-dog" is the result of the animal and his human victim merging through the bite in a mutual becoming against. Making the Jew or the black an edible commodity is the sine qua non condition of turning the human into an animal, and the dog takes an active part in this agenda. The Cartesian tradition deems reason the main differentiator of humans and animals, but, as the utilitarian philosopher Jeremy Bentham argues, the newborn or the mentally challenged individual may show very little—if any—trace of reasoning, and yet no one would ever question that they are human. Instead, human consciousness, namely feeling human as opposed to animal, could very well be based on the taboo of cannibalism. Humans eat animals but do not let other animals eat them, including the human animal. However, the dog bite, a somewhat mundane occurrence in our society, is a constant reminder that the human being is also an animal that can be eaten. As Coetzee writes in *Diary of a Bad Year*, "animal flesh looks much the same as human flesh (why should it not?)."[78] The bite brings to mind the fetishistic nature of human nonedibility; it shows that human consciousness is based on the disavowal of being an (edible) animal. The dog, in this sense, is essential to the process of dehumanization since it is the only animal that dares bite humans on a regular basis, thereby constantly confirming the fragile nature of the human condition.

The fact that the dog bite not only dehumanizes but also, and more importantly, commodifies the human victim by making her fit for animal consumption, is all the more poignant in a racial context. In such a context, species dominates race, making blackness an indicator of species rather than a racial marker. The white fantasy of cannibalism is a mental strategy that demotes the black race to the level of animal species, thus banning the so-called black race from human taxonomy. The dog bite, when orchestrated by the white against the black, is a racially driven kind of cannibalism that uses fangs as a means of transference. In his essay "Going to Meet the Man," James Baldwin gives a vivid picture of this cannibalistic fantasy, as the author revisits the question of edibility and blackness within the context of the civil rights era. The essay is supposedly based on Bull Connor, the commissioner of public safety responsible for the use of fire hoses and police dogs against the civil rights protestors in 1963 in Birmingham, Alabama. In the story, Baldwin portrays Jesse, who has been said to be based on a young Connor: a bitter deputy sheriff with an atavistic hate for, mixed with uncontrolled sexual attraction to, black people. "They were like animals, they were no better than animals, what could be done with people like that?" Jesse thinks.[79] Baldwin revisits the primal scene likely responsible for the deputy sheriff's complex relation to the black body. In his childhood, Jesse witnessed the lynching of a black man in the company of his parents. Jesse initially thought that he was going to a picnic, but, instead of a pleasant family outing, the young boy became the witness of a violent mobbing and castration scene:

> The man with the knife took the nigger's privates in his hand, one hand, still smiling, as though he were weighing them. In the cradle of the one white hand, the nigger's privates seemed as remote as meat being weighed in the scales; but seemed heavier, too, much heavier, and Jesse felt his scrotum tighten; and huge, huge, much bigger that his father's, flaccid, hairless, the largest thing he had ever seen till then, and the blackest. . . . Then the crowd rushed forward, tearing at the body with their hands, with knives, with rocks, with stones, howling and cursing.[80]

After the show came to an end, Jesse's father said, "Well, I told you, . . . you wasn't never going to forget *this* picnic."[81] The lynching scene is very similar to the real-life event that Rochambeau organized in the Saint-Domingue arena. Publically turning the black into flesh is a spectacle for which each attendee must take responsibility. But here, unlike with Rochambeau, the mob grabs their cannibalistic fantasy literally by the balls and does not hide behind a canine proxy. Baldwin superimposes this lynching scene, published in 1965, with the canine repression of black rioters led by Bull Connor in Birmingham, Alabama, two years prior. In Baldwin's superimposition, the dog bite and the white's knife become one.

Because black edibility is a fantasy that has been sublimated through the use of dogs in lieu of cannibalistic humans, the idea of dogs attacking black people has become a haunting and unresolved image in the collective memory of both slavery and the civil rights movement. As a result, dog fangs digging into black flesh is a recurrent image that first appeared in testimonials and then became deeply ingrained in popular culture. In a public address in 1846, the former slave Frederick Douglass recounts the role of dogs on plantations:

> If any man has a doubt upon it, I have here the "testimony of a thousand witnesses," which I can give at any length, all going to prove the truth of my statement. The blood-hound is regularly trained in the United States, and advertisements are to be found in the southern papers of the Union, from persons advertising themselves as blood-hound trainers, and offering to hunt down slaves at fifteen dollars a piece, recommending their hounds as the fleetest in the neighborhood, never known to fail.[82]

Dogs hunting down unsubmissive, colonized blacks is also a recurrent image in *A Short Account of the Destruction of the Indies* by the sixteenth-century Dominican friar and defender of the

Indians Bartolomé de Las Casas. Las Casas's report about the inhumane treatment of Indians in the early stages of the Spanish colonization of the West Indies includes a significant number of incidents involving Native Americans thrown to dogs, torn into pieces, and eaten alive. The most distressing incident involves a mother and her infant, chased by wild dogs:

> One woman, who was indisposed at the time and so not able to make good her escape, determined that the dogs should not tear her to pieces as they had done her neighbours and, taking a rope, and tying her one-year-old child to her leg, hanged herself from a beam. Yet she was not in time to prevent the dogs from ripping the infant to pieces, even though a friar did arrive and baptize the infant before it died.[83]

Some historians have questioned whether Las Casas exaggerated and even fabricated stories concerning the inhumane treatment of Indians by Spanish colonists in the early Americas. What is of value here is not the accuracy of his reports of dog-related events but rather the repetitive and almost compulsive pattern of his stories of dogs eating humans. Historians have no doubt that dogs chasing and tearing Indians and black slaves to pieces is factual in the history of the Americas, but the extent of this hunting practice is unknown. As the Haitian historian Michel-Rolph Trouillot says, history is a hegemonic power "that makes some narratives possible and silences others."[84] As early as 1542, Las Casas, as the voice of historiographical hegemonic power, chose to make the image of dogs chasing and eating slaves a predominant emblem of atrocity. In his account of colonization in the Americas, dogs took center stage.

Karen Delise addresses the discrepancy between the documentation of bloodhounds chasing runaway slaves and the real extent of these incidents. As she says, "How much of these images [dogs chasing slaves] was fiction and how much was based on truth was a highly contentious topic even in the era in which these incidents were reportedly taking place."[85] Delise uses the case of Harriet Beecher Stowe's novel *Uncle Tom's Cabin* as an example of potential factual inflation. Stowe's novel holds a famous passage of a runaway slave, Eliza, crossing the frozen Ohio River with her baby in her arms while being chased by a slave merchant and two slaves. Sam, one of the slaves, recounts the scene: "I saw her, with my own eyes, a crossin' on the floatin' ice. She crossed most 'markably; it was n't no less nor a miracle; and I saw a man help her up the 'Hio side, and then she was lost in the dusk."[86] In the recounted scene, there is no mention of chasing dogs. In a preceding scene, the slave merchant did mention the possibility of using dogs to catch Eliza but quickly retracted as he realized that "the dogs might damage the gal" and, as he explains, "for this sort that's to be sold for their looks, that ar won't answer."[87] In other words, the book explicitly states that deploying an arsenal of dogs was impractical since physical scarring or crippling would negatively impact a slave's market value and thus would constitute a blow to the owner's investment, already at stake with an escapee. The Eliza scene is redolent of Las Casas's aforementioned depiction; both scenes draw on the extreme pathos of mothers and infants devoured by wild dogs, though in Eliza's case the use of dogs is only a threat. As Delise explains, by 1880, all productions of *Uncle Tom's Cabin* included a pack of ferocious-looking dogs for dramatic effect. The recurrence of the canine prop gave people the impression that Stowe's book was filled with dogs chasing slaves when, in reality, the Eliza scene is the only incident in the book involving the *idea* of chasing dogs. Although the frequency of stories of dogs devouring slaves may be exaggerated, the question remains as to the motivation behind and the effect of those potential inflations.

Delise's main claim in *The Pit Bull Placebo* is that the dog—from the bloodhound during slavery, to the German shepherd after World War II, and to the pit bull since the 1980s—has always been the victim of a fearmongering ideological apparatus that fabricates "vicious breeds." Since Vicki Hearne's *Bandit*, many have written in defense of the pit bull. But because the reputation of the dog is indissociable from the human presence accompanying it, the rehabilitation of the dog is incomplete without addressing the stigmatization of its human companion. The human and the dog compound each other's constructed viciousness in a mutual "becoming against," the consequence of which is that the image of the vicious dog pursuing the slave has become part of a collective consciousness that compulsively recreates—and each time reignites—the association of the vicious dog with truant blacks. The best example of this, since *Uncle Tom's Cabin*, is Andy Warhol's 1964 "race riots" series. In 1963, the photographer Charles Moore took pictures of the German shepherd police dogs attacking black rioters in Birmingham, Alabama. Moore sold the photographs to *Life* magazine, a weekly photojournalism magazine widely read by the white middle-class in the 1960s. The photographs were part of a larger project that also included pictures of children being fire-hosed by the police. Moore titled his photo essay, "They Fight a Fire That Won't Go Out." The *Life* issue containing Moore's riot photographs was released May 17, 1963. In the summer of the same year, for a 1964 exhibit in Paris at the Galerie Ileana Sonnabend, Warhol made paintings of Moore's dog pictures. Like his rendition of Marilyn Monroe's portrait or the Campbell's soup cans, Warhol's paintings faithfully reproduced the original photograph but with a significant added difference in colors, tones, and hues. One painting, titled *Race Riot*, consists of four panels reproducing the same photograph showing a German shepherd tearing the trousers of a black man who is attempting to walk away. The same year, Warhol made additional paintings based on Moore's dog photographs for the Wadsworth Atheneum Museum in Hartford, Connecticut. One of those pictures presents a pixilated and highly contrasted version of the photograph of two police dogs attacking a protester. The interesting fact about the "race riots" series is that, like the many renditions of Stowe's *Uncle Tom's Cabin*, the vicious dog attacking the black person is the only image that Warhol chose to single out in Moore's otherwise multithematic photo essay.

In "Warhol Paints History, or Race in America," Anne M. Wagner makes a distinction between Warhol's *Marilyn Diptych* (1962) and *Campbell's Soup Cans* (1962) and *Race Riot*, arguing that the first two represent a system of commodification where the image of the soup or Marilyn are only referential, while the latter has more depth. "Marilyn 'means' the entertainment industry the way a mirror in a seventeenth-century Dutch painting 'means' vanity,"[88] Wagner explains. The same is true for the can of soup that signifies mass consumption. Wagner argues that *Race Riot* does not follow Warhol's usual signature because the painting does not iconize pop culture with an empty and purely referential picture. Instead, the reproduction of Moore's photograph tells a true story anchored in a temporal framework and populated with real characters. For Wagner, the unique nature of *Race Riot* lies in the temporality of the original photograph (the narrative) and the topic, racism. As she says, "because race is a different kind of historical object than the 'commodity' or 'celebrity' or 'mass production[,]' [i]t cannot be allegorized. The mirror may be vanity; Marilyn, Hollywood;

but what are black and white men? They emerge as scripted narrative, no matter what Warhol does."[89] However, what Wagner has not taken into account in her assessment of *Race Riot* is the presence of police dogs. The dog is centered in the photograph, and the other actors—the black protestor and the police—are perceived only in terms of their relationship to the dog. What is being iconized in this narrative is the central position of the dog. As a result, the dog alone comes to "mean" racism, no need for the actualization of the black and white men.

Likewise, artist James Drake felt the urge to literalize the allegorical nature of the dogs in his 1991 life-size, interactive iron sculpture. Located in Ingram Park, in Birmingham, Alabama, Drake's hyperreal sculpture is composed of two walls forming a hallway, with snarling dogs on both sides, jumping out of the walls. When crossing the hallway, visitors are made to relive the African American experience of Connor's dog attacks. In the sculpture, the white and black men are nowhere to be found. Drake's sculpture brings the image to a point: The dogs are the last ones standing in a narrative of racial tension between black and white men. Dogs attacking blacks haunts American collective consciousness, as it reveals a compulsion to represent (in the sense of making present again) this particular image of racially invested aggression. As mentioned earlier, photographs of dogs attacking protesters were only one portion of Moore's *Life* photo essay. Warhol's choice to select only the dog attacks is pregnant with meaning. Warhol singled them out because the dogs in those pictures have the same effect as the Eliza scene in *Uncle Tom's Cabin*. The image of dogs attacking blacks haunts American collective consciousness, as it reveals a compulsion, in the history of the black diaspora of the Americas, to represent (make present again) this image. The dog attacking the black is the ultimate simulacrum, in Fredric

Jameson's sense of photorealism,[90] where a painting copies a photograph, itself a copy of reality. The iterative logic in photo-realism, doubled with Warhol's repetition (four panels of the same picture in *Race Riot*), empties the subject of its content and gives it an allegorical surface, similar to the *Marilyn Diptych* or *Campbell's Soup Cans*. In other words, one no longer needs to see the black man next to the dog's fangs or the white man holding the leash in order to know that the attack dog *means* racism.

Jean-Claude Baker, in his biography of Josephine Baker, finds a correlation between black freedom of movement and "fierce" dog ownership. Talking about Josephine Baker, his adoptive mother, in the Paris of the mid-1920s, the author writes:

> For a long time, I couldn't figure out why every black entertainer who came to Europe bought dogs. Fierce dogs, like wolves. Jose-phine had one so savage she had to board it in a kennel. Finally, a friend put it all together. "During slavery, blacks were hunted with dogs. In Europe, they could take a kind of revenge, they could own the same kinds of dogs that chased their ancestors." So there they were in little hotel rooms and they had these huge dogs.[91]

James Baldwin also, in the midst of civil rights unrest, experi-mented with dog ownership while living in Turkey, adopting a dog named Andromache. There is no doubt that black emanci-pation could have resulted in a rise of any type of ownership by blacks, including dog ownership. As Weaver explains, in the nineteenth and twentieth centuries, dog fighting was mainly a practice in the white rural South, but in the 1980s, "there was an influx of urban men of color into breeding circles."[92] The 1980s saw the first black, emancipated generation after the Civil Rights Act of 1964 as potentially the first generation of blacks able to move freely around in the company of dogs. That being said, unlike Jean-Claude Baker's suggestion, the association of blacks and attack dogs in American collective consciousness is not based on an actual "revenge" of the black race but rather on the white fantasy of black revenge. Blacks do not own "fierce" dogs as retribution for slavery, but those who do own dogs are unconsciously perceived as vengeful due to the lingering fantasy of the "Cudjoe Effect." Blacks owning big dogs enacts Justice Brown's double fear: the black and the dog together on the loose, without the white master. We may dare to make a symbolic connection between the 2005 pit bull ordinance and black men losing their lives (Michael Brown, Tamir Rice, Trayvon Martin, or Eric Garner) at the hands of policemen and self-appointed authority figures: Blacks jaywalking or roaming the streets are like "dangerous" dogs on the loose, threatening and to be contained at all costs.

3

THE COMMENSAL DOG IN
A CREOLE CONTEXT

From the Arabic *kish* ("scram" or "get out of here"), *kishta* is a Hebrew and Yiddish interjection commonly used to drive away unwanted animals. *Kishta*, with a dismissive gesture of the hand, is the equivalent of the English "shoo" or "hoosh," from the German *husch*, meaning "(move) quick." In Israel, where feral cats feeding off trash and living among humans abound, *kishta* comes in handy. *Kishta*, and its equivalent in other languages, is the only cross-species word in the vocative case exclusively designed to speak not *about* the animal (Derrida's *animot*), but *to* the animal.[1] A childhood friend, a French Israeli citizen who spent every summer in Israel, once told me that animals are naturally more responsive to the sound *kishta* than to the onomatopoeia *pschtt*, the French equivalent. In other words, *kishta*, as a Hebrew-Arabic hybrid word semantically tainted with the history of the Wandering Jew in close contact with the Arab, is best fitted to speak to what is made not to feel at home, be it the Jew, the Arab, or the feral animal.

Coincidentally, there is another Arabic word that combines the idea of man speaking to animals with not feeling at home.

In "Dog Words," Moroccan writer Abdelfattah Kilito explains that *mustanbith* in Arabic refers to "he who imitates the dog's bark."[2] When a Bedouin loses his way in the desert at night, the lost man imitates the dog's bark in hope that a village is nearby. Since feral dogs usually live in the vicinity of a human habitat in Morocco, the animals will bark back to the nomad, thereby indicating the direction of the closest village. Dogs are hospitable to the one who imitates their bark by kindly showing the putative canine wanderer the way home. Yet, Kilito portrays the cynanthropic nomad not as a man grateful for help but rather as a mischievous trickster, a "hypocritical simulator."[3] Kilito elaborates, "the barker is certainly very clever, and dogs are easily tricked. . . . Thus he kills two birds with one stone: he finds people and cheats dogs."[4] However, the joke is on the nomad since, soon enough, the prodigal son realizes that the village is not home. Even worse, no longer able to use his human language, his bark becomes his only means of communicating with the villagers. The moral of the story is that, according to Kilito, foreignness is always defined in terms of animality. "When two languages meet, one of them is necessarily linked to animality. Speak like me or you are considered an animal."[5]

Edgar Allan Poe draws a similar comparison in "The Murders in the Rue Morgue," a short story in which a detective, Monsieur C. Auguste Dupin, is assigned a double murder case with no visual witnesses. There are several aural witnesses, however, who indicate that the unfamiliar sounds that they heard during the time of the killing came from a foreign (human) language. This presumed foreign language, as Dupin eventually discovers, is that of an orangutan, the perpetrator of the double murder. Poe's story completes Kilito's axiom: the animal is a foreigner to man, just as much as the foreigner is an animal to the native. The human-animal divide is put into question when the unfamiliar intrudes upon the familiar in a sort of *unheimlich* (uncanny) effect. But the most interesting aspect of Kilito's story lies in the man's self-assuredness when it comes to the verisimilitude of his imitative dog bark. How can the nomad be so sure that he tricked the dog? Did the dog naively think that it was responding to a dog's bark? Or, instead, did the dog bark back to the human imitation of a canine bark only because the animal sensed the desperation of the human wanderer who resorted to animal language to seek help? Either way, there is something dismissive, just like *kishta*, in the man's attempts to talk directly *to* the feral animal—an animal that like himself, as a Jew or as a Bedouin, is nomadic and diasporic.

MACH AND THE CREOLE DOG

Antilleans from Guadeloupe, Martinique, and Haiti (formerly Saint-Domingue), also part of a diasporic history due to the slave trade, have a very particular relationship to feral dogs. "Va-t-en chien des nuits va-t-en" (Go away, night dog, go away), Martinican poet Aimé Césaire cries as the night approaches. The poet, like the Jew and the Bedouin, addresses the animal directly but with a human-to-human language, *va-t-en* meaning "go away." The atavistic memory of the bloodhound of slavery chasing the maroon and devouring the wretch alive upon capture is haunting. As described in detail in chapter 2, the French Rochambeau expedition in Saint-Domingue (1801), which was led against the leader of the slave rebellion, Toussaint Louverture, notoriously used slaves as dog food. The image of fangs biting into the flesh of the slave takes over Césaire's poem entitled "Des crocs" (Fangs),[6] while the archipelagic memory of the slaves' blood dripping from the dog's mouth makes an unwelcome nocturnal visit to the poet again in the poem "Va-t-en chien des nuits." The poet's cry for the dog to go away is a plea to release the Caribbean people from the fangs of history:

> Go away, night dog, go away
> Unexpected and major in my temples
> You hold between your fangs
> A bloody flesh that I recognize all too well[7]

And yet, the dog will not go away. The animal is an accessory to the black's dehumanization. As Martinican Frantz Fanon would later say in *Peau noire, masques blancs* (*Black Skin, White Masks*), "le nègre est une bête" (the Negro is an animal).[8] As it roams the streets of Port-au-Prince, Fort-de-France, and Pointe-à-Pitre, the now stray animal has stopped running, even though the canine still follows the black man. The race (as in racial and as in "chase") of the black man with the dog has made the two one. Credited with being one of the first important voices to draw attention to the sense of alienation inherent to black consciousness in America, W. E. B. Du Bois writes, "it is a peculiar sensation, this double-consciousness, this sense of always looking at one's self through the eyes of the others. . . . One ever feels his two-ness,—an American, a Negro; two souls, two thoughts, two unreconciled strivings."[9] But there exists another form of double-consciousness for the universal black folk, which is the feeling of being both human and animal in the eyes of the others.

Martinican novelist Patrick Chamoiseau, in *L'esclave vieil homme et le molosse* (The old slave and the hound), offers a parable of the primal mutual becoming between the dog and the slave. The author recounts the story of a cynanthropic metamorphosis, one that can explain the modern-day relationship between the black man and the stray dog in the Caribbean. A big, threatening dog is launched against an old slave, who abruptly decides to run away from the plantation. Chamoiseau follows the chase of the dog after the slave as the latter feels the pressure of the canine swift steps tailgating him, which forces the maroon to "get in tune with its gallop . . . adjusting his steps to the thump of its paws."[10] The story focuses on the theme of momentum through speed. "Cette vitesse," "this speed," is the premise of the interspecies entanglement, this monumental event about to take place in Martinique. Gilles Deleuze and Félix Guattari talk about the "zone of proximity."[11] When two particles, or rather two "fugitive speeds," synchronously near each other, this proximity "makes it impossible to say where the boundary between the human and animal lies,"[12] Deleuze and Guattari explain. Their mutual becoming feeds on the motion rather than the destination.[13] The zone of proximity in Chamoiseau's text is the interstice, a place where the dog and the slave are neither in the plantation nor completely outside, a liminal state that is still inherent to the Martinican condition in the postcolonial era. At the end of Chamoiseau's book, the dog catches up with the slave. This is when the completion of the mutual becoming takes place. As Deleuze and Guattari say, a mutual becoming is not a simile, words are not "'like' animals," but they literally bark, being properly "linguistic dogs, insects, and mice."[14] In other words, a mutual becoming is not the *mustanbith* of a "hypocritical simulator," as Kilito would phrase it, but rather a true becoming-dog similar to what the Bedouin nomad underwent.[15] Say that the village dog in Kilito's "Dog Words" was not fooled by the cynanthropic trick. By barking back, the dog incidentally misled the nomad into the wrong, non-native village, and thus turned the simulator into a real barker. By barking back, the village dog created the zone of proximity that completed the nomad's becoming. *Mustanbith* is therefore not merely about the nomad but also about the clever dog, the one that responds to the human call for canine metamorphosis.

At the end of Chamoiseau's story, after a physically draining pursuit, the dog finally finds its moribund human prey. The mutual metamorphosis that has been gaining momentum during the whole chase/story reaches a climax when the dog gets near the fugitive slave and realizes that the old man has already embarked on a new becoming by becoming stone. The dog feels drawn to the histories, peoples, and collective sufferings engraved in the human stone. Soon after, the animal starts licking the old man become stone. The dog licks the slave as an animal licks its wound, as if the pain that the dog saw in the man/stone were its own pain. Chamoiseau proceeds to demonstrate that there is no more distinction to be made between dog and man in their conjoined diaspora. Dog and slave follow the same Creole fate in a mutual becoming.

In *Silencing the Past*, Haitian Michel-Rolph Trouillot argues that historiographical omissions are an important part of a narrative apparatus that shapes "History" as we know it. The oft-overlooked historical fact that not only humans but also animals were transplanted to the New World during the slave trade is part of this historiographical silencing process. The nonhuman animal diaspora does not fit into the design of Creole poetics for the very reason that Caribbean writers seek to make the interspecies entanglement inherent to the history of slavery go away, *va-t-en*. Martinican Edouard Glissant's body of work is well known for what comes across as a Creole continuation of *A Thousand Plateaus*. The author has used the image of the rhizome and chaos as the main fodder for his poetics. Chaos is an important concept in *A Thousand Plateaus* that Glissant has creolized and turned into a poetics of *chaos-monde* (world chaos),

where all cultures connect in a poetics of relation.[16] Also, starting in the 1990s, the mangrove has been a recurrent Caribbean
metaphor.[17] Deleuze and Guattari's rhizome is like the Caribbean mangrove, a multidirectional root that is not singular and
vertical like the root symbolizing the Western teleological system
of thought, but rather heterogeneous and diverse like Creole
culture. Guadeloupean Maryse Condé's novel *Traversée de la
mangrove* (*Crossing the Mangrove*) solidified the identification of
the Creole culture with the mangrove rhizome.[18] While most
Francophone Caribbean writers have capitalized on the scientific
image of chaos and the vegetal paradigm of the rhizome, the animal paradigm—an important, if not the most important, part of
Deleuze and Guattari's theory—has been left almost untouched.
The "animal rhizome," as Deleuze and Guattari call it, however,
is the central part of their theory.[19] The pack, the molecular
animal approach of looking at the history of the Caribbean, is
unavoidable in the haunting presence of the stray dogs that
live in close proximity to the Caribbean population. In the last
pages of Chamoiseau's canine tale, the dog finally returns to
the master, but it is now a changed and defiant animal. The
slave has died, but not before leaving his legacy to the dog. The
returning dog is ready to shed its European status as a watchdog and become a modern (pack) stray dog, a nomadic animal
with no master. The pack animal is what is left of the slave;
this animal-human combination is the embodiment of modern Creoleness.[20]

In the French Antilles, the stray dog is commonly referred to
as *chien créole*, "Creole dog." Créole comes from the Spanish *criollo*, which is itself derived from the Latin *creare*, meaning "to
produce," "to raise." *Créole* signifies being born and raised in the
master's house, in contrast to the *bossale*, who was born in Africa
and later brought to the Americas as a slave.[21] *Créole* can denote

both black and white, with either a master or slave lineage, but it also refers to all that was initially imported to the Caribbean and has become endemic to the land through a process of acclimation. The Creole designation includes therefore also plants and animals. Martinican Creole linguist Jean Bernabé is interested in how, and in what order, the word *créole* became all encompassing. Bernabé argues that *créole* first referred to whites, and then it extended to other categories—blacks, plants, and animals, which leads him to wonder what came after whites in the Creole designation. Did blacks or did nonhumans (plants and animals) come right after whites in the evolution of the Creole designation? Since the word *créole* now applies indiscriminately to whites, blacks, and nonhumans, it is legitimate to question in what chronological order this indiscrimination, or as Bernabé calls it "undifferentiation," occurred. As the linguist says, "we do not know whether this undifferentiation in the opposition of human (white) traits versus nonhuman (animal and vegetal) is anterior, simultaneous, or posterior to the undifferentiation from the opposition between white and black traits."[22] What we do know is that, according to Bernabé, blacks and nonhumans *together* came after whites in the chronology of Creole taxonomy. Dogs and blacks, therefore share not only a historical but also a semantic bond.

In terms of diaspora, we also know that the master's dog came after the slave in terms of re-territorialization since dogs were historically shipped to the French islands from the Black Forest and Cuba with the purpose of chasing fugitive slaves. Since the master's dog came to the French Caribbean after the slave, we can say that, genealogically speaking, the dog comes after the black in what Deleuze and Guattari call the "line of escape."[23] Yet, as Jacques Derrida shows in *The Animal That Therefore I Am*, the chronological "coming after" does not necessarily imply that the animal metamorphically *takes after* what it follows.[24] On the contrary, the followed can *take after* the follower, which is the case in Chamoiseau's parable since the slave takes after the dog in his becoming-dog.

Because of the conjoined diasporic history of the dog-slave impacted by the slave trade, the black Antillean cannot relate to the *chien créole* with a dismissive *kishta* or hypocritical *mustan-bith*. The black is too aware that the dog will go nowhere without its human counterpart. Césaire uses the French *va-t-en*, the human-to-human language of colonization, to address the dog, thereby indicating that the dog-black bond is like French itself, a matter of irreversible postcolonial assimilation. Césaire could have also used *mach*, the Creole human-to-animal language equivalent to "shoo," but by staying clear of the Creole language, the Martinican poet indirectly suggests that *va-t-en* addresses the slave master's dog embodied in the nocturnal canine ghost, and not the nomadic Creole dog with no master following his daytime activities. *Mach* carries a different connotation than *va-t-en*. This Creole injunction, meant to address only dogs, comes from the French *marcher*, which means "to walk." Because *marcher* denotes a slow and gentle movement, the *mach* injunction does not sound as dismissive as "shoo" (from the German "[move] quick") or *kishta*.[25] By saying *mach* to the dog, the Creole subject acknowledges his inextricable bond with this animal. The stray canine is not asked to move quickly or go away but only to walk, potentially alongside man in a Creole synchronous pace. Unlike the fast-paced "shoo" or *kishta*, *mach* carries the Caribbean indolence of Jeanne Duval, Charles Baudelaire's Haitian-born mistress, who walks with the pace of a baby elephant.[26] *Mach* is to some extent a request only for space, it does not ask the dog to go away since the *chien créole* will tag along anyway.

COMMENSALISM

Aimé Césaire was a poet and one of the forefathers of Negritude, the pan-Africanist movement that he founded in the 1930s alongside the French Guyanese Léon-Gontran Damas and the Senegalese Léopold Sédar Senghor. A lesser-known fact is that the poet was also a politician. As a member of the French National Assembly, Césaire was instrumental in the decision to turn the French colonies Martinique, Guadeloupe, and French Guyana into French overseas departments. Unlike Saint-Domingue (now Haiti), which declared its independence from France in 1804, the three colonies chose the path of departmentalization in 1946, thus turning the then colonial subjects into French citizens. This citizenship has been a double-edged sword. On the one hand, the departmentalization has allowed the ex-colonies to maintain some semblance of political and economical stability, unlike what has happened in Haiti. But on the other hand, again unlike Haiti, the French overseas departments have lost all sense of accountability, as they have fallen into a state of what some have called apathy. The famous line from Césaire's 1947 epic poem, *Cahier d'un retour au pays natal* (*Notebook of a Return to the Native Land*), "Haiti where Negritude stood on its feet for the first time and declared to believe in its humanity,"[27] retrospectively sheds a bitter light on Césaire's own island, which seems never to have stood on its feet since its departmentalization. Should we then also conclude that, unlike Haiti, Martinique has yet to claim its humanity?

All things considered, the question should not be whether the once chattel slave should claim his humanity since the concept of humanity is itself tainted with a racio-anthropocentric perspective that is part of a Western hegemonic and imperialistic design responsible for slavery and colonialism in the first place. The question is rather how the once chattel slave may be in the best position to challenge this so-called humanity and, in the process, redefine the meaning of existence beyond the human-animal divide. In other words, how can the black diasporic subject in the Americas abide by a different set of identifications, one that would not consist of refuting a putative inhumanity, since such refutation validates the accepted (racially invested) norm of humanity's signification? Refuting black inhumanity perpetuates the archaic colonial psychology that conditions the black to look at himself (even by way of opposition) through the white's anthropocentric eyes. To think outside of this Sartrean racial *pour-autrui* (for-the-other) dynamic, one must reject the human-animal divide.[28]

Borrowing from a gender paradigm, we could say that the Martinican case allows for the contemplation of a species-fluid (as in "gender-fluid") condition, a nonbinary identity with the privilege of unspecification and the possibility to reposition one's "human" identity at will. Race fluidity is not unlike racial passing, a condition that consists of shifting away from the fixed racial denomination assigned at birth, with the exception that racial fluidity allows for a chameleonic to-and-fro between races rather than a single and permanent shift from one race to the other. Anatole Broyard (1920–1990), a celebrated literary critic for the *New York Times*, was one of the most striking cases of racial passing in the twentieth century in America.[29] He was born black and passed for white his entire adult life in order to fit in the white, East Coast, country club lifestyle he had chosen for himself. Broyard was, as the saying goes in Louisiana, a *blanc passé*. But his parents, who moved from New Orleans to New York City during the Great Depression and who, on a daily basis, had to pass for white at work and revert back to their self-defined blackness at home, introduced the premise of racial fluidity, an undetermined racial composition that can flow either way. Today though, racial fluidity is more prone to flaunt an undeclared racial identity as a resistance against, rather than a way to fit into, the obsolete hypodescent (one-drop) rule.

Species fluidity differs from racial fluidity in that the former does not involve a question of biological hybridity. Human-animal fluidity is evidently not biological but cultural, it is a way to live by different standards and in synchronicity with animal living. In Guadeloupe, the *mofwazé* is a person who, through *quimboiserie* (Guadeloupean voodoo), can shed his or her human skin and become a dog. Colin Dayan, in *The Law Is a White Dog*, mentions a similar Haitian voodoo tradition of canine metamorphosis.[30] However, cynanthropy is not only about black magic in the Antilles. Taking the "skin of the dog" (the title of a chapter by Dayan) is also about sharing the life of the dog, in what we may refer to as "commensalism." In ecological terminology, commensalism, from the Latin *cum* (with) and *mensa* (table), meaning "sharing a table," refers to a class of relationship in which two organisms mutually benefit without adversely affecting each other. Like a bird of prey feeding off a carcass after a lion ate the best part of the dead animal, the commensal animal has a perfect understanding of how to share life with its provider. The hunter does not seem to mind the so-called parasite since both animals agree on the sequence of eating. Commensalism, therefore, is an organic philosophy built on the act of sharing without being owed and taking without being indebted since the various organisms share a table with no strings attached.

Sue Donaldson and Will Kymlicka have raised a important point about the nature of animal rights advocacy. As they argue, "reflecting the prevalent domestic/wild dichotomy, animal rights (AR) theorists have talked about domesticated animals who need to be liberated from humans and about wild animals who need to be left alone to get on with their lives, but have not talked about liminal animals."[31] Liminal animals are those who are neither domesticated nor feral, like urban deer, pigeons, or squirrels. They live within human communities, and, even though they are not threatening or dangerous to humans, they are often considered to be pests and are shooed away because they destroy yards, defecate on urban architecture, or allegedly spread diseases. In "How Pigeons Became Rats," Colin Jerolmack documents the passive-aggressive relationship that humans entertain toward New York City pigeons.[32] The urban pigeon is a liminal animal against which the city launched a nonfeeding campaign with the goal of suppressing this putative avian nuisance in the city. The campaign, which gained momentum in the 1990s, was meant to incite New Yorkers to shift their perception of the bird, from an animal that people enjoyed feeding with leftover bread in public parks to a "rat with wings." Even in cases when they are not vermin who spread diseases, liminal animals are usually perceived as nuisances because, unlike domesticated animals, they do not return the favor of being fed by humans. They only take but do not partake in a pet relationship with humans. As Donna Haraway points out in *The Companion Species Manifesto*, being a pet is "a demanding job for a dog, requiring self-control and canine emotional and cognitive skills matching those of good working dogs."[33] Pets work for their food; they are docile, loving, and loyal animals at a cost. Likewise, cattle pay the price for being fed by humans; they eventually become human food and, in this manner, repay their debt of having been fed. Some humans are not wont to feed animals without expecting something in return. If there is no return, the animal is then vermin, a pest, and a parasite, which explains the clear correlation in the New

York City campaign between the feeding ban and framing pigeons as vermin. Jerolmack mentions many articles that portray pigeons as rats, vermin, and nuisances, but the most interesting is a 1959 article that draws a direct connection between feeding and unrequited attention. This article, Jerolmack writes, "while recognizing that 'feeding the pigeons is universal' and that pigeons offer 'city folk a chance to participate in outdoor life,' called pigeons 'free-loaders at heart' and 'panhandlers.'"[34]

A commensal relationship does not carry the negative sense of freeloading since in commensalism there is truly nothing to owe. "Free" in freeloading means costing nothing, but it does not mean not owing anything. In that sense, the "free" in freeloading is not freedom. In *Humiliation*, William Ian Miller draws a parallel between the hidden rules of social exchanges in archaic honor-based societies and the social value of kind gestures in our modern society. The Saga Icelanders have a complex system of honor in which the reception of gifts can be a burden since they require a return of significant value. In archaic societies, nice gestures and gifts are never debt-free, and the same is true in our society. As the author says, "like them, we rarely fail to keep a mental accounting of who owes what to whom."[35] Our society still carries remnants of a potlatch economy in which kind gestures and gift giving have strings attached. The human-animal bond in Creole culture does not resemble a potlatch economy but, rather, is based on a commensal relationship in which the Creole dog is like the bird of prey that feeds on the carcass but does not owe the lion retribution for its subsistence. In Mexico, according to Eliza Ruiz-Izaguirre, village dogs are referred to as *criollo* (Creole) and, more commonly, *callejero* (street dog). As the author argues, village dogs are not strays. They live with humans and are fed by them but with no particular strings attached: "Villagers only take advantage of dog's natural abilities as agricultural aids, . . . dogs can leave when they wish, or decide not to work at all."[36] Whether the *callejero* chooses to work or not, the animal will not starve to death. The dog's means of subsistence is not dependent on the work or the companionship it can provide to man. Likewise, the Creole dog, like the *callejero*, is not necessarily perceived as parasitic since, in Creole culture, there are no clear expectations of return for living alongside humans and being fed by them. In some cases, the *chien créole* may choose a specific human household, and, in others, it may be itinerant and feed from human refuse.

THE BEAST IN CALIBAN

Commensalism is not only proper to the Creole dog or Creole animal. Human relationships in Creole culture may also be said to abide by a sort of commensal ideology. American novelist Truman Capote gives a very interesting rendition of Creole culture in a piece entitled "Music for Chameleons." The American narrator is in Martinique and pays a visit to an old, aristocratic lady who lives in Fort-de-France and also owns an apartment in Paris. The narrator sits on the terrace in this elegant and open house, which reminds him of old New Orleans architecture. Creole houses (*maisons créoles*) are known for their airy and open space with no windowpanes, and with large terraces as the epicenter of the house. As the old lady speaks to her guest, green chameleons chase each other on the terrace. One sits at the lady's feet, as a house cat or dog would do. The old lady tells her guest that chameleons like music, a statement that the American seems to doubt. The Martinican goes to her piano and plays a tune: "Soon the music lovers assemble, chameleons scarlet, green, lavender—an audience that, lined up on the floor of the terra-cotta terrace, resembles a written arrangement of musical notes. A Mozartian mosaic."[37] After this event, the American guest understands that the nature of human-animal relations is different in Martinique, not only because of the open space concept of the Creole house that blurs all distinctions between the outside and the inside of a domestic space, but also because the old lady and the chameleons seem to be sharing the house as pets and pet owners do, yet not quite so. When done playing, the lady invites the chameleons to retreat by stamping her foot, making the chameleons "scatter like sparks from an exploding star."[38] The foot stamping is like the *mach* Creole injunction, it asks the commensal animal to give man some space but not necessarily to go away.

In this short story, Capote not only gives a glimpse of the Creole understanding of proximity and distance between humans and animals in Creole culture, he also draws an important parallel between the animal and the human way of life in a Creole context. The guest will soon realize that, in Martinique, human subjects act very much like their liminal animal counterparts. The old lady tells her American guest that Martinicans rely on France for subsistence: "The price of everything is double what it should be, because everything has to be imported," the lady explains. "If the troublemakers here got their way, and Martinique became independent of France, then that would be the close of it. Martinique could not exist without subsidy from France. We would simply perish."[39] The old lady blames the natives for Martinique's demise: "As I remarked, everything is imported. We don't even grow our own vegetables. The natives are too lackadaisical." As the lady concludes her statement, a hummingbird penetrates the terrace and, as Capote writes, "lackadaisically balances in the air." There is no doubt that

Capote, like Baudelaire describing his Creole mistress walking with the nonchalant pace of a baby elephant, hints at the stereotypical Creole temperament impacted by the tropical climate. But even more than that, the author draws a gentle connection between the lackadaisicalness of man and that of the animal. Both seem to move and live in synchronicity, effortlessly sucking the readily available nectar from the flower of life.

Not much has changed since 1979, the publication year of Capote's "Music for Chameleons." Due to massive subsidization from the *métropole* (the mainland), the overseas departments have developed a modern culture of economic tutelage, what Martinican author Edouard Glissant calls "habitudes d'irresponsabilité passive,"[40] "habits of passive irresponsibility." Martinican novelists Raphaël Confiant and Patrick Chamoiseau have condemned what they describe as a collective apathy exacerbated by a French regime of economic assistantship (*assistanat*) that the two authors see as responsible for an alarmingly low level of local production. Ironically enough, Confiant and Chamoiseau look back with nostalgia on the 1940s Vichy era, when General Pétain sent Admiral Robert to be the leader of the French occupation in Martinique.[41] For the two authors, Vichy in Martinique was a blessing in disguise. During the French occupation, the island was cut off from external support due to a blockade, which forced Martinicans to explore their capacity for resourcefulness and self-sufficiency. In that sense, the "Robert years" (the Creole Vichy years) brought out in Martinicans an aptitude for what Chamoiseau calls "débrouillardise du compère lapin des contes du soir,"[42] *débrouillardise* referring to ingenuity and the aptitude for making do, and *compère lapin des contes du soir* being a popular rabbit protagonist in Creole folk tales known for its cleverness. During the French occupation, people started seeing their piece of land as their only means of subsistence, which explains the explosion of *jardins créoles* (Creole gardens with local "native" produce) during those years.[43] The Martinican soil and soul never had as much value as during the "Robert years." In a way, the Martinican people became like their animal counterparts, the *chiens créoles*. The people had to make do with what was at their disposal, just as Creole dogs had to fend for themselves after breaking away from their masters in the postslavery era.

Assistanat, a French type of welfare and tutelage, has a negative taint and a slight colonial connotation when used in a Martinican context because it resonates with what Octave Mannoni calls the "dependence complex." In *Prospero and Caliban*, Mannoni presents the colonial and the colonized mind within a psychoanalytical framework that measures colonialism in terms of phylogenic development. Mannoni models the colonial after Prospero, Shakespeare's protagonist, who, in *The Tempest*, was stranded on a desert island. Mannoni argues that colonialism fosters a stage of permanent infantilism because the colonizer looks at colonialism as a projection of his childhood fantasy, namely a desert island populated by fantastical figures (the colonized). Likewise, Mannoni models the colonized after Caliban, the colonial native at the service of Prospero in *The Tempest*. Mannoni sees Caliban as the epitome of the colonized because instead of seeking independence, the colonized wants only a better master. For Mannoni, the colonized suffers from a dependence complex that makes him or her incapable of wanting to cut the umbilical cord with the master. As Mannoni writes, "Caliban, in his hopeless situation, begins plotting against Prospero—not to win his freedom, for he could not support freedom, but to have a new master whose 'foot-licker' he can become. . . . It would be hard to find a better example of the dependence complex in its pure state."[44]

Mannoni uses the example of the Malagasy people and his own experience interacting with them in Madagascar to posit that if a European makes a nice gesture toward a native, the latter will surprisingly not feel indebted to the European. On the contrary, in the native's scheme of things, it is the European who should feel indebted to the native. In this logic of reverse indebtedness, the native swears loyalty to the European: "You are now my white man. I shall always come to beg of you."[45] Mannoni sees this reverse loyalty as a form of infantilization. The colonized cannot break from the patriarchal figure due to a putative dependence complex fostered by the colonial context.

Mannoni's (dated) analysis is controversial in its presentation of the colonizer and the colonized as naturally predisposed to fulfill their respective positions in the slave-master dialectic, but what remains as food for thought in *Prospero and Caliban* is the reserve sense of indebtedness inherent to the putative "dependence complex." The colonized is perceived as ungrateful because he acts as if he owed nothing to the white man for the gift. And, according to Mannoni, the white man is made to feel indebted to the Malagasy because the white man should feel the responsibility of not failing in his initial promise (through the gift) to care for the native. But what Mannoni does not take into account in his study of colonial psychology is that the European is *always already* indebted to the native given his guest status in Madagascar. The native is the host (albeit against his will) and therefore expects the colonizer's gratitude and indebtedness. Showing surprise at the native's lack of gratitude upon receiving a gift or nice gesture only shows that the white man is oblivious to his initial debt. It is as if an uninvited and unwanted dinner guest undertakes to clear the table after dinner and expects accolades for his initiative while taking the dinner itself for granted. We could therefore argue that there is no reverse indebtedness, as Mannoni claims, but only a colonial due.

That being said, we could also look at this "dependence complex," or "Caliban complex," as Mannoni also calls it, as an illustration of commensal psychology, as opposed to a potlatch economy. Gratitude, debt, and the pressure to return the gesture are the premises of colonization, husbandry, and domestication. The chattel-slave, the cattle, and the animal are fed for the sake of profit through work, animal meat, or companionship. What seems like an attentive gesture of providing food and board inevitably comes with expectations of profitability. In *The Gift*, French sociologist Marcel Mauss addresses the potlatch (gift-giving) economy of exchange and reciprocity in so-called archaic societies. The rules of gift exchange are based on three obligations: giving, receiving, and repaying. As Mauss explains, "the prestige of an individual [is] closely bound up with expenditure, and with the duty of returning with interest gifts received in such a way that the creditor becomes the debtor."[46] As cynical as it may sound, and as Miller would argue, this ritualistic exchange presents the gift as what it truly is, a burden of debt with an obligation of return.

Mannoni's surprise at the Malagasy's ingratitude is symptomatic of the complacent nature of the colonial mind. On the basis of Jean de La Fontaine's seventeenth-century animal fables, Michel Serres in *The Parasite* gives a very interesting illustration of the colonial and imperialistic logic of gift giving. In La Fontaine's fable ("The Villager and the Serpent"), the serpent is stiff, cold, immobile, and exhausted, as it stretches out on the snow, probably in hibernation. A villager walks by and brings the serpent to his house, putting it next to the fire to warm up. The serpent awakes from its frozen slumber and asks the villager for further assistance in the form of food and board.

As Serres says, La Fontaine's snake "asked for but did not negotiate; it is not a question of price,"[47] and the villager's hospitality is understood to be free. However, the villager does not see it that way. As Serres writes, "as his action is meritorious—charity, my good sir—it is a question of rent. Rent, that is to say, a price for a space, a payment for territory. The one who is at home is my lessee."[48] The serpent, having warmed up next to the fire, has recovered its heated temperament and starts hissing and attacking. The villager feels duped and exclaims, "such is my pay."[49] The villager eventually cuts the serpent into three pieces, a mutilation intended to teach the serpent some manners. La Fontaine's fable warns against being charitable to the wrong person; one should beware of ungrateful people.

Serres's take on the story is different. La Fontaine tells the story through the eyes of the villager, while Serres chooses to retell the fable through the snake's eyes. As Serres argues, the villager should not expect to be paid for a charitable gesture. Here is Serres's interpretation:

> But he figures wrong. The serpent is not a lessee; he was not looking for a haven; he was answered without having been called. He was given an uncalled-for opinion. Someone made himself the serpent's benefactor, savior, and father. You are sleeping quite peacefully, and when you wake up, you find yourself in debt. You live with no other need, and suddenly, someone claims to have saved your country, protected your class, your interests, your family, and your table. And you have to pay him for that, and other such grimaces. Thus the serpent awakens obliged to another.[50]

Serres's take not only addresses how man treats nature, it also carries colonial undertones. The villager invades the space of the serpent, de-territorializes the reptile, and creates a meta-narrative of benevolence to tie this uprooting with a logic of repayment. There is a great similarity between the villager hosting the serpent and the white man's gesture toward the Malagasy. Both Mannoni and Serres tell a story of a recipient who did not ask for assistance and yet expects continued assistance after the initial gesture. The additional requests are perceived as ungratefulness on the part of the recipient who should know better than to burden the generous giver with the pressure of further assistance. It is understood that the recipient should be the one carrying the burden of debt, even though the snake and the Malagasy did not ask for anything initially. In addition, in both stories, the free gift comes with a lien, which allows the charitable person to possess the recipient in a relationship of debt.

Serres's rereading of La Fontaine's fable, echoing Mannoni's text, ultimately repositions the question of exchange within an intersectional context where the animal and the colonizer are seen to be both, equally, the lessee of the white man. In *Animal Rites*, Cary Wolfe addresses the importance of understanding the pattern of entangled oppressions, with the animal at the center of this entanglement. As he says, as long as the discourse of speciesism goes unchallenged, as long as one refuses to accept the intersectionality of species, race, gender, and sexuality, "the humanist discourse of species will always be available for use by some humans against other humans as well, to countenance violence against the social other of whatever species—or gender, or class, or sexual difference."[51] Speciesism essentially breeds other forms of -isms. In his interpretation of La Fontaine's fable, Serres indirectly hints at the entanglement of oppression and the layering of human and animal abuse. Imperialism begins with a hold on nature, on a territory, and ultimately on the animal. As Serres argues, the serpent may have felt at home on the snow, and yet the villager took it upon himself to bring the reptile into his own home, thereby forcing the serpent into de-territorialization through domestication. Moreover, when the serpent was brought into the villager's home, the villager assumed that the snake was not at home there and therefore had to *pay* for the hospitality. Yet, when the villager was walking in the snow, this man never felt not at home outside of his house. As Serres says, "history hides the fact that man is the universal parasite, that everything and everywhere around him is a hospitable space."[52] Serres's argument weaves into the colonial thread. Both the villager and Mannoni's white man treat the animal and the Malagasy native, respectively, as their lessees, even though Madagascar and nature are not their property.

As Serres suggests that anthropocentrism breeds colonialism, it becomes evident that the anthropocene cannot be addressed only at the macro-level of the so-called *human* relation to the environment. Intersectionality—race, class, gender—plays an inevitable part in man's relation to nature. Like the colonial, the villager is home everywhere. If the snake could talk back, he would tell the villager, as Serres ventriloquizes:

> *You* are the ingrate. We'll go to the cow; let he be the judge. She says: I give my milk and my children to man and he has never given me anything but death. The steer, a new third party who will judge, says that he works and is beaten in return and that his life is ended with a sacrifice on the altar of gods. All of them give to man, then, who never gives anything in return. But let us descend to the level of the tree. It gives shelter, decoration, flowers, fruits, and shade. And in return for its wages or more accurately for its rent—for it shelters and produces a territory—it is felled.[53]

La Fontaine is a jester who uses animal figures in his human comedy of manners. Besides the fact that each animal typifies a human trait, the use of animals in the fables reminds us of how closely connected humanity is to its animal counterpart. As Wolfe says, "we all, human and non-human alike, have a stake in the discourse and institution of speciesism; it is by no means limited to its overwhelmingly direct and disproportionate effects on animals."[54] In other words, anticolonialism and anti-racism cannot hold the course without an anti-anthropocentric approach to matters of power, domination, and oppression.

Whether it is the villager or the colonizer, there is always a question of "litigation," as Serres puts it, in how the human relates to the other human and the nonhuman. Who owes what to whom is the essential question. Fanon argues that decolonization requires violence. This is how one reclaims one's humanity, as Césaire says. But in the case of a revolution long past its call, another option could be, inversely, to purposely not reclaim one's humanity. Because man has an all-too-human predisposition for trading, commensalism could be an antidote to this humanistic potlatch economy. As Serres argues, there is something eminently human about a contract and a fair deal: "In the torrential flow of the irreversible and the abusive, contractual equilibrium is unique. It is only human history to want to create it."[55] The contract is man's way to reaffirm his or her human nature. The human contract can be said to be a pleonasm; only humans make contracts, and contracts are a human's way to stay human. On the other hand, an economy based on an ecological model, like commensalism, will not follow a contractual approach. Commensalism does not require a return for a given since it invites participants to share a table (*cum*/with, *mensa*/table) independently of whether a participant has something to bring to the table or not.

Even though, as Donaldson and Kymlicka point out, liminal animals are understudied, those animals are pivotal figures in human-animal relations because, as they reach the point of (literally) no return, they manage to blur the human-animal divide. Based on their research in a Mexico City garbage dump, Raymond and Lorna Coppinger call the liminal dog the "archetypal dog." As with the bird of prey and the lion's leftovers, the dog in the dump waits for human refuse and feeds on it. The archetypal dog is a commensal animal. The archetypal dog is not the domesticated animal, the pet as we know it, but the village and street dog, the one that is uniform in size, shape, and, often, color everywhere around the world. Just as pigeons look the same whether one visits Milan, Paris, Istanbul, or Central Park, liminal dogs also look alike (light-colored fur and neither big nor small) in Mexico City, South Africa, or the Caribbean, hence the Coppingers' axiom of an archetypal dog, or what we may also refer to as a "world dog." The particularity of the village dog is its adaptive ability. The authors define "domestication" as simply the ability to live in the presence of humans. While transitioning from a wild to a so-called domesticated animal, the archetypal dog has learned to eat in the presence of humans, which a wild animal is not inclined to do. Dogs hold a symbiotic relationship with humans because they rely on humans for their subsistence. As Coppinger and Coppinger write:

> The reason dogs make good pets is in large part because they have this innate behavior of finding somewhere to sit and wait for food to arrive, which is exactly what our pets do. Their niche is scavenging food from humans. . . . Dogs find some food source that arrives daily and they sit here and wait. Being somebody's "pet" isn't all that different from being a dump dog or a street dog or a village dog.[56]

Yet, it seems that what makes a village or street dog ultimately different from a pet is the former's ability to be fed by humans without the provider necessarily expecting something in return. The street dog may or may not become of assistance to the human who fed it; the liminal animal may or may not engage in an exclusive relationship with a human individual. Between dogs and humans, the rules of free ranging are clear. The word "symbiotic" refers to two organisms living in proximity with each other in a form of cohabitation. In that, there is no doubt that humans and village dogs have a symbiotic relationship since the dogs feed on human waste and therefore need to live in a human niche. But often, as Coppinger and Coppinger point out, people think that "symbiotic" is synonymous with "mutualistic." And yet, the relationship between humans and village dogs is symbiotic but not mutualistic in the sense that it is not meant to be beneficial to both parties.

The *Encyclopaedia Britannica* defines commensalism as a "relationship between individuals of two species in which one species obtains food or other benefits from the other without ever harming or benefiting the latter."[57] In commensal relationships, one species gives, or rather lets the other take, without expecting to benefit from this transaction. In a Creole context, the animal and human species share a commensal relationship where animals obtain food or other benefits from humans with no strings attached. The Creole human subject lets the Creole animal benefit from living within human communities without expecting to domesticate the animal and to get personal satisfaction from this domestication. Like the *callejero*, the Creole dog does not need to work for humans or be a companion to humans. The chameleon enjoys the music, and yet the Creole lady does not expect domestication, companionship, or any sort of return for the animal's enjoyment in her house. When the animal overstays its welcome, the old lady stamps her foot; no harm, and yet, no benefit either. As Giorgio Agamben says about animal and human *Umwelten*, even though they come across as uncommunicating, "they are equally perfect and linked together as if in a gigantic musical score."[58]

LACKADAISICAL

I see commensalism as a human-to-animal and human-to-human relationship that carries an anticolonial, antihegemonic, and anti-anthropocentric resonance. Creole commensalism shows that claiming one's humanity—as the Haitian people did heroically during the Haitian Revolution against the French—may not be the only option for the Caribbean people to reclaim their autonomy. Refusing to be defined "through the eyes of the others," as Du Bois phrases it,[59] requires positioning oneself not in relation to—or in opposition to—the white gaze, but rather living and thinking outside of the human-versus-animal box. Double-consciousness is then reclaimed, or rather auto-interpellated,[60] to embrace the entangled humanity and animality of black folk. The Negro is an animal, indeed.

Saying that the Martinican relates *commensally* to the dog, by not expecting anything in return for feeding the animal, gives agency to the one who is on the giving end of the cross-species commensal relationship. The Creole dog is not a pest since the Martinican agrees on the one-way nature of giving. But *commensalism* is also useful in understanding the relationship between Martinique as an ex-colony and France as the colonizer. Using ecological semantics to speak about slavery, blackness, and colonialism carries political weight since it allows revisitation of the question of so-called humanity within an anticolonial context. Joshua Rothman, in a 2016 *New Yorker* piece entitled "The Metamorphosis," mentions a quote from primatologist Frans de Waal addressing our inclination to compare all animals to ourselves: "even the term *nonhuman* grates on me since it lumps millions of species together by an absence, as if they were missing something."[61] Indeed, the word "human" is ideologically tainted with hues of entangled anthropocentrism and (neo)colonialism. Nonhuman animal species are defined in relation to the normative "human," as much as the black is defined in opposition to the compounded "white human." The intersection of race and animality is based on a shared status of nonrelevance as nonhuman and nonwhite. To grapple with colonialism means to first acknowledge and embrace the inextricable compoundedness of race and animality in order to then defiantly inhabit or transcend it. Looking at the relationship between Martinique and France in terms of commensalism is a way to first inhabit and then transcend the history of slavery, a history that has defined the black as nonwhite and nonhuman.

Of particular interest in Capote's "Music for Chameleons" is the parallel drawn between the animal and the Creole human subject. While the old lady talks to her American guest and asserts that Martinicans are too lackadaisical to support themselves, a hummingbird enters the terrace and "lackadaisically," as Capote writes, balances in the air. The Creole animal is not the only "species" in Martinique seen as commensal, it is not the only group said to be taking from the other. Like the animal species, Martinicans seem to be profiting from the other, from France. They eat off the carcass and do not seem willing to work for their own food. The long-lasting system of French welfare and tutelage (*assistanat*) gives the commensal culture in Martinique a bad image. Yet, just like the Malagasy (Madagascar was a French colony until 1960), the way that Martinique, as an ex-colony of the French, takes from the "white man" without the intention of return could be perceived as postcolonial retribution—"I shall always come to beg of you,"[62] as Mannoni writes. Or another way to look at it would be through the lens of anticolonial defiance. The Martinican shares a table with the French, and yet, this time, in a postslavery era, the island chooses not to bring anything to the table—political commensalism.

In 2010, a referendum proposed by then French president Nicolas Sarkozy asked Martinique if it wanted more local governance by switching from a department to an overseas territory status. The referendum was massively rejected by 79 percent of Martinican voters. In spite of an overall discontent with the French government in Martinique based on the low standards of living on the island (hence the 2009 massive strikes), the rejection of the proposal shows that the French department seeks neither more autonomy nor more responsibility. Frantz Fanon in *The Wretched of the Earth* says that a revolution, like in Haiti and Algeria, is the only way to reverse the course of colonization. As the Martinican author writes, "the naked truth of decolonization evokes for us the searing bullets and blood-stained knives which emanate from it. For if the last shall be first, this will only come to pass after a murderous and decisive struggle between the two protagonists."[63] Independence cannot be granted, it has to be taken, often with violence. Martinique seems therefore to be in a state of limbo. It has been granted freedom through French citizenship (*liberté, égalité, fraternité*), yet it is still in a colonized state of mind due to a freedom that was never snatched away from the French. Not to mention the fact that, as French citizens, Martinicans have no legal recourse under French law against the very fate of being French citizens, a conundrum that Jean-François Lyotard has raised in *The Differend*.[64]

While, as Césaire says in his poem, Haiti was the first black republic to stand its ground and to voice its humanity through the Haitian revolution, Martinique's Achilles' heel—as Martinican separatists would argue— lies in the fact that the island never got to claim its own humanity. In the midst of an ever-growing postdepartmentalization apathy pervading Martinique, Césaire published, in 1969, *A Tempest*,[65] which is a postcolonial rewriting of Shakespeare's play. As the civil rights movement raged in America, Césaire sketched a new Caliban after Malcolm X. No longer the "foot licker" mentioned by Mannoni, Césaire's revolutionary black figure has overcome his "dependence complex." Two decades after Martinique became a French department, the writer turned Caliban into a defiant black who stands his ground in the face of Prospero's colonial aspirations. By turning Caliban into a Toussaint Louverture figure, Césaire reasserts the Haitian model as the universal source of black pride. But what Césaire has failed to explore is Caliban's original hybrid identity. In Shakespeare's play, Caliban is portrayed as an animal-human hybrid monster. De-animalizing Caliban follows the Haitian model of claiming the former chattel-slave's humanity. But as Mannoni says, "Caliban, it is true, asserts himself by opposing, but he is mere bestiality."[66] In other words, even though Caliban as the emblematic colonized figure proudly opposes Prospero, the French (Mannoni) see in this opposition nothing more than a beast grunting, something that can be easily dismissed. What if, then, Caliban started acting like the beast he is portrayed to be? What if the colonized no longer tried to prove his humanity to the white man?

Dominique Lestel, in *Apologie du carnivore*,[67] offers an interesting rebuttal to ethical vegetarianism. As the French philosopher says, not eating meat to avoid causing pain to animals reinforces the idea of the "human exception," namely the belief that humans are not animals. According to him, ethical vegetarianism carries the paradoxical effect of reinforcing the human-animal divide by disavowing that which makes humans and animals fundamentally alike. As Lestel says, "It is therefore important to reverse the ethical vegetarian rationale by showing that eating meat is rather an ethical duty. Let's call it the *carnivorous imperative*."[68] Carnivorism is, for Lestel, what makes us fundamentally animal. But while eating animal meat can make us feel less strictly or *exceptionally* human, being eaten as a human is an even more radical way to become animal; this is the anthropophagic imperative. Cannibal as an anagramic distortion of Caliban blurs the divide between the human and the animal in fundamental ways. Anthropophagy emphasizes the fact that it is a human who eats another human, and yet, at the very moment that this human eats human flesh, it is the animal that prevails over the human. Humanness and animality are all at once attracting and yanking each other apart. Caliban, the archetype of species fluidity, devours the human while incorporating it. It is Caliban's way to be one with nature. As Serres says:

> The tree and the cow told us that man never returned or recognized the gifts of flora and fauna. He uses and abuses them but does not exchange with them. He gives food to the animals, you say. Yessir, he gives flora to the fauna, fauna to the fauna, gives inert material to the flora. What does he give of himself? Does he give himself to be eaten?[69]

In a posthuman fable, man gives himself to be eaten, like an animal, and becomes only half man and half animal, in a sort of posthuman fluidity.

DECENTERING THE HUMAN

When Christopher Columbus traveled for the first time to the Caribbean in 1492, the explorer thought that he had landed in the Indies and that the natives were Indians, when in fact he had discovered a new world. Because of the utterly unfamiliar nature of the experience, the colonial encounter was marred by misunderstandings and misidentifications, one of them being that Columbus thought he heard the word "cannibal" instead of "Carib," the name of a local tribe mentioned to him. Echoing Daniel Defoe's *Robinson Crusoe* and the famous footprint, Columbus's Carib/cannibal amalgam voices the mistrust of the Other on an island that the colonial would rather keep to himself. And yet, this wish for solitude is what makes the colonial lose sense of himself, as a person and as a human as well. The island stands at the far end of the human world, where the human is bound to, like Columbus, get lost. Cannibal/Carib also reveals the preconditioned idea of the Other as a human predator. Caliban embodies the Caribbean, as both the tribe (Carib) and the archipelago. The cannibal Caliban preys on the human and, by so doing, exposes humanness as mere artifact. By preying on the human, one preys on one's well-constructed humanness. Cannibalism goes against the ideal of the "human exception" because it presents the human as something that can be eaten as well. As seen in chapter 2, in the Rochambeau case, the Caribbean is where the clear divide between the human and the animal loses some of its clarity. The land of the Carib feeds on the anthropophagic imperative: eating or being eaten, either way, one is an animal. Rochambeau's French army ate the slave (through canine proxy) before the slave could eat them. The dog that incorporated the slave returned to the plantation, as Chamoiseau shows, as half man half animal (dog), like Caliban. After its/his various transformations through Shakespeare, Mannoni, and Césaire, Caliban is now a self-assured human beast who will not start a revolution since his/its cross-speciesness *is* the revolution.

The Caribbean island as, if not the archetypal site of the posthuman, at least the place where humanity comes into question, is something that Chamoiseau has explored in *L'empreinte à Crusoé* (Crusoe's footprint). After *L'esclave vieil homme et le molosse* (The old slave and the hound), Chamoiseau again takes on the human-animal question within a Caribbean context with his rewriting of Daniel Defoe's classic *Robinson Crusoe*. *L'empreinte à Crusoé* tells the story of a man struck with amnesia and stranded on a desert island for over twenty years after being the only survivor of a shipwreck. Chamoiseau's story is an existential parable about the meaning of humanity, individuation, and subjectivity: How is one to maintain human consciousness when one is the only human living on a desert island? What is the significance of the human in the exclusive presence of the nonhuman? The stranded man's first reaction is, as expected, to try to recreate human civilization on the island. With the support of miscellaneous tools and objects salvaged from the shipwreck, the marooned man pieces together a thread of human rites, traditions, and habits, the "recommencement d'une civilisation,"[70] the "restart of a civilization." His instinctual goal is to build a conceptual wall around his humanity, a desperate attempt to distinguish his humanness from other nonhuman organisms populating the island: "Man's life only makes sense if lived under the strictest demand; to be neither an animal nor one of those savages who infest the world."[71] For the narrator, animal domestication is, as for Defoe's Crusoe, a sine qua non condition of human civilization. The animals are kept in enclosures, parks, and pastures. And like Serres's villager, the narrator as the master of the island becomes the provider for animals that used to provide for themselves before his impromptu presence.

And then comes the life-altering moment, "c'est ainsi que je la vis" (this is when I saw it): the human footprint.[72] Henceforth, the fear of being eaten as a human by a human colonizes his mind and becomes monomania, an uncontrollable fear of the cannibal Other: "My imagination about cannibals would turn even more abominable when it would unleash without the restraint of a bit of conscience."[73] The narrator understands then that the survival of mankind is not about the bits and pieces of human civilization, but what Chamoiseau calls *en dehors*, "from the outside." *En dehors* is symbolized by the footprint. When the stranded man discovers the footprint, it is the moment when he starts seeing the island through the Other's eyes: Everything he sees and touches has potentially been seen and touched by the Other. The man is no longer locked within his own mind; he is no longer trying to salvage his humanness from within his human self. Chamoiseau's parable carries a strong Sartrean resonance, except that in Chamoiseau, the *pour-autrui*, the specular "for-the-other," is not alienating but rather all encompassing. The idea of the Other is not simply about the other human being but rather about the outside of oneself, namely the surrounding environment, the *Umwelt*. The realization of the Other frees the narrator from all enclosures. The narrator is now fully *en dehors*: "I was living outside—and no doubt even *in* the outside—, I would eat outside, work outside, sleep outside, dream outside, piss and defecate outside; I was avoiding all the retreats, and stayed exposed to the fullest."[74] No longer interested in domestication and agriculture, the narrator eats whatever he can catch, grab, or pick. The narrator no longer fears his animality, no longer needs to enclose himself and sequester his domesticated animals in separate enclosures. He is *en dehors* on the island in the sense that he is intrinsically part of the island. He is no longer the human exception.

As previously mentioned, when Martinican writers introduced a philosophy of Creoleness starting in the 1980s with Edouard Glissant that was further developed in the early 1990s with Jean Bernabé, Patrick Chamoiseau, and Raphaël Confiant, the animal presence was very much subdued in favor of a vegetal (mangrove) and scientific (chaos) paradigm that pervaded their poetics.[75] As mentioned above, with *L'esclave vieil homme et le molosse*, first published in 1997, Chamoiseau paved the way for an animal consciousness within Creole ideology. In 2007, Chamoiseau published with Glissant *Quand les murs tombent* (When walls fall down), an essay addressing the controversy around the existence of a putative "French national identity" as suggested by then French president Nicolas Sarkozy. It was the beginning of Chamoiseau's call for the all-encompassing *en dehors*: "Walls threaten everyone, from one to the other side of their obscurity. It is the relation to the Other (to the whole Other, in its animal, vegetal, environmental, cultural, and human presence) that guides us to the highest, most honorable, and enriching part of ourselves."[76]

In *Le discours antillais* (The Caribbean discourse), published in 1982, Glissant introduced for the first time what is now known as his "poetics of relation." As Glissant explains in the essay, Creoleness is a rhizomatic and centrifugal line of thought that relates to the outside. This is what the author names the *pensée relais*, meaning a "relay thought" that "relie (relaie), relate," (links [relays], relates) stories together.[77] Glissant's *pensée relais* is evocative of the French expression *donner le relais*, which, in hunting terminology, means "launching the dogs." The animal has already been launched with the *pensée relais*, it is now a question of feeling this animal presence in Creole poetics, feeling that humanness, within a Caribbean context, is *en dehors*, like the Creole lady's house in Capote's story, outside with the chameleons, the dogs, the plants, and the entire environment unconstrained by walls.

In *The Companion Species Manifesto*, Donna Haraway praises the art of sculptor Andrew Goldsworthy. The author writes, "Scales and flows of time through the flesh of plants, earth, sea, ice, and stone consume Goldsworthy. For him, the history of the land is living; and that history is composed out of the polyform relatings of people, animals, soil, water, and rocks."[78] The Caribbean, with the house (*maison créole*) open to the world, with a commensal relationship to the environment, with a *mach* injunction antithetical to the *kishta/hoosh/husch* approach, is the embodiment of this history composed of polyform relatings. The Caribbean is, to paraphrase Haraway, the house of "companion species," in which all species are mutually constitutive without human exception. When Haraway says that "companion species . . . must include such organic beings as rice, bees, tulips, and intestinal flora, all of whom make life for humans what it is—and vice versa,"[79] it also needs to be stressed that this companionship goes both ways. Humans are also a companion species to the rice, bees, tulips, and intestinal flora, just as the old lady is a companion to the chameleons in this Caribbean cross-species symphony.

As the island is a piece of land separated from the continent, its geography is pregnant with the idea of isolation. The Caribbean archipelago was formed by volcanic irruptions, which, some eighty million years ago, arched from South America to the Yucatan Peninsula (from a bird's-eye view, the arc is still visible today). The islands today are populated with endemic organisms, and one may wonder how, given the isolation from the mainland, those organisms happen to be there. It is easy to imagine that the flora and flying fauna came to the Caribbean islands through dispersal (flying and seed spreading). Yet, it has been more complicated for scientists to account for the presence of the nonflying vertebrates that are also endemic to the islands. The current hypothesis, among geologists, is that because of intermittent tectonic and sea-level fluctuations, the Caribbean arc at one point formed a land bridge that allowed those nonflying vertebrates to walk from South America to the archipelago. Tectonic fragmentation has since isolated the species that had crossed the land bridge, preventing them from exchanging with species on the mainland. The theory of vicariance, the interruption of a gene flow due to the separation of lands, explains why similar endemic species can be found in different parts of the world, even though those parts are no longer directly connected. Vicariance is an interesting hypothesis that can be applied to the world of explorers. In "Historical Phytogeography of the Greater Antilles," biologist Alan Graham calls the geological process that has isolated species due to tectonic fragmentation "genetic isolation."[80] Genetic isolation, however, does not necessarily mean genetic difference. In *Essay on Exoticism*, French author and explorer Victor Segalen addresses the underwhelming experience of world exploration and calls it "in-oticism."[81] In-oticism is the opposite of exoticism, and, for Segalen, it refers to the idea that in spite of the long road traveled, the traveler will discover things seen before. Likewise, in *Tristes tropiques*, French anthropologist Claude Lévi-Strauss travels to Brazil and expects to be struck by the blow of exoticism. Instead, species look the same in Brazil as in other parts of the world, except that their names are different. As he writes, "I would have been quite surprised if someone had told me that an animal or vegetal species could have the same aspect on both sides of the globe. Each animal, each tree, each grass, should be radically different and expose at first glance its tropical nature."[82] His attempts to "reconstituer l'exotisme" during his trip to Brazil are, as he says, in vain.[83] The theory of vicariance shows the interconnection of everything in spite of the lack of visible land bridges. It also explains why, in the Coppingers' observation, the village dog looks identical whether one travels to the Caribbean, Brazil, or South Africa. Vicariance informs Chamoiseau's poetics of *en dehors*. Everything is connected, interrelated, ultimately not that different. The island, as the epitome of isolation, is in fact the very place where everything comes together. It is the very place where, whether seen through the lens of Defoe, Shakespeare, Césaire, or Chamoiseau, the human can understand his companionship with his environment, his intersectionality with the vegetal and animal worlds.

In *L'empreinte à Crusoé*, Chamoiseau reveals the real reason behind the shipwreck at the end of the book. The narrator's name turns out to be Ogomtemmêli, and he comes from a family of glorious hunters from an African coast. A slave merchant had taken him under his wing and made him a ship's boy. The boy lent a helpful hand for many years in the commerce of slaves before hitting his head and losing his mind. As the mentally deranged boy became aggressive and dangerous, the slave merchant resorted to abandoning him on a desert island. The boy was knocked unconscious by the crew and put on a ship drifting toward the shore of a desert island. When, years later, the merchant's ship arrived at the same island, the captain was utterly surprised to see that Ogomtemmêli was still alive and well. The captain invited the stranded man onto his ship for a celebratory dinner and marveled over the grace, posture, and serenity of the boy who used not to possess those qualities. The captain offered to take the man back with him to civilization, but the islander declined the invitation, claiming that the island was his home. The dinner, however, took a turn for the worse when Ogomtemmêli realized that the captain's ship was a slave ship full of chained, captive slaves. Ogomtemmêli attempted to free the slaves by force and was shot to death by the captain's order. The captain was sad to have lost Ogomtemmêli and decided to explore the island in order to see how the stranded man survived all those years. To his surprise, there was no sign of human presence on the island, no enclosures, no huts, no sheds, as if no humans had ever lived there. In an ironic twist of events, Chamoiseau ends the story with the captain's diary. The captain started his diary on September 30, 1659, four days after having found and killed Ogomtemmêli. The captain is now the one stranded in the island as the sole survivor of a shipwreck after a heavy storm. In the diary, we learn that the captain has named the desert island the "Island of Despair," and that his name, finally revealed to the reader, is Robinson Crusoe. Here begins Daniel Defoe's story, the story of the archetypal colonial. As we know, Crusoe will not adhere to the ideology of *en dehors*. The desert island will no longer be connected to the world, and the human-nonhuman divide will be stronger than ever. It is the beginning of colonialism.

4

DOG OWNERSHIP IN
THE DIASPORA

What does it mean to own an animal—a sentient being—in the way that one owns a car or a house? The controversy over the question of animals as property is best illustrated in the most recent changes to the legal French system. Since February 18, 2015, a new amendment (Article 515–14) to the French Civil Code defines animals as "des êtres vivants doués de sensibilité" (living and sentient beings).[1] The French owe this amendment partially to the efforts of Fondation 30 Millions d'Amis (Thirty Million Friends Foundation), the largest animal rights organization in France, a group that started a petition in 2013 asking the government to cease identifying the animal as a thing and to acknowledge animal sentience in the French Civil Code. The amendment was proposed at a time when the French government was looking to simplify and modernize the Napoleonic French Civil Code, created in 1804. After an initial rejection by the Senate, the proposed amendment was approved by the Assemblée Nationale. By explicitly indicating in the Civil Code that the animal was a sentient being, France was aligning itself with other countries that had already ratified progressive animal rights legislation, including Germany and Switzerland. But while Fondation 30 Millions d'Amis hailed this amendment as an unprecedented achievement, La Fondation Droit Animal, Éthique et Sciences (LFDA) (the French Animal Law, Ethics, and Sciences Foundation) expressed some reservations about the nature of their campaign. The LFDA criticized the Fondation 30 Millions d'Amis for using misleading rhetoric to rally people to their cause. The popular mainstream organization had indeed presented a simplified and erroneous version of the "animal as a thing" problem in the French Civil Code. The truth is that, in 1999, LFDA had already succeeded in passing an amendment to the Civil Code, the aim of which was to distinguish animals from things. Since 1999, and through LFDA's efforts, the animal is no longer described as a "thing" in the French Civil Code, even though it is still defined as *meuble* (chattel). The 1804 version of the Civil Code reads, "Are deemed moveable (*meuble*) by nature, the bodies that can move from one location to the next."[2] In this initial Napoleonic version, animals are implied to fall within *corps* (bodies). The 1999 amended version reads as follows: "Are deemed moveable (*meuble*) animals *and bodies* that can move from one location to the next."[3] By adding the mention "animals" next to "bodies," it is meant to suggest that animals are not equivalent to the said "bodies." Fondation 30 Millions d'Amis was aware of the inexactitude of its claim but, according to its president, Reha Hutin, the priority of the organization had been to transmit its message to a large audience, even if that meant opting for a "journalistic vulgarization of the message."[4]

LFDA's reaction to the Fondation 30 Millions d'Amis campaign may come across as persnickety in the larger scheme of what Fondation 30 Millions d'Amis has been able to accomplish for the sake of animal rights in France. But LFDA's objection brings attention to pertinent questions about human-animal relations. The result of the Fondation 30 Millions d'Amis campaign was to deemphasize the humanist paradox that struggles with a knowledge that animals are not like things and the continual practice of treating them as such, in spite of that knowledge. The animal rights foundation circumvented the crucial issue of humans' aptitude for fetishistic disavowal that allows for the routine reification and commodification of the animal body. In "The Problem with Commodifying Animals," Gregory R. Smulewicz-Zucker posits that, with animal-based products, "the commodity conceals the animals used to produce it."[5] But even more than concealing the animal, this commodification conceals our own awareness of the animal as a product. Fondation 30 Millions d'Amis' distorted campaign gives the illusion that the fate of the animal depends on the animal no longer being considered a thing, when the animal has already been considered in this liberatory light under French law—not only in the post-1999 Civil Code but also in the French Penal Code and the Rural and Marine Fishing Code, which serve as complements to the Civil Code and which have always differentiated the animal from things. As LFDA vice president Jean-Marc Neumann explains in *Le Monde*, under French law, there is no legal recourse on behalf of a chair if one purposely breaks the leg of a chair. On the other hand, if one purposely and cruelly breaks the leg of an animal, under the Penal Code one is liable to two years in jail and a 30,000-euro fine.[6] Further, since 1976, the French Rural and Marine Fishing Code has shown its commitment to animal sentience with Article L214–1, stipulating that "every animal, *as a sentient being*, must be placed by its owner in conditions compatible with the biological requirements of its species."[7] The problem lies, therefore, not in the fact that French law considers the animal as equal to a chair, but rather in that even though the law does not consider the animal to be a thing, it still makes allowance for treating the animal as such. In France, the animal is still subjected to cruel, yet legal, treatments. The law does not condemn, for example, bull and cock fighting or the production of foie gras. But more important, one could also ask, following legal scholar Gary Francione's vegan abolitionist argument: If animals—like slaves in history—are now recognized as sentient beings, how can they still be legally treated as property?[8]

THE ABOLITIONIST APPROACH TO SENTIENT PROPERTY

Fondation 30 Millions d'Amis' erroneous claim about the French Civil Code was facilitated by the frequent misunderstanding of the word *meuble* in the French language, a word that is often taken to mean "furniture," when in reality it refers to the condition of mobility and transferability of a possession. In its petition, the organization states that, "the Civil Code still considers animals as moveable property [*meuble*], just like a *dresser* or a *chair* (LFDA's emphasis), . . . it is therefore incomprehensible that the Civil Code continues to consider them as 'things.'"[9] The English translation does not do justice to the semantic complexity at stake in the French wording of the petition. When used as a substantive, *meuble* means furniture, but if the word is used as an adjective, which is the case in the judicial language, *meuble* refers not to a piece of furniture, but rather to the mobility of a given property. The adjectives *meuble* and *immeuble* are accordingly used in judicial language as references to succession and inheritance. *Meuble*, in the Civil Code, designates personal property that can be moved, as opposed to *immeuble*, which is property that is fixed to the ground, like a pigeon coop or a beehive. *Meuble* and *immeuble* are both adjectival and refer to the removable or nonremovable nature of a property. The slippage from *meuble* (moveable property) to *un meuble* (a piece of furniture) is what has allowed Fondation 30 Millions d'Amis to misleadingly argue that the animal is described as a piece of furniture in the French Civil Code. Since most laypeople are not acquainted with this adjectival nuance, the association of *meuble* with the word "animal" inevitably leads to the assumption that the animal is legally viewed as no more than a chair.

Interestingly enough, the same is true for the legal language used in relation to the status of the slave in the Code Noir. The Code Noir is a French slave code that was created under Louis XIV with the goal of policing slavery. It was implemented in Martinique and Guadeloupe in 1685, spread to Saint-Domingue in 1687, and reached Louisiana in 1724.[10] The infamous Article 44 in the Code Noir includes the phrase "déclarons les esclaves être meubles" ("Let us declare that slaves are chattel [or movable property]"), another usage of *meuble* that has led many Francophones to understand that the slave is literally defined as a piece of furniture, and thus as a thing, in the Code Noir.[11] Slave codes in the English language have not been as confusing since "chattel," the English equivalent to *meuble*, has a straightforward meaning. The English equivalent to *meuble* denotes a state of being mobile property but does not imply that the slave's body is furniture. The Slave Code of South Carolina (1740), one of the main Slave codes composed in English, declares slaves to be "chattels personal in the hands of their owners and possessors, and their executors, administrators."[12] Unlike *meuble*, "chattel" refers unequivocally to a moveable item of property.[13]

In 2006, French president Jacques Chirac declared May 10 to be the annual day for the remembrance of the slave trade and for the celebration of the abolition of slavery. Chirac explained to a young crowd gathered for the occasion at the Champs Elysée that slaves were considered as *biens meubles*. To get his point across, the president added "comme ma chaise" (like my chair), thereby revealing that the president of France was incognizant of the adjectival meaning of *meuble*.[14] Likewise, French Guyanese politician Christiane Taubira delivered a speech on February 18, 1999, to the Assemblée Nationale in which she mentioned that the Code Noir "stipule que l'esclave est un meuble," which in English would translate as "the Code Noir stipulates that the slave is a piece of furniture [*un meuble*]."[15] Taubira herself, who helped pass a law in 2001 denouncing slavery as a crime against humanity (the Taubira Law), could not avoid the mix-up, though there is no indication as to whether the politician intentionally used this rhetoric to ratify her law or whether it was an unintentional confusion. French law and its misrepresentation in public discourse exemplify an aspect of the complexity of the animal question through the relationship of the animal to the slave in legal history. The linguistic confusion of the chair-yet-not-a-chair description of sentient beings reveals the blurring of the frontier between living beings and inanimate objects in our collective consciousness.

Stating that the animal and the slave are *un meuble* in the Civil Code and the Code Noir, respectively, is grammatically and semantically incorrect. However, it could easily be argued that the difference between being considered as *meuble* (moveable property) as opposed to *un meuble* (furniture) is a thin line. In both cases, the result is an absence of personhood and, ultimately, a form of reification. As moveable and transferable possessions, animals and slaves have no say in the handling of their bodies, and, in that, they are comparable to things. In "The Case Against Pets," Francione advocates against pet ownership, positing that, "if animals matter morally—if animals are not just things—they *cannot* be property."[16] Francione's argument is based on an abolitionist approach to personhood that sees similarities between human slavery and animal exploitation. Francione and Anna Charlton open *Animal Rights: The Abolitionist Approach* with a manifesto structured around six principles, the first of which states: *"Abolitionists maintain that all sentient beings, human or nonhuman, have one right—the basic right not to be the property of others."*[17] According to Francione, animals should be granted the same moral consideration as human slaves. One has no rights at all if one—human or animal—does not have the fundamental right not to be property. Francione's argumentation partially refers back to utilitarian philosopher Jeremy Bentham's approach, discussed in more detail in chapter 1. In his 1789 *Introduction to the Principles of Morals and Legislation*, Bentham suggested that abolitionism and animal welfare activism are interrelated in that animals, like slaves, deserve rights as sentient beings. But for Francione, it is not sufficient to consider animal suffering. There is no such thing as "happy exploitation," which means that animals also have a right, like humans, to be free. In response to Francione, Wesley J. Smith, a senior fellow at the Discovery Institute's Center on Human Exceptionalism, says that Francione's case against pet ownership is the result of an absolutist, abolitionist approach in which "what is done to an animal [is] viewed in the same way as if the same thing were done to a human."[18] In other words, if slaves and animals were at one point both deemed *meuble*, to what extent should animals be granted the right (the only meaningful right, as Francione claims) not to be property, just as former slaves were granted such rights? Francione's literal take on "animal rights" forces us to envision life without animal companionship: "Animal rights, properly understood, is not about treating animals more humanely. This is the welfarist approach. No, the goal of animal rights is to end all animal domestication, including depriving us of our beloved dogs, cats, and other pets," Smith argues.[19]

Francione takes a radical stand that most animal rights organizations would not entertain. Fondation 30 Millions d'Amis, like many other groups, is not willing to argue for the end of animal domestication, let alone pet ownership. Fondation 30 Millions d'Amis is aware that the question of property is enmeshed in the word *meuble*, but the intentional slip from "moveable property" to "furniture" is one way for the organization to avoid the question of animals as property altogether. LFDA, on the other hand, has been more forthcoming about the question of animals as property. In a piece addressing the controversy over the Fondation 30 Millions d'Amis campaign published in its journal, also called *LFDA*, the LFDA concedes that it would be "utopian" to believe that the law could one day cease to consider animals as property. For this reason, in its 1999 proposed amendment, the scientific organization asked that animals be viewed as "biens particuliers protégés" (distinctive protected property), a compromise on the property status of the animal.[20] While the 2015 amendment furthered the progress made in the 1999 changes to the Civil Code—namely, the suppression of the word *meuble* regarding animals—the new amendment stipulates that "unless there are special laws protecting them, animals are submitted to the legal regime of property."[21] Animals are no longer liable to identification as furniture, but no organization would go so far as to request that they be liberated from being considered property.

In a chiasmic turn of events, animals are still property yet no longer *meuble*, whereas blacks are still *meuble* (as former slaves) yet no longer property. Unlike animals, black slaves remain forever *meuble* since the designation cannot be amended in the now obsolete Code Noir. Because the Code Noir's unamendable status results in the impossibility of ever retracting the *meuble* or chattel personal designation, the unalterable Code Noir and other slave codes will forever attest to the slave's chattel status. In other words, blacks' irrevocable ownable-ness confines them to an irremediable "previously owned" status.

PRE-OWNED

The Code Noir cannot be amended, but it can be reinterpreted, a task that some slavery scholars have taken to heart. French philosopher Louis Sala-Molins released an important book in 1987 entitled *Le Code Noir ou le calvaire de Canaan* (The Black Code or Canaan's ordeal). The book has been celebrated in the French Antilles for having presented the Code Noir as the most monstrous judicial text ever produced in modern times.[22] For Sala-Molins, the Code Noir represents "the darkest of horror, the worst refinement in evil, the coldest technicality in the market of human flesh and genocide."[23] The monstrous nature of the Code Noir lies in its representation of slaves as not fully *Homo sapiens*; as part human, part animal, and part object. The writer questions the status of slaves: "Des hommes [men]? Des bêtes [beasts]?"[24] He will later conclude that "the slave is neither a person, nor an animal. He is personal property [*bien meuble*], one of those things that are stipulable and transferrable, like some sort of money or any other movable property."[25] Sala-Molins shows that the status of the slave inevitably boils down to a question of fungibility that becomes even more salient in light of the nuance of the word *meuble* and its controversial interpretation in contemporary discourse.

In 2015, Jean-François Niort, a French historian and faculty member at the Université des Antilles et de la Guyane in

Guadeloupe, challenged Sala-Molins's allegations regarding the Code Noir. In his book *Le Code Noir*, Niort argues that, from a French perspective, the Code Noir was "monstrous" in the sensu stricto of "out of norm" only in that slaves did not exist in France during the era that slavery was in practice in the Americas and so applied only to the black body in the Americas. According to the "Freedom Principle," if a slave stepped on French soil, she or he would become free upon entering the slavery-free country.[26] Slavery was not permitted in France, and the Code Noir—which was purposely created for the colonies—represented the legal indicator of slavery, a colonial excrescence meant to stay outside the French monarchy. In that sense the document and its referent were indeed, from a French continental perspective, judicial and colonial monstrosities.[27] This is, according to Niort, the only so-called monstrous aspect of the Code Noir; he bases his conclusions on the etymological meaning of "monstrous." The word "monster" derives from the Latin *monstrare*, meaning "to show" or "to point the finger," as one points at a man or an animal in a circus or at a fair that appears abnormal and malformed. For Niort, it would be erroneous to claim, as Sala-Molins and his followers have, that the Code Noir was in itself monstrous in the sense that the word means "contradictory and incoherent with itself because [the Code Noir] acknowledges simultaneously the humanity of the slave and its being a thing, its reification."[28] Niort instead argues that, in those days, the reification of the slave did not exclude his or her humanity. It is precisely because the slave is a human in the slavery economy, rather than a thing (a plow) or an animal (livestock), that the Code Noir was created. By addressing the right to marry, to be baptized, or to be freed, the Code Noir acknowledges that the slave is not merely an animal or an agricultural tool. In other words, there would have been no need for the creation of the Code Noir if slavery had involved an equation of the human body with the animal or things alone, since animality and objecthood are, legally speaking, two clear categories. According to Niort, there is no incoherence between recognizing a slave's aptitudes as a *Homo sapiens* while simultaneously defining him or her as property, because in 1685, when the Code Noir was first created, personhood was not intrinsic to the human condition. Only with the French Revolution and the drafting of the 1789 Declaration of the Rights of Man and of the Citizen did humanity become synonymous with personhood: "Men are born and remain free and equal in right."[29] Essentially, Niort argues that, besides the fact that Continental France may have seen the slavery of the American colonies as monstrous compared to their own legal restrictions against slavery in the mainland, the monstrosity mainly comes from the modern perspective pointing back to the Code Noir as an abnormality.

By denying the overall and unrestricted judicial monstrosity of the document, Niort has been anathematized by a number of Guadeloupeans who accused him of revisionism,[30] even though the author did concede in his book that, on moral and philosophical grounds (as opposed to legal grounds), the Code Noir can undoubtedly be said to be monstrous. One bone of contention between Niort and his opponents lies in the question of historical perspective. Niort argues that the document cannot be read through the lens of our modern concept of humanity, while, for his opponents, the Code Noir is not a matter of humanity but rather a question of race. Indeed, by arguing that the historical era of the Code Noir simultaneously allowed for humanization and reification, Niort overlooks the role of race as a vector of reification. And this holds true not only for the Code Noir but also for all the slave codes in use in the Americas at the time. The Slave Code of South Carolina explicitly mentions that "all Negroes and Indians, . . . mulattoes or mustizoes" were chattel property (and hence reified), while the white race was exempted from the doom of being considered legal property. The co-existence of humanity and reification was within the so-called norm only when it came to the black condition. Even though the law was not per se "monstrous" in the sense of being contradictory and incoherent with itself, the law nonetheless made not necessarily the legal document but at least the black himself or herself monstrous by excluding him or her from the (white) human norm. The slave under the various slave codes was a Caliban—the polymorphous Shakespearean monster: a human, animal, object hybrid in his own secluded island.

Despite Niort's claim that interpreting the Code Noir requires contextualizing it within a historical perspective, there is no doubt that the frontier between pre- and post-1789 is porous and that the Code Noir cannot be assessed exclusively through its antiquarian purpose. Today the racial monstrosity of all the black codes lingers, as modern blacks drag along the weight of their pre-owned status. The ghastly presence of *meuble* makes blacks imperfectly free or, more precisely, "imperfect property"; they are like stray animals, essentially defined by the fact that they once had owners. In *What Is a Dog?*, Raymond Coppinger and Lorna Coppinger go to great length to show the difference between a village or street dog and a stray dog. As discussed in chapter 3, according to the two authors, the village dogs of Vietnam, India, Africa, and Mexico represent the archetypal dog responsible for its own breeding and genetic evolution. The village dog is a *domestic* animal—in that he lives in a human environment to sustain himself—but this canine is not *domesticated* in the sense of being subjected to a human-controlled reproduction. It is very important, for the Coppingers, to communicate the idea that the village dog is distinct from a stray dog. They write, "our beautiful village dogs are neither the result of artificial selection nor the result of mongrelization of stray pet dogs."[31] The two authors rebut the common assumption, one made even by experts, that village dogs are previously owned dogs that have become feral.[32] Instead, they argue that those dogs are their own, undomesticated breed. What the Coppingers show is that all dogs are by default perceived as owned or pre-owned and it requires much effort to prove otherwise. On the other hand, the black in the Americas, though once *meuble*, would never be said to be "pre-owned" today, although the modern black is indeed a stray.

THE STRAY

According to Teju Cole,[33] what defines blacks in America is that Ellis Island was not their entryway, as it was for Americans of European descent. They are defined by their transit across the Middle Passage in a slave ship, which Paul Gilroy describes as their chronotope.[34] The slave ship chronotope pinpoints the birth of a new identity. Because the concept of blackness was brought to the Americas through the Middle Passage where black bodies were cargo, being black in the Americas initially refers to a condition of being owned. As Saidiya Hartman says, "The slave trade required that a class of expendable people be created."[35] Blackness has become a class of its own, a class that, as Frank B. Wilderson writes, is "'off the map' with respect to the cartography that charts civil society's semiotics,"[36] hence the challenge of accounting for the seemingly oxymoronic condition of being both human and property. Unlike Niort's claim, one cannot look at slavery as a historically autonomous system of thought.

The way slavery first shaped blacks in America has ramifications for our modern experience and perception of blackness. One of the many nuances of blackness today is the relationship of the black body to the idea of pre-ownership; the black is not a free man, but a stray in the legal and historical imaginary. This state of being brings us back to *The Law Is a White Dog*, in which author Colin Dayan shows us, indirectly, that the ghost of the Code Noir is central to an understanding of modern blackness in America. Dayan brilliantly juxtaposes two Louisiana cases with uncanny similarities: one case addresses the free mobility of the black, the other the free mobility of the dog, and both cases reached the Supreme Court one year apart.[37] In his juxtaposition, Dayan shows that the "free" (postabolition) black is legally perceived in terms comparable to a dog on the loose in a state still haunted by the Code Noir.

In both cases, Justice Henry Brown arrived at the conclusion that blacks and dogs should stay, literally, in their place. As we know, in *Plessy v. Ferguson* Justice Brown upheld the constitutionality of racial segregation under the legal doctrine "separate but equal," and in *Sentell v. New Orleans*, Justice Brown argued that dogs, by default, represent a threat to public safety and are therefore liable to destruction by the police power of the state when they are not properly restrained. Justice Brown ultimately ruled that Sentell would not be compensated because signs showed that the owner was not in complete possession of his dog, the dog was not registered. Justice Brown explains at length the nature of property in relation to dogs: the property of a dog is conditional in Louisiana. If the dog does not fulfill specific conditions (being registered with a collar, for example), the animal can be destroyed by the state if deemed a risk to society. And even if the dog were to be considered personal property, Justice Brown argues that the police have a right to destroy the animal if they see fit. As he elaborates, "even if it were assumed that dogs are property in the fullest sense of the word, they would still be subject to the police power of the state, and might be destroyed or otherwise dealt with as in the judgment of the legislature is necessary for the protection of its citizens."[38] As Justice Brown argues, his ruling is not novel, since all types of private property can be destroyed by the police power of the state if the destruction is justified. For example, meats, fruits, vegetables, rags, clothes, and homes—though they are private property—can be destroyed if they represent a public health hazard. But the point on which Justice Brown does not elaborate is the fact that the dog is not an inanimate object and, as such, is more liable to be destroyed on impulse and without recourse to the legal process due to the animal's capacity to instantaneously attack a human victim. Justice Brown mentions the hydrophobic nature of the dog in his report, which indicates that he sees the dog as distinct from a house or a fruit. Dogs can be seen only as imperfect property, as Justice Brown argues, due to their propensity for *active* mischief. The dog is unpredictable and never fully under human control, and therefore liable to be destroyed.

The coincidence of both the dog and the black being discussed within the context of their out-of-place-ness in the State of Louisiana, a state once under the French Code Noir legislation, is pregnant with meaning. Both cases raise questions about the incompleteness of the property status of both the dog and the black: the dog, in terms of its legal existence as imperfect property and its propensity for mischief; and the black, in terms of his or her existence as a stray. After the Louisiana State Constitution abolished slavery in 1864, the 1896 *Plessy v. Ferguson* demonstrated the white man's struggle to adjust to the former slave's relatively recent freedom. *Plessy v. Ferguson* stands in the shadow of Louisiana's Code Noir as the legal process tries to negotiate the transition from *meuble* as moveable (as opposed to mobile) property to a partial restraint on personhood through racial segregation. The Code Noir confirms that the black slave was once perceived like the dog described by Justice Brown: naturally mischievous, unpredictable, and dangerous. As Sala-Molins points out, the Code Noir is a punitive legal document in which "the black slave exists judicially when he disobeys, society focuses on cruelly reprimanding this part of his existence. On the other hand, he *is not deserving* when he complies to the whims of his master or of society as a whole."[39] The fact that the slave has a judicial existence proportional to his propensity for mischief recalls Brown's ruling on the legal status of the dog in Louisiana. The slave's legal existence as mischievous descends from the perception of the black in the context of the so-called curse of Ham. In the book of Genesis, Canaan, Ham's son, is doomed to eternal slavery because of his father's insubordination. And since Ham is alleged to be black, the primal black slave biblically already carries the scarlet letter of insubordination. As Sala-Molins says, "it is the mark of misdeed that defines them [black slaves], the seed of viciousness."[40] Slave law reveals the white fear of the rebellious, unruly, and potentially retaliative black subject who needs to be kept at bay by the police power of the state, which can destroy with impunity the black no longer restrained by ownership and the chains of slavery.

LIKE DOGS

In *Animal Rights*, Francione and Charlton advocate for the end of *all* domestication because, Francione writes, we have a "moral obligation to not use animals as things, even if it would benefit us to do so. With respect to domesticated animals, that means that we stop bringing them into existence altogether."[41] Let us envision a world where Francione's position on animal rights is embraced by the majority and eventually leads to the abolition of all animal domestication. Stray dogs and feral cats would be remnants of an animal population once securely domesticated. Seeing them might stir domesticating impulses in us again; the drive, for example, to capture and imprison one in our home. Or, more likely, their uncontained, undomesticated presence within our human-dominated habitat would inspire the fear and disgust induced by a phobia of animal reproduction on an exponential scale.

In *A Thousand Plateaus*, Gilles Deleuze and Félix Guattari point at the voracious and quasi-anthropophagic nature of vermin proliferation. The two authors use the example of Daniel Mann's 1972 movie *Willard*, in which the protagonist has a rat fetish and is eventually devoured by the rats whose proliferation he was unable to contain. As Deleuze and Guattari explain, "the proliferation of rats, the pack, brings a becoming-molecular that undermines the great molar powers of family, career, and conjugality."[42] In other words, animal proliferation is a threat to domestic stability. There is a subtle connection to be made between the sight of the roaming animal and the phobia of the proliferation of that which is uncontained, previously owned, or meant to be owned. The best example of this phenomenon occurs in Detroit, a city where both blacks and stray dogs are presented as abandoned, on the loose, and roaming the streets. Detroit is the quintessential space for addressing the nexus between blacks and dogs as two previously owned entities. Detroit, a city with numerous abandoned homes, is particularly prone to the proliferation of stray dogs. After a third of Detroiters were forced to leave the city under bankruptcy and abandoned their homes, dogs were left behind to fend for themselves. Stray dogs thrive particularly well in areas that are unpopulated yet proximal to human trash. Because of its stray dog population, Detroit has been depicted in the media as a postapocalyptic canine city with packs of stray dogs prowling through neighborhoods. Despite the undeniable threat that packs of stray dogs represent for the human population in terms of health and safety, however, the extent of the problem of stray dogs in Detroit has been blown out of proportion and sensationalized in the media. A 2012 piece in *Rolling Stones* magazine and a 2013 piece in *Bloomberg* inflated the number of stray dogs in Detroit to 50,000,[43] while the World Animal Awareness Society has put the number closer to 3,000.[44] Images like the one in *Rolling Stone* of a pit bull tugging "long, rubbery strands from a bloody mass in the snow" and eventually pulling out a frozen puppy alert readers to the possibility that the pit bull could have been licking the blood of a human being instead of that of a puppy.

In 2013 as well, a new TV drama, set in Detroit and titled *Low Winter Sun*, was released on the AMC channel. As the *New York Times* writes, "the series presents a dystopian view of urban decay that makes the Baltimore of 'The Wire' look almost like Monte Carlo. This Detroit is a fetid no-man's-land that law-abiding citizens fled long ago, leaving whole blocks abandoned, houses boarded over and feral dogs roaming empty streets."[45] The representations of Detroit's dog population in visual media reveal that the majority of those dogs are abandoned pets avoiding human contact, rather than feral animals preying on residents. Yet the dogs' status as previously owned and on the loose stigmatizes these animals as feral, aggressive, dangerous, and unrestrained. The media's misrepresentation and amplification of this stray dog presence additionally depicts Detroit as a predatory and savage city. Given that Detroit is a predominantly black city, the emphasis on the fierce dog on the prowl subliminally connects with the image of the unchained black in the postslavery era, making both the black and the animal appear dangerously on the loose and eerily alike in their unbridled existence.

Sentell v. New Orleans returns to haunt a society in which it has become routine for the police power of the state to destroy with impunity the (black) stray regarded as a public threat. In an open letter to his nephew, published in *The Fire Next Time* in 1963, James Baldwin writes about the demise of America, positing that the country is oblivious to the fact that racism destroys both blacks and whites: "I said that it was intended that you should perish in the ghetto, perish by never being allowed to go behind the white man's definitions . . . those innocents who believed that your imprisonment made them safe are losing their grasp on reality."[46] In the 2015 *Between the World and Me*, Ta-Nehisi Coates crafts his own open-letter essay to his son, as a response to Baldwin's writing, picking up where Baldwin left off. Assessing institutionalized racism in present-day America, the author writes to his son:

> I write you in your fifteenth year. I am writing you because this was the year you saw Eric Garner choked to death for selling cigarettes; because you know now that Renisha McBride was shot for seeking help, that John Crawford was shot down for browsing in a department store. And you have seen men in uniform drive by whom they were oath-bound to protect. And you have seen men in the same uniforms pummel Marlene Pinnock, someone's grandmother, on the side of a road. And you know now, if you did not before, that the police departments of your country have been endowed with the authority to destroy your body.[47]

In the context of Coates's writing, Baldwin's letter takes on a prophetic dimension. We are reminded, in reading Coates, that Baldwin had warned us about "those innocents who believed that [black] imprisonment made them safe." In spite of the mass incarceration of blacks in the country, whites do not feel any safer around blacks today. On the contrary, as more blacks are imprisoned, white insecurity increases.

As Justice Brown argues in *Sentell v. New Orleans*, some animals exist in the condition of "*ferae naturae*, in which, until killed or subdued, there is no property." Within the phenomenon of mass incarceration of black bodies, which some argue constitutes a modern form of slavery, the police power of the state performs a ritual reclamation of its lost property wherein the unchained black man who has been walking (too) freely in the streets of America is subdued and killed.

THE FRENCH ARAB AND THE AFRICAN AMERICAN

Coates has been vocal about his admiration for Baldwin. Like Baldwin, Coates chose to move to Paris, and, like Baldwin, he discovered that blackness carries a different meaning in France. Baldwin was arrested in Paris for *l'affaire du drap*,[48] as he calls it in in his essay "Equal in Paris." Baldwin was aware that in France, the underdog, so to speak, is the Arab and not the French black. He had an idea of how the police might treat him since he had seen, he writes, "what Paris police men could do to Arab peanut vendors."[49] Here Baldwin refers to his witnessing the French police violently beating an Arab peanut vendor in the street, one example of the treatment of Arabs in France at a time when France was losing its grip on its colonies.

After the loss of Indochina, France justifiably feared that Algeria was next, a fear that translated itself into random acts of violence against Arabs by the police. Baldwin explains in *No Name in the Street* that institutionalized violence "is the way people react to the loss of empire."[50] The Algerian War (1954–62) prompted the practice of what the French call *ratonnades*. The term derives from the word *raton*, which means "little rat," where the rat represents the Arab. *Ratonnades* refers to the racial act of preying on and killing Arabs, which is imagined as a rodent extermination. As Baldwin soon came to realize, "Algerians *were* being murdered in the streets, and corralled into prisons, and being dropped into the Seine, like flies,"[51] while blacks from Senegal and Martinique were spared in spite of the fact that—as surprising as it sounded to an African American— their skin was darker than that of Arabs. In Frantz, from "an American frame of reference" (as Baldwin phrases it), the Arab *is* the black.

Coates also encountered this phenomenon of French distrust of the Arab during his more recent residency in France. Coates was in France when the January 2015 terrorist attack by Islamist extremists took place at the *Charlie Hebdo* journal headquarters. It occurred to Coates that, in order to even begin to understand the situation of Arabs in France as an American, it was useful to consider the condition of blacks in America.[52] As Coates would further explain in an interview in the *New York Times*, it would be "dangerous to make a one-on-one comparison between black folks there [America] and black folks here [France]." The real comparison, as he came to understand through his discussions with French Algerian anthropologist and sociologist Nacira Guénif-Souilamas, should be made between the French Arab and the American black. "Her [Guénif-Souilamas's] experience sounded a lot more similar to African-Americans," Coates reveals, "with the Algerian war being a rupture, in the same way the Civil War was a rupture."[53]

This parallel between the French Arab and the American black explains why, in France, the idea of the stray and the phobia of proliferation are most provoked by the image of the Arab (rather that the black) roaming the streets, hence the inclination of the police to contain the Arab through *ratonnades*. Today, the new generation of French-born people of Algerian descent is pejoratively termed *zonard*, a substantive derived from the word *la zone*, which initially referred to a space outside of the medieval walled city of Paris used as a buffer against military attacks. Though off-limits, *la zone* had many informal dwellings inhabited by those who could not find their place within the city walls. The verb *zoner* in familiar French means "loitering" and "wandering aimlessly," and *zonards* refers to the young population, a large part of which is of Maghrebian (including Algerian) descent, who are perceived as having no aim in life and who live on the outskirts of big cities like Paris or Marseilles.[54] This population is defined not only by the space they inhabit, but also, and more importantly, by the kind of displaced, roaming movement that they generate: *zoner, zonard*. The *zonard* is a sour reminder of the loss of national control over colonial property. Similar to the signification of the black in America, the Arab *zonard* stands as the pre-owned and ex-colonized subject who represents a public threat when in the street.

In 1993, the Interior Minister Charles Pasqua reinforced a controversial law designed to contain and regulate the flow of immigration into France. In addition to weakening the *jus soli* (right of the soil) principle, the Pasqua Law requested random police identity checks for potential illegal immigrants. This initiative necessitated that all people living in France carry residency cards, or *cartes de séjour*, with them at all times. Since the law targeted potential immigrants, mostly from North Africa, it resulted in the legalization of racial profiling and intensified the antagonistic relationship between the police and Arab-looking subjects. Published two years after the passage of the Pasqua Law, French Algerian author Azouz Begag's novel *Les chiens aussi* (The dogs too) portrays the condition of Algerian immigrants in France under this law. Begag offers a parable that figures the Arab immigrant as a stray dog, chased by the police, who are imagined as the Animal Control Service. As the author says, "les chiens et les zimmigrés, c'est kif-kif,"[55] meaning "dogs and immigrants are the same." In this dystopian fantasy of France under the Pasqua Law, Begag describes the police car as "la Brigade Anti-Chiens-Errants" (an anti-stray dog brigade).[56] In the book, the stray Arab generation prepares for a rebellion; they want an end to the mandatory duty to carry "the residence card, the end of random police control, no more leashes, collars, or muzzles."[57] The threat of rebellion that Begag envisions in the book became a reality in the 2005 French riots following the accidental deaths of two young Maghrebians who had been chased by the French police. The rioters, a majority of whom were Arabs, burnt cars and public buildings. It was the French version of Baldwin's warning about blacks in America: "the fire next time." The rat, like the hydrophobic dog, was ready to fight back.

All this to say that blackness is not necessarily a matter of pigmentation. As Hartman has argued,[58] it is determined by class, wherein a class of expendable people are perceived, in the new postcolonial order, as misplaced and constituting a public threat; those who are imagined as pests. In the framework of institutionalized white supremacy, the French Arab (rat) is just as black as the African American (dog) and must be recaged or eliminated by the police power of the state.

DOG OWNERSHIP

In *The Fire Next Time*, Baldwin explains how his views on the future of America differ from those of Elijah Muhammad, the leader of the Nation of Islam. In Muhammad's view, blacks should form a separate nation by claiming the southern states, while Baldwin believes that blacks and whites should work through their shared history together toward a united country. But Baldwin agrees with Muhammad in that "no people in history had ever been respected who had not owned their land. . . . For everyone else has, *is*, a nation, with a specific location and a flag—even, these days, the Jew."[59] And indeed, colonization and repression raise a question about the nature of ownership not only in terms of the right not to be owned but also in terms of the right to own. Baldwin's comparison between the American Negro and the Jew is pertinent in that both peoples have suffered a diasporic trauma of uprootedness, homelessness, and persecution. Additionally, at the darkest times of their persecution, both groups were treated like animals,[60] and both, oddly enough, have been, at times, barred from owning dogs.

Stripping Jews of their rights to own pets was part of a series of Third Reich animal welfare laws referred to as *Tierschutzgesetz*. The laws, initiated in 1933, the very year Hitler rose to power, paved the way for institutionalized Jewish discrimination. The anti–animal cruelty law prohibited the slaughter of animals for food without prior anesthesia or stunning. The law indirectly targeted Jews through the practice of Kosher slaughter since the Jewish (*Shechita*) procedure required butchers to kill the animal through exsanguination, severing the jugular vein while the animal was still conscious. The Jew's interaction with blood during the exsanguination procedure may have galvanized Richard Wagner's theory of the relation between blood contamination and human degeneration, a theory that very much appealed to Hitler. In *Hero-dom and Christendom* (*Heldentum und Christentum*),[61] Richard Wagner argues that the degeneration of the human race is the result of blood contamination through the absorption of animal meat and sexual intercourse (miscegenation). Hitler, supposedly influenced by Wagner, became a vegetarian later in life.[62] As Boria Sax explains in *Animals in the Third Reich*:

> The enormous symbolic significance that the Nazis attached to blood made death by bleeding seem perverse. From their point of view this was not simply a matter of being killed but also being deprived of primeval vitality. Jews were called "bloodsuckers" and "parasites." The animal being slaughtered in a kosher manner would twitch. . . . This is a muscle spasm, but many people interpreted the reflex as a sign of torment. Kosher slaughter was called a form of ritualistic torture practiced by a coarse and unfeeling people.[63]

Tierschutzgesetz, which included close to thirty different decrees and laws for the protection of animals and nature, was meant to show compassion for all animals. Conversely, the 1850 French Loi Grammont prohibited only the public mistreatment of pets and provided no protection for pets outside of the public sphere and no protection at all—either public or private—for nondomesticated animals. In contrast, the Third Reich legislation for animal protection was nondiscriminative—at least, when it came to animals. The underlying anti-Semitic goal of this anti–animal cruelty law became more explicit in the February 15, 1942, decree that prohibited Jews from owning pets, presumably on the grounds that Kosher-abiding Jews were unfit to care for dogs. Within the context of Nazi eugenics experimentation on dog breeds and their ideals concerning the human superiority of the Aryan race, however, banning Jews from owning dogs could also have been a way to curb a so-called Jewish dog population that could have contaminated the pure Nazi dog.

Austrian-born writer Hans Fantel recalls the first time in his early teens that he heard the expression "Jewish dog."[64] Fantel witnessed the Gestapo arrest his neighbor and shoot the neighbor's dog as the animal came to the defense of his owner. Fantel did not know his neighbor, but he knew the dog and was upset that the dog had been killed. Fantel's housekeeper, a Nazi sympathizer, comforted the young Fantel by telling him that the dog was only "a Jewish dog." Fantel recalled his puzzled reaction then, wondering what does it mean to be a "Jewish dog"? The Austrian teen did not believe in the concept of "Jewish dogs," which made him distrust the man who propagated such fallacies. Fantel's housekeeper's logic demonstrates the Nazi ideology of extermination: If the Jewish dog exists in the Nazi mind, those dogs would be euthanized, just as their Jewish owners soon would be.[65]

The adjective "Jewish" in the phrase "Jewish dog" contains both a possessive and adjectival nuance acquired through a perverse kinship: The dog becomes Jewish through ownership by a person of Jewish faith, as possession and identification merge in a tragic fate of abuse.[66] French author Hélène Cixous teases out a similar cognitive ambiguity found in the combination of possessive and adjectival nuances in her autobiographical short story, "Stigmates."[67] As mentioned in chapter 2, Cixous claims to have been the victim of anti-Semitic abuse after the death of her father, in the years following World War II. Algerians would throw stones at her house as Fips, Cixous's dog, snarled and barked in response to the abuse: "'Am I Jewish?,'" Fips

wondered. "'But what does it mean to be Jewish?,' the dog suffered, not knowing the answer."[68] Fips internalized the ordeal
of his family's presence being unwanted and as such became a
sort of Jewish *Pied-Noir* dog—hence the story's title, "Stigmates," which refers to the dog carrying the wounds of his
owners.

As Emmanuel Lévinas shows in "Nom d'un chien ou le droit
naturel" (The name of a dog, or natural rights), for the victim
of anti-Semitism, owning a dog is also a way to reclaim one's
humanity. Bobby, the dog that wags his tail to greet Jewish prisoners during the morning call in the Nazi concentration camp,
reverses the process of dehumanization for the Jew: "For him
[Bobby]—there was no refuting it—we were men."[69] Because
the Jewish dog is a marker of humanity, Nazi legislation stripping Jews of animal companionship sought to impact the perception of them as human.

Hitler was fond of dogs, particularly of his beloved female
German shepherd, Blondi, to whom he gave a cyanide capsule
in a group suicide (with Eva Braun) when the Russians captured
Berlin. His love of German shepherds was coupled with a fascination with wolves. Adolf in Old High German means "noble
wolf" (*Athalwolf*), and Hitler took pride in the lupine identification. In their respective fictional rewritings of World War II
history, authors Asher Kravitz (*The Jewish Dog*) and Jonathan
Crown (*Sirius*) capitalize on Hitler's known weakness for dogs
to present the Jewish dog as the Führer's Achilles' heel. In both
stories, the Jew-owned dog stealthily infiltrates the Nazi regime
in support of the Jew. *The Jewish Dog* tells the story of a dog
named Caleb, who, due to the Third Reich ban on Jewish dog
ownership, loses his Jewish owners. Caleb is a wandering Jew
with a strong sense of "Jewish blood flowing through [his]
veins."[70] Despite being owned by a series of anti-Semitic people,

Caleb shows unwavering loyalty to his initial Jewish family. The dog eventually betrays his SS officer owner in the Treblinka Nazi camp when he catches sight of his original owner, Joshua. At the end of the story, Joshua says of Caleb, "his dog is no less Jewish than you and I. Our nation (Israel) is his, and our God is his."[71] In *Sirius*, Crown pushes the question of Jewish loyalty even farther, as Levi, the Jewish-owned fox terrier, becomes the undercover personal dog of Hitler. After having gained the Führer's trust, Levi single-handedly leads the Führer to his downfall by playing a double agent. Crown ironically substitutes the Jewish dog, whom Hitler sees as unfit to represent his race, for Blondi.[72] In these two books, the authors redeploy the so-called Jewish dog as a means of empowerment. Like Lévinas's Bobby, the dogs are able to vindicate the Jew in the face of the dehumanizing Nazi design, finally proving the primacy of interspecies loyalty over a pet ownership system that depends on a hierarchy of beings. Despite their being owned by a series of anti-Semitic humans, Caleb and Levi remain Jewish in a sort of auto-interpellation reversal in which what was deemed condemnable, their Jewishness, becomes the source of their pride.

For Joseph to take Caleb along with him to Israel carries a powerful symbol of conjoined salvation that transcends the Nazi ban on companionship with animals. But for blacks—to paraphrase Romain Gary in *Chien blanc*—there is no such thing as a "Black Israel." Additionally, Baldwin's previous comment about the analogy between black and Jewish land ownership and the respect it confers upon the owner also applies to pet ownership. Blacks in American history have had their right of dog ownership suspended as a form of racial oppression, just like Jews in Europe. During the slavery era, however, banning blacks from owning dogs was not, technically speaking, perceived as a dehumanizing practice since slaves, as chattel property, were already less than human, already dehumanized. As John Campbell explains in "My Constant Companion," "viewed ever in law as a piece of property and only slightly less so in reality, it was impossible, if not illogical, for black slaves to own their property: for how could chattel own property? how can one object be said to own another?"[73] Were a slave to own a dog, it would have been viewed as an aberration and, as such, an act of defiance against the various slave codes. As Campbell pursues, "the very fact of having a dog represented a vital assertion and demonstration of slave humanity in defiance of what slaveholder law and daily practice proclaimed to the contrary."[74] Owning a dog, for the slave, was a Lévinasian moment of human recognition: "there was no refuting it—we were men."[75] In *Pit Bull*, Bronwen Dickey mentions the 1833 treatise *Detail of a Plan for the Moral Improvement of Negroes on Plantations*, in which a Georgia rice planter named Thomas Savage Clay recommends that dogs be outlawed in slave quarters because "blacks were not morally sophisticated enough to care for animals properly,"[76] an argument similar to the Nazi rationale behind the decree banning Jews from owning dogs. Even though slaves used their dogs mainly for hunting, planters feared that slaves' dogs would be used as weapons against their masters. South Carolina, as Campbell points out, passed an antidog law in 1859 for the very purpose of preventing the weaponization of dogs by slaves.[77] Even free blacks, Dickey says, were legally prohibited from owning dogs in Virginia, South Carolina, Maryland, and Arkansas. The irony of the ban on dog ownership for slaves lies in the fact that canine weaponization was a specifically white practice, used by plantation owners to discipline recalcitrant slaves; blacks were the victims of dog attacks, not the perpetrators. The fear that the slave will use the dog against the white is similar to the white fear of the black rapist on the plantation; both fears are based on projections: the master is the one using dogs against blacks, just like he is the one raping the (black) woman on the plantation.

The main reason behind the ban was that roaming slave-owned dogs were a threat to the master's cattle, to the sheep in particular. The dog was also a potential facilitator for slaves' mischief, such as theft. President George Washington ordered that "all dogs belonging to slaves (on his plantation] be handed in immediately, because they 'aid[ed] them in their night robberies.'"[78] But behind the guise of the slave's dog as simple nuisance looms the fear of the white fangs of slave retaliation.

Chien blanc (*White Dog*) by French author Romain Gary takes place in Los Angeles in 1968 and, as mentioned in chapter 2, tells the story of a so-called white dog rescued by a white couple.[79] The phrases "white dog" or "nigger dog" refer to dogs trained by white southerners to discriminately attack blacks in a manner reminiscent of the dog-training practices of slave owners. The story ultimately reveals that a black dog trainer secretly reconditioned the "white dog" to attack only whites instead. At the end of this autobiographically based fiction, Gary, a white man, becomes the victim of the vicious white dog. With this surprising twist, Gary's narrative pinpoints the persistent white phobia, even after the abolition of slavery, of the racially reversed attack, the fear that the lingering plantation-based system of racial repression will turn back on them.

Interestingly enough, in the 1982 film adaptation of Gary's novel, also titled *White Dog*, director Samuel Fuller presents the white dog as an attack dog not only against blacks but also against sexual predators—a sexual component that is not present in Gary's original story. In the movie, young actress Julie Sawyer rescues a white German shepherd on the road. Given her frail body, young appearance, and the fact that she lives by herself in a house in the Hollywood hills, the company of a watchdog proves to be a blessing when a rapist breaks into Sawyer's house at night and attempts to rape her. The dog viciously attacks the intruder and saves Sawyer. In a following scene, the dog growls at Sawyer's boyfriend when the latter initiates physical contact with the young lady. It then becomes apparent that the dog is the protector of the young woman against any type of sexual predation.

After these two preliminary scenes, the movie follows Gary's original storyline about a racist dog that exclusively attacks blacks. Fuller's extrapolation in adding sexual predation to blackness highlights the prevalence of white guilt. The dog functions as a historical trigger, recalling the plantation-based connection between dog attacks, rape, and blackness. The storyline in Fuller's movie changes the course of history, as it justifies the use of canine weaponry against the black, who is subliminally portrayed as a rapist. With Keyes reconditioning the white dog, the black embodies the role of both the sexual predator and canine tormentor. The dog is a reminder of the archetypal white phobia of poetic justice: What if the attack dog turned on the white, the same way that the white fears the black might start raping the white woman?

The ban on dog ownership for blacks in America occurred during the plantation era, but it could easily be argued that there are insidious remnants of the racially oriented ban on dog ownership in our modern society. A number of scholars have looked at how breed-specific laws and state bans on dog ownership in America have targeted the so-called pit bull, a dog inclined to be stigmatized as dangerously urban and black-owned.[80] Erin C. Tarver explains that the criminalization and racialization of the pit bull dates back to the 1980s, "when reports surfaced connecting dog bite attacks by 'pit bulls' to gang violence by urban youths. . . . This image was, it seems, propped up at least in part by the association of 'pit bulls' with the hip hop music scene—itself a strong racialized genre in the United States." [81] As Tarver looks at the contagion effect of the dog and his human companion through dog ownership, she argues that the criminalization of one (the owner or the pit bull) leads to the criminalization of the other. It has been shown, as Tarver points out, that the pit bull owner is often perceived as "thuggish,"[82] a word that is racially and criminally suggestive for the owner but also, by association, for the dog. It is no coincidence, according to Tarver, that at the same time that the pit bull and his owner were stigmatized as "thuggish," the word "wilding" (a reference to group or "pack" violence committed by blacks and Latinos) became popular. Looking at the contaminating effect of dog ownership in a racial context helps us understand how breed-specific crackdowns (discussed in detail in chapter 2) could have coincided with the tough-on-crime laws that massively targeted blacks in the early nineties, a synchronous phenomenon that Dickey also addresses in her book *Pit Bull*. When one becomes aware of the racialization of the pit bull through putative black ownership, pit bull bans across America take on the appearance of a modern version of the plantation-era ban.

Tarver, like Claire Jean Kim in *Dangerous Crossings*,[83] has raised some racial questions about football star Michael Vick's conviction for his role in a dog-fighting ring. The two scholars have argued that the way the black athlete was anathemized for his participation in a dog-fighting ring needs to be examined within a historical context of conjoined animalization, criminalization, and racialization in America. Tarver goes as far as saying that active participation in the foie gras industry in America, through imports and consumption, has been treated as a noncontroversial matter of fact only because this type of animal cruelty is part of a wealthy, white, mainstream culture—unlike the type of animal cruelty in which Vick engaged. But what has not been addressed yet about the quarterback's case are the historical undertones related to the controversy over Vick's right to possess a dog. Vick's felony sentence included twenty-three months in prison and a three-year ban on the possession of a dog. After Vick's sentencing, the Virginia Legislative Assembly amended the law to make bans on dog possession a mandatory sentence in dog-fighting cases. Five years after his sentencing and two years after the expiration of the ban on his possession of dogs, Vick admitted to owning a dog again, which created a public uproar and prompted some to question whether his ban could be extended or become imposed for a lifetime. Advocating for a lifetime ban for Vick recalls the oft-overlooked historical connection between bans on dog ownership and blackness. Making an appeal to extend Vick's ban to possess dogs past the duration set by a court is an indirect way of reinstating a special kind of sentencing for a special kind of people, one that happens to be black in this case. The public's reaction, their desire to see Vick's dog ownership ban become lifelong, feeds into a logic of a criminal system that already deprives ex-convicts—who are massively disproportionately black—of their rights, as Michelle Alexander shows in *The New Jim Crow*.[84] Admittedly, the human right to own property is, as vegan abolitionist Francione would argue, different from the right to own a dog since the property status of animals can be debated. Racially invested dog ownership bans, be they through breed-specific bans in given locations or Vick's extended ban, however, echo the plantation era, in which blacks unequivocally had no right to own property, given that they were themselves property.

Dog ownership is historically and, more often than not, racially charged because of a recurrent history, on both sides of the Atlantic, of canine weaponry used against the oppressed. In

1974, the epic boxing event in Kinshasa, Zaire, referred to as the "Rumble in the Jungle," brought two heavyweight champions face-to-face: George Foreman and Muhammad Ali. Foreman was undeniably the contender, but Ali's colorful and feisty personality stole the show before the boxing match even started. When Foreman descended from the plane with his German shepherd, his fate was sealed. The sight of Foreman with a German shepherd on a leash reminded Zairians of the repressive tactics used by the Belgian police against the populace during the colonial era, when the Belgians had used German shepherds to keep blacks on their toes. Ali tauntingly calling Foreman a "Belgian" capitalized on the colonial fear of dogs in Zaire and drove the crowd to support him instead of the "white man."[85] This anecdote shows that the racial dimension attached to dog ownership far exceeds the history of the Americas. Because of a cross-Atlantic colonial history impacted by the widespread use of canine weaponry against blacks, the alliance between dogs and blacks is often tainted by the idea of repressive tactics, even when the interspecies relationship seems to be mainly one of companionship, as with Foreman in Zaire.

Few and far between are the cases in history in which the relationship between blacks and dogs includes an uncomplicated story of companionship. The 1859 slave narrative by Charles Ball, *Fifty Years in Chains*, is one exception.[86] The author talks about his heart-wrenching experience of having to leave his beloved dog behind when he attempted to escape from the plantation.[87] The same is true of Harriet Wilson's *Our Nig*, which tells the story of Nig, a free black woman who becomes very close to a dog that the white son of her employer gives her to comfort her from the mistreatment that he knows she endures in the house.[88] The moment the son leaves the house, the dog is taken away from Nig by the white matriarch, a sign that the possession of this dog was only guaranteed by the presence of the white son. Canine companionship is a white privilege.

John Berger, in "Why Look at Animals?," posits that animal companionship is different from human exchange because it is a "companionship offered to the loneliness of man as a species."[89] Man alone can claim to own animals because man is alone in his human claims. But by slightly distorting Berger's claim, one could also say that dog companionship is offered to the loneliness of man, not as a species, but as a (white) race. In a colonially impacted system of thought, the white man alone claims the right to animal companionship, because he alone claims a right to be fully human.

5

THE NAKED TRUTH ABOUT
CATS AND BLACKS

A nimals offer companionship to lessen the solitude of the human species, but along with this companionship comes a living presence endowed with a pair of eyes that observes and takes notes. In his 1980 essay "Why Look at Animals?," John Berger posits that the animal holds secrets about man and that the latter becomes aware of those secrets the moment that "he intercept[s] an animal's look."[1] Looking at the human reflection in the animal gaze and seeing it as a phenomenological epiphany is a concept that has become more mainstream since French philosopher Jacques Derrida's 1997 lecture, "The Animal That Therefore I Am (More to Follow)."[2] But what makes Berger's earlier version particularly pertinent is the idea that only the animal knows man's secrets. In German, Martin Heidegger refers to animal silence as *Sprachlosigeit*, "speechlessness."[3] The incapacity to speak, however, is not synonymous with ignorance; in his essay, Berger disentangles the association of silence with ignorance in a powerful way. The animal is the silent eyewitness to human existence and the only one who knows about man. But the particularity of *Sprachlosigeit* is its inevitable connection to secrecy since the secret is that which cannot be told. As Berger writes, "animals are always the observed. The fact that they can observe us has lost all significance."[4] But in Berger's essay, the animal gaze regains its significance, which the author describes as a humbling experience for man. The glow of human exceptionalism, due to the exclusivity of the logos, pales in contrast to animal silence. For the secret holder, having no access to the logos is incidentally a strength. The animal has something on man and will not give it away. "Such an unspeaking companionship," Berger writes, "was felt to be so equal that often one finds the conviction that it was man who lacked the capacity to speak with animals."[5] To paraphrase one of Vinciane Despret's book titles, What would animals say about us, if we could ask them the question?[6]

Blacks have a secret too, a secret specifically addressed to (the white) man. The difference here, however, is that the white man knows about the nature of this secret and will go to great lengths to keep it concealed. The Bible (Gen. 9:25) is where to find the secret. Noah plants a vineyard, gets drunk from his wine, and lays naked in his tent. His son Ham enters the tent, sees his father uncovered, and leaves the tent to tell his two brothers, Shem and Japheth, about their father's exposure; after which the two brothers take a garment, enter the tent walking backward in order to avoid seeing their father in the nude, and cover their father's body. Once Noah awakens from his slumber, the two brothers tell their father what Ham has done. Noah, infuriated, throws a curse at Ham's son, Canaan, and his descendants, vowing them to eternal servitude. Ham is the holder of the naked truth, but servitude will guarantee that the story never gets out.

Because it is believed that Ham was black, this biblical story seems to explain and justify black slavery. As the story has it, people from Africa have been enslaved because they saw what they should have never seen. In *Curse of Ham*, David M. Goldenberg attempts to retrace the common assumption that slavery was the God-given fate of blacks as told in the book of Genesis. There is no clear indication that Ham's bloodline was incidentally black, except for the speculation that *Ham* in Hebrew means "burnt," "swarthy," "black." According to Goldenberg, there are no semantic anchors that can convincingly tie the word *Ham*, as it is spelled in Hebrew, to "black." Yet, the curse of Ham has been one of the most persistent and commonly shared justifications for black slavery in the Americas. As Goldenberg explains, "the belief that Ham was the ancestor of black Africans, that Ham was cursed by God, and that therefore Blacks have been eternally and divinely doomed to enslavement has entered the canon of Western religion and folklore, and it stayed put well into the twentieth century."[7] The curse of Ham is the story of the primal encounter between the white and the black. The former has been seen fully naked; it is a question now of making sure that the black will not use the shame of this exposure against the white. As Noah suggests in his curse, slavery is the way to keep the eyewitness quiet. Yet, how can one guarantee that the black will not eventually speak? How can one be so sure that there will never be an Olaudah Equiano or Frederick Douglass to tell on the white man?[8] If the chattel (as in cattle) slave were truly an animal, the white would have no need to feel exposed—or would he?

THE NAKED TRUTH

"Everything begins as if we were only two,"[9] Emmanuel Lévinas says in an interview—two as in a face-to-face. In human encounters, the eyes, nose, and ears are essential receptors to becoming familiarized with the unknown other. The face is also a crucial body part, as it is the only part, generally excluding the hands, that is not covered with a garment, making first contacts a true and bare experience. "The skin of the face is that which stays most naked, most destitute,"[10] Lévinas argues. Because all human faces are equally destitute, first contacts are a vulnerable experience for both parties. When the face-to-face occurs between an animal and a human, however, one is more naked than the other since the animal's face is by nature covered. A face-to-face encounter between men and animals remains possible, even if what we call "face," as Lévinas explains, is different in an animal fully covered with fur than in a man whose face is utterly naked. In *The Animal That Therefore I Am*,[11] Derrida playfully teases out the polysemic nature of the French expression *à poil*. When the animal is *à poil*, the French expression means "covered with fur," but when man is *à poil*, the expression refers to being stark naked. When faced with the animal, humans are at a disadvantage since they alone, and more specifically their face alone, is *à poil*. It is a shameful premise for the interspecies encounter: man's face is irremediably exposed, while the animal stays covered.

Within an interracial encounter, the chattel/cattle slave can also be said to be figuratively *à poil*, not because the slave is naked, but rather, and on the contrary, because the slave looks covered in contrast to the exposure of the master; in that, the black is indeed an animal (cattle). The inception of slavery in the Americas seen through the lens of Ham's curse allows us to understand nakedness as the constitutive taboo of plantation society. In his study of the psychology of colonialism and racism, *Peau noire, masques blancs* (*Black Skin, Whites Masks*), Frantz Fanon posits that blacks are alienated by the fact that they have been conditioned to see themselves through the eyes of whites.[12] Fanon's theory is somehow a racial adaptation of Jean-Paul Sartre's concept of *pour-autrui* (for-the-other). *Pour-autrui* is based on the idea that self-perception is shaped through the eyes of the other.[13] But the fate of Ham shows that whites, as Noah's descendants, are equally alienated in the way that they see their disavowed, exposed, self through the eyes of blacks. Just like Berger with the animal secret, it seems that the white man is reminded of the existence of the secret the moment that "he intercepts the black's look." Laconic in the simplicity of its style, the story of Ham's curse in Genesis has been subject to much speculation, not the least of which, aside from the putative blackness of Ham, is the sexual innuendo in Ham's action. Why should Noah react so strongly to his son seeing him naked if it were not because of an abominable infraction? How do we explain the extent of Ham's sentence? Jennifer Knust, in "Who's Afraid of Canaan's Curse?," alludes to the potential taboo of incest,[14] but ultimately argues that in an ancient Israelite context, seeing someone naked was perceived as an act of shaming.[15] And not just in an ancient context, because nakedness, the postlapsarian fate of Adam and Eve, is the quintessential expression of man's vulnerability, gazing at a senior or superior's naked body would be shameful in any context where not losing face (not being exposed) would be vital to the maintenance of the hierarchical structure.

Not losing face is what ultimately defines the primal encounter with the other; and this applies to both the archetypal interracial and interspecies relationships. Lévinas argues that animals do not have a face in the same way that humans do. "The phenomenon of the face," Lévinas writes, "is not in its purest form in the dog. In the dog, in the animal, there are other phenomena. For example, the force of nature is pure vitality. It is more this which characterizes the dog."[16] For Lévinas, only humans have a face in the ethical sense since only they can understand the "Thou Shall Not Kill" command on the other's face. "I am concerned about justice because the other has a face,"[17] Lévinas says. But more important than ethics is the question of perception. Animals do not have a face because, to repeat Berger, "the fact that they can observe us has lost all significance."[18] The animal's face is inexistent and unaccounted for due to man's unwillingness to face the existence of the secret in the animal's eyes. Berger does not give any clues as to the nature of man's secrets, but Derrida, in *The Animal That Therefore I Am*, names nakedness as what stands between man and the animal. Human nakedness is what man fears to see in the animal's eyes: "I have trouble repressing a reflex of shame. Trouble keeping silent within me a protest against the indecency. Against the impropriety [*malséance*] that can come of finding oneself naked, one's sex exposed, stark naked before a cat that looks at you without moving, just to see."[19] Derrida later explains that this sense of impropriety comes from the fact that animals, in contrast to man, are not naked because they do not have the consciousness of the shame of nakedness. The human species is therefore the only one *à poil*, "naked," while the animal species is not vulnerable to that kind of shame. The animal's look resting on the human body is a reminder of the human exception—exceptionally naked.

As Derrida explains, man does not return the animal gaze as a way to not feel *à poil*, naked. The same can be said about the archetypal interracial relationship. Accordingly, in Genesis, slavery is the white man's attempt not to return the gaze that would remind him of his nakedness. So the absence of face is not only an ethical issue but also, if we follow Berger and Derrida's logic, the result of a denial to see the gaze, to see the eyes that can redress you. Martinican-born Frantz Fanon depicts being looked at as a black man in a French train: "Mama, see the Negro! I'm scared!,"[20] Fanon reminisces. Racial interpellation (in Louis Althusser's sense of the term, see note 117 in chapter 1) has led Fanon to understand his self-consciousness as defined by the white man's gaze in a racially invested kind of *pour-autrui*: "I found that I was an object in the midst of other objects."[21] But, while this passage from *Peau noire, masques blancs* has been extensively quoted, and many scholars have commented on the black's objectification, the fate of the white boy who interpellates Fanon in the train has been mainly ignored. What does it mean to see a black in contrast to being seen as black? It is understood that the boy fears a face that does not look like his. But what if the boy's fear did not lie simply in a difference of complexion but in the experience of seeing no face at all in the other? What if the boy had just come face-to-face with pure alterity identified not only as a lack of sameness but also, and more importantly, as a ghost-like absence of being, hence the fear? Lévinas says in his interview about the human face:

> Alterity is not at all the fact that there is a difference, that facing me there is someone who has a different nose than mine, different colour eyes, another character. It is not difference, but alterity. It is alterity, the unencompassable, the transcendent. It is the beginning of transcendence. You are not transcendent by virtue of a certain different trait.[22]

Indeed, the encounter with the black is not a question of a "different trait" in the sense of a different pigmentation; it is rather a question of absence of face, an unencompassable face-to-no-face experience with the black other. The absence of face is the result of the silence, the hushed secret, imposed by slavery at

Noah's request. The parable of Ham's curse allows us to understand the boy's fear in the train as an atavistic reaction to seeing the white's reflection in the black's eyes. Soon enough, the boy will learn to avoid that gaze and thus ignore the existence of his shameful secret reflected in the black man's eyes.

In his short story "L'homme qui ne parlait pas" (The man who did not speak),[23] Haitian Canadian writer Dany Laferrière envisions a scene in which performers are on stage, ready for opening night, when the director decides to add a last-minute prop on stage: a silent and motionless black man. Through his silence and immobility, the black is more of a disturbance than if he had done a lousy job at performing. In this short story, Laferrière tries to convey, with a slight touch of magical realism, the experience of black presence as an unidentified, silent uneasiness. The black, as "the man who did not speak," cannot have a face since, as Lévinas says in the interview, the face is what speaks, "I think that the beginning of language is in the face."[24] Lévinas explains that, when one sees the other's face, the frailty and nudity of the face on the one hand and the power of spoken command on the other, one understands that there is something larger than their own individual existence, something that they need to respect in the other, and not annihilate. As a nonspeaking being, however, as a man silenced by slavery, the black does not have a face in the ethical sense either; the black is seen as not participating in the Thou Shall Not Kill command, which explains the reaction of the frightened boy who fears for his life. Fanon, interpellated as black—"Mama, see the Negro! I'm scared!"—has no voice. So the mother speaks for the black man, in front of him and on behalf of him, as if he were not there listening: "Look how handsome that Negro is,"[25] she says to the boy. Yet, Fanon does answer back, "Kiss the handsome Negro's ass, madame!"[26] The "Negro" is in the third person; he is not meant to address but only to be addressed. "Shame flooded her face,"[27] Fanon writes, as the mother unexpectedly hears the black man talk back. The mother, for her part, has a face, which is "flooded with shame."

Not having a face would technically suggest the absence of blushing, an animal phenomenon that Charles Darwin addresses in *The Expressions of the Emotions in Man and Animals*. The exposed part of the human body, mainly the face and the neck, can blush. Animal bodies do not blush since they have no exposed skin. Darwin writes, "blushing is the most peculiar and the most human of all expressions. Monkeys redden from passion, but it would require an overwhelming amount of evidence to make us believe that any animal could blush."[28] Instead of blushing, dogs, for example, put their tails between their legs as an expression of embarrassment. Now, if we argue that the black does not have a face either, does it mean that, like the animal, the black does not blush? Ironically enough, this is a question that Darwin has also raised in his book. From the German explorer Alexander Von Humboldt writing in his personal narrative about Australian natives, "How can those be trusted, who know not how to blush"?[29] and to some informants insisting that the Kafirs of South Africa never blush, Darwin claims to have repeatedly heard that blacks do not blush. Ultimately, Darwin argues in the book that all races blush, even though "in the very dark races no distinct change of colour can be perceived."[30] Of importance here is obviously not Darwin's conclusion but the question raised. The capacity to blush is subject to question in the animal and the black alike, somehow confirming that, for white consciousness, the black does not have a face; or at least, that the animal and the black face are not meant to be exposed (since it is *à poil*), unlike the white face. Darwin explains that it is not the feeling about exposure that makes one blush but rather, and more precisely, "the thinking about what others think of us, which excites a blush."[31] The fact that the white is said to be the only one who can unequivocally blush reveals a heightened sense that self-consciousness is an exclusive aspect of whiteness. In return, the black and the animal do not unequivocally possess this hypersensitivity to "thinking about what others think of us," this self-attention to exposure. As Fanon exposes the mother in the train, she becomes aware of his presence in the car, now fully conscious that he has been here, looking, *all along*, which makes her blush. This exacerbated sense of self is triggered by the black's unexpected return of the gaze, something that the white has been avoiding all along.

In sum, if the human face is deemed *always already* white, it is because the white is the one who expects to speak. But more importantly, the human face is white because it is the one exposed, the one that blushes. Seeing a nonface in the animal and the black ultimately reveals the anguish of not knowing what the animal and racialized Other think of us. The black and the animal are nonfaces that do not blush in return, as if they did not even care about what the Other—white and human—may think of them, as if they did not fear being caught naked.

ALL ALONG

Jacques Derrida is in the bathroom and notices that his cat has been looking at his naked body, "I am seen and seen naked, before even seeing *myself* seen by a cat. Before even seeing myself or knowing myself seen naked."[32] At stake in this situation is evidently the shameful nakedness of man, but more important and even more shameful is the sudden realization that one's naked body has been observed for an undetermined amount of time without one being aware of it. This interstice, the very moment when Derrida leaves his state of oblivion and enters the knowing, is the quintessential experience of shame. As with Noah, the disadvantageous situation lies not only in one being dressed (*à poil*, with animal fur) and the other naked but also in the unawareness of being seen naked. This experience entails a sequence of specularity in which one takes note belatedly of having been seen all along, the "all along" temporal marker being key. Belatedness is unavoidable in human exposure since animals are silent onlookers who cannot verbally alert humans to their presence in the room.

In *The Animal That Therefore I Am*, Derrida deplores the fact that none of the philosophers who have addressed the animal question in their work have evoked the possibility of being looked at by the animal that they, for their part, observe, and of which they speak. "No more than Descartes does any of them evoke or take into account the problem of nakedness and modesty operating between animal and human."[33] The main reason for the oversight resides in the fact that philosophers have been too busy talking about the animal's incapacity to speak, *Sprachlosigeit*. While Descartes views the animal simply as comparable to the mechanism of a clock or automation (*automatica mechanica*), Heidegger and Lacan have the merit of ascribing agency to the animal. Yet, Derrida considers the latter philosophers' inclination to present the human-animal divide in terms of logos versus instinct to be limiting in its humanistic approach. Whether it is Descartes's "I think," Heidegger's "*Dasein*," or Lacan's "subject," the assumption remains, in all cases, that humans alone have the capacity to respond (reason), while animals only react (instinct). As the anti-Cartesian sounding title suggests (*The Animal That Therefore I Am*), Derrida's approach essentially consists of refuting the human-animal distinction.

Instead, Derrida chooses to blur the interspecies frontier by casting doubt: How can one be so sure of knowing what the animal has on her mind precisely because the animal cannot speak?

It can be a source of comfort to remind ourselves that animals cannot speak since, unlike with Ham, the cat cannot tell about our shameful acts committed behind closed doors. That said, Derrida's tour de force in *The Animal That Therefore I Am* is to transmit the idea that, though she cannot speak, the cat, his cat, may have the capacity to think, and even more troublesome, to judge him. In response to Lacan's claim that the animal is incapable of second-degree deception such as "pretending pretense," an aptitude deemed exclusively human, Derrida asks, "in the name of what knowledge or what testimony . . . one could calmly declare that the *animal in general* is incapable of pretending pretense?"[34] As Derrida suggests, however slim it may be, there is still a chance that our self-assured knowledge makes us blind to the manipulation of animals, who may know more than they care to share. Pretending pretense, as Derrida explains, is as follows: "Why do you tell me that you are going to X in order to have me believe you are going to Y whereas you are indeed going to X?"[35] By questioning Lacan's infallible certainty, Derrida opens the door to an ontologically altering "what if?" situation. What if animals, at least some of them, were endowed with the capacity for deceit, lies, sarcasm, and even contempt? What if François, my German shepherd, had always been one step ahead of me in his knowledge of me? François, pretending not to care about the steak left on the kitchen table, waits for me to leave the room in order to grab it and eat it. Yet, how can I be so sure that my dog did not pretend to pretend, only to give me the impression that he fears me to the point of only stealing when I am not in the room, when in fact my dog is fully aware

THE NAKED TRUTH ABOUT CATS AND BLACKS ⟨R 169

of his capacity to overcome me and even use me as a piece of meat if he so wishes? By pretending to pretend, my dog feeds my ignorance, comforting me in the assumption that I have the upper hand in our interspecies relationship.

Suffice it to say that Derrida has successfully cast a doubt on the animal question, a doubt that he semantically conveys with the word *animot*. The neologism addresses two important axioms: first, that "animal" is a word arbitrarily imposed on a complex set of species (ani-mot from the French *mot*, meaning "word"); and second, that the animal question should be addressed in the plural (from French plural *animaux*, which sounds like *animot*) in order to reflect the incommensurability of singular animal experiences. And indeed, what does François, my pet dog, have to do with a lion in the wild, or a whale in the ocean? This is where Heidegger comes into play, with his emphasis on the domestic animal (*Haustier*). In his 1929–30 lectures,[36] Heidegger argues that the animal is "poor in world" (*weltarm*), whereas man is "world-forming" (*weltbildend*). Animals are not "worldless" (*weltlos*) like a stone, but because they cannot speak, they can only be "captivated" or "taken" (*benommen*) by their environment without the capacity to comprehend their world with analytical perspective. It goes without saying that the animal's absence of language in Heidegger is presented as an impoverishment only in comparison with man's capacity to speak. This impoverishment, or at least the awareness of it, is aimed at the household animal, the one exposed to human language. In a similar vein, Sartre has argued that the dog has learned the experience of boredom and frustration from living with speaking humans. In a study of Flaubert,[37] Sartre argues that going from nature to culture has taught the dog to experience his or her life as a limitation. Living in the human household, as Florence Burgat paraphrases Sartre, raises the dog "toward an impossible understanding even as his bewildered intelligence collapses into stupidity."[38] The dog understands that humans are talking about him, yet the frustrated animal cannot make out the words. Enlightened ignorance is therefore the lot of the household dog. The domesticated animal is aware of his human-impacted environment while also cognizant of his limitation in it (*weltarm*). In sum, had he stayed in nature, the dog would have not suffered from his incapacity to comprehend language. Strictly speaking then, the domesticated animal's world is not poor (*arm*) but impoverished, his world having become less fulfilling once in contact with the speaking human.

Yet, it would be too simple to conclude that the animal, as a houseguest, is strictly poor in the company of human beings. It is also important to point out that, as a trade-off for her domestication, the animal has in turn gained the advantage of being able to see it all. Even more to the point, the incapacity of animals to share what they see is not necessarily experienced as a disadvantage to them. On the contrary, as previously mentioned, the *Sprachlosigeit* (muteness) of the animal may be a disadvantage to humans more than to animals. In the presence of the animal gaze, humans are lacking in their capacity to know what the nonhuman animal thinks and, even more troubling, what the animal thinks of *them*. Humans are left wondering not what domesticated animals are saying about them (like with Sartre's dog) but, more precisely, what they are *not* saying. The proximity between speaking human animals and silent nonhumans has created a discomforting imbalance between the human who has said it all and the nonhuman animal who has yet to speak. Heidegger, in his 1929–30 lectures, writes about living with household animals:

> We keep domestic pets in the house with us, they "*live*" *with us*. But we do not live with them if living means: *being* in an animal

kind of way. Yet we *are with* them nonetheless. But this being-with is not an *existing-with*, because a dog does not exist but merely lives. Through this being with animals we enable them to move within our world. We say that the dog is lying underneath the table or is running up the stairs and so on. Yet when we consider the dog itself—does it comport itself toward the table as table, toward the stairs as stairs? All the same, it does go up the stairs with us. It feeds with us—and yet, we do not really "feed." It eats with us—and yet it does not really "eat." Nevertheless, it is with us! A going along with . . . a transposed-ness, and yet not.[39]

Domestication has enabled creatures who act like us (going up the stairs with us) but who may not think like us or share a similar *Umwelt* (seeing the stairs as stairs) to share our daily life. As the only silent one in a speaking group, the dog comes across as an inconspicuous presence in our daily life. Yet, his silent gaze could become disconcerting if we allowed ourselves, for one minute only, to consider the possibility that this dog may be capable of pretending to pretend, a doubled pretense that would also imply a potential for manipulation, deceit, and contempt. Precisely because they cannot speak, animals can be thought only in terms of "what if?"—What if they did judge us?—the uncertainty of which makes us lose our usual composure.

In Sartre's *Being and Nothingness*, a man, overtaken by jealousy, looks into a room through a keyhole. As he hears footsteps in the hallway, the jealous man becomes aware of his shameful position. This example does not only depict shame as the experience of seeing one's vulnerability through the other's gaze, but it also and more broadly addresses self-consciousness as a state only accessible through the other's gaze (*pour-autrui*, "for-others"). *The Animal That Therefore I Am* is Derrida's pendant to Sartre, it is his way of questioning what happens when the footsteps are either not audible or not minded. What are the phenomenological implications of not minding the animal footsteps and looking on through the keyhole just as the cat keeps staring at our pathetic posture? What difference would it make in terms of the framework of our self-consciousness if we did return the cat's silent stare, if we did become aware of their having been in possession of our naked truth *all along*?

CAN THE SUBALTERN SPEAK?

The premise of the curse of Ham and Derrida's cat is that of a silent or silenced one who has seen the exposure and will not tell about it. The difference between these two cases, however, is that one (human) can technically speak and the other (animal) cannot. Yet, the threat of feeling exposed is equally poignant in both cases since shame has more to do with wondering what the Others think of us than wondering what they will subsequently tell about us. "Can the Subaltern Speak?" asks postcolonial scholar Gayatri Chakravorty Spivak, arguing that Western intellectuals, with their "politics of the oppressed," often speak on behalf of subalterns as a homogeneous whole with the unacknowledged result of muting their individuality.[40] Derrida asks "Can the animal respond?" with a similar intent to show that humans have for too long spoken for animals and reduced their existence to species, thus not giving justice to individual animals. The curse of Ham parable and Berger's and Derrida's contributions put emphasis not on the black or the animal but rather on the white or the human who becomes aware of being seen and judged by this once-innocuous presence.

What we have addressed so far is the way in which the human or the white situates himself when *faced* with the so-called animal or black, two projections that share the comparable experience of being perceived as permanently silent (*Sprachlosigeit*). And equally important is the question of "blackness" and "animal" as they relate to the experience of feeling naked (*à poil*) next to an all-too-covered onlooker. Derrida has raised a unique phenomenological question with the unreciprocated gaze of the silent one, a question that addresses the role of silence—be it human or animal—in the history of Western consciousness. When Heidegger asserts that the animal cannot speak, using the German word *Sprachlosigeit*, what he means by this "voicelessness" or "speechlessness" is different from the idea of black silence. The black can technically speak but has been prevented from doing so. For the slave, silence is imposed by culture, and not nature. And yet, I argue that Heidegger's concept of *Sprachlosigeit* applies also to black silence. Heidegger's *Sprachlosigeit* is a permanent condition, and, while human silence is reversible, the slave was meant to be forever silent: Ham's descendants were doomed to eternal servitude. The extent of the horror of slavery could have happened only if the slave owner was assured that the dirty secret would never come out. Horror thrives in a context other than the ordinary life of language, in a context where the act of perversion can never be communicated. Auschwitz survivor Charlotte Delbo writes in her memoir, *Auschwitz et après* (*Auschwitz and After*), that when prisoners were sent to the camp by train, they expected the worst, not the unconceivable.[41] The Holocaust surpasses the worst thing imaginable; it enters the realm of the ineffable. As such, the purpose of ethnic cleansing is literally an act of irrevocable silencing. How can one testify to a wrong when the very essence of this wrong is, through death, to divest the victim of the means to talk? As Jean-François Lyotard explains in *Le différend*, "a wrong," or a *différend*, occurs when only one voice can speak, the voice of the perpetuator.[42] The prisoner is in a state of permanent silence (*Sprachlosigeit*) because the tragedy will never be told by the dead victim. It was the same for the horror of slavery: Plantation life was sustainable only when there was a guarantee that what happened there could never be told. Slavery necessitated the death of the black author, the *always already* silent black book.[43]

But when, during slavery, former slaves started writing their stories in an effort to bring awareness to the horrors of human bondage and in the hope of ending slavery, the impact of their voices was comparable to the experience of the philosopher realizing that his naked body was exposed all along. The slave narrative genre broke the assumed permanence of the black *Sprachlosigeit*. Olaudah Equiano, an African slave also known as Gustavus Vassa, worked for British captains of slave ships and British Navy vessels as a slave. He is the author of *The Life of Olaudah Equiano*, published in 1789. In this autobiography, Equiano depicts a situation where he, as a slave, would witness his master reading a book out loud, which would give him the impression that the book was in conversation with his master. When Equiano would grab the book to start a conversation with it the way he had seen his master do, the book would fall silent in his hands. He writes:

> I had often seen my master and Dick employed in reading; and I had a great curiosity to talk to the books, as I thought they did; and so to learn how all things had a beginning; for that purpose I have often taken up a book, and have talked to it, and then put my ears to it, when alone, in hopes it would answer me; and I have been very much concerned when I found it remained silent.[44]

Equiano's account is one of the best-known slave narratives, alongside those by Mary Prince, Frederick Douglass, and Harriet Jacobs, and it is also one of the earliest ones. According to Henry Louis Gates Jr., the passage above is not, however, unique to Equiano. The nontalking book or the talking to the book episode appears in four other early slave narratives, those of James Gronniosaw in 1772, John Marrant in 1785, Cugoano in 1787, and John Jea in 1811. For Gates, this recurrence shows that early slave authors were accustomed to reading and revising each other's books. As Gates says in an interview for *Slate Academy*, "it's absurd to think that they all had this experience. They're all taking the experience from Gronniosaw, and revising it."[45] Those early slave narratives pinpoint the birth of the black literary genre, with the literary trope of talking to the book as a trademark. As an alternative to the silent white book, Gronniosaw created a book that literally *speaks to* the black.

What is important to keep in mind in the successive nontalking book episodes is that this trope is meant to present the book as racially discriminative, since the book speaks only to whites. The slave narrative genre, from its inception, carries a retaliative purpose. After putting his ear close to the book and realizing that the book would not speak to him, Gronniosaw felt that, as he says, "every body and every thing despis'd me because I was black."[46] By giving a voice to both the slave and the book in the slave's hands, Gronniosaw and his followers "write back with a vengeance," to paraphrase Salman Rushdie.[47] The nontalking book trope takes on a whole new dimension in John Jea's 1811 autobiography, *The Life, History, and Unparalleled Sufferings of John Jea*. In this version, the book in question is the Bible—something that one may already have suspected in the earlier versions of the trope since the Bible is a book commonly read out loud. John Jea, an African slave and preacher owned by a cruel master in New York since the age of two and a half, grows up despising the word of God, used too often by his master to justify his bondage and physical abuse. "I had seen so much deception in the people that professed to know God, that I could not endure being where there [*sic*] were, nor yet to hear them call upon the name of the Lord,"[48] Jea writes. As he grows older, Jea becomes intimately acquainted with Scripture through his frequent visits with the minister. The slave eventually becomes truly devout. Some magistrates, who were convinced that Jea was a real man of God, granted Jea his freedom, which his master immediately disputed. The master tried to convince Jea to remain his slave by telling him that the Bible, meaning the actual book, talked to him:

> So [the master] used to tell me that there was a time to every purpose under the sun, to do all manner of work, that slaves were in duty bound to do whatever their masters commanded them, whether it was right or wrong; so that they must be obedient to a hard spiteful master as to a good one. He then took the Bible and showed it to me, and said that the book talked with him.[49]

In Jea's version of events, the talking book episode shows how white Christians were wont to use Scripture to fit their interests, a tendency that brings us back to the curse of Ham. The Bible is supposed to have told the white that the black should be doomed to servitude, words that the black has not heard—or technically speaking, has not been able to hear—from the Bible. Jea's story puts an end to the talking book trope, exposing it as a sham at the service of the master. Paradoxically enough, even though Jea shows that he is not gullible (the way that Gronniosaw and the others may have appeared to be), he ends the episode expressing his disappointment at not hearing the book:

> My master's sons also endeavoured to convince me, by their reading in the behalf of their father; but I could not comprehend

their dark sayings, for it surprised me much, how they could take that blessed book into their hands, and to be so superstitious as to want to make me believe that the book did talk with them; so that every opportunity when they were out of the way, I took the book, and held it up to my ears, to try whether the book would talk with me or not, but it proved to be all in vain, for I could not hear it speak one word, which caused me to grieve and lament.[50]

There is a sense of necessary disavowal, what Octave Mannoni has referred to as the "I know but nevertheless,"[51] in Jea's concluding remarks, a disavowal that has pushed him and others in his condition to write their own books. The talking book trope in the slave narrative genre translates a need for a resounding voice. A book is commonly seen as silent, reading being an activity more often associated with the mind. Yet, the slave has taken the book to be a public affair. The black book, as a narrative that should have remained silent, is inopportune par excellence, it is the work of a subject who should have known better than to talk. Equiano mentions a house slave who had a particular iron machine in her head that "locked her mouth so fast that she could scarcely speak, and could not eat or drink."[52] This iron machine in the plantation is a reminder that Noah's inebriated nudity should remain secret and that if not muzzled, the slave could talk.

The plantation is an enclosed space where various transgressions are in the open within the realm of the plantation yet never meant to become public outside of this enclave. Many of the slave narratives contain moments of extreme violence, cruelty, barbarism, and sexual perversions on the part of the master. Solomon Northup, in *Twelve Years a Slave* (1853), describes in extreme detail the daily physical abuse that he received while in bondage, particularly at the hand of John Tibeats: "He was my master," Northup writes, "entitled by law to my flesh and blood, and to exercise over me such tyrannical control as his mean nature prompted."[53] Additionally, the story of Patsey in Northup's narrative gives a glimpse into the sexual perversions permeating the plantation.[54] Mary Prince's narrative, *The History of Mary Prince*, reveals a similar world of sexual perversions. The Marquis de Sade wrote *120 Days of Sodom or the School of Libertinism*, published in 1785, only a few years before the slave insurrection in Saint-Domingue, at a time when the island was still very much a so-called libertine colony.[55] Sade's book tells the story of four wealthy men retreating to an isolated castle for four months with forty-six young men and women used as sex slaves. Doris Garraway writes, "Sade's most horrific scenarios of terror and pleasure may have in fact been inspired by the French colonial slave societies of his time,"[56] a suggestion that Joan Dayan also makes in *Haiti, History, and the Gods*.[57]

But while Sade's *120 Days of Sodom* is a disturbing work of fiction that uses narrative props to give the semblance of truth (such as the diary narrative format), the slave narrative tells a true and equally disturbing story traditionally presented, through forewords and prefaces, as needing some convincing to be believed as true. The forewords and prefaces commonly found introducing slave narratives are meant to contradict the presumption of untruth, but while doing so, those paratexts also *reaffirm* the presumption of their untruth. Autobiographical accounts of living in bondage penned or dictated by former slaves of African descent were usually written under the sponsorship of abolitionists from Britain or the northern states and meant to expose the extreme cruelty and barbarism of slave owners in the South. Those narratives, mainly written between 1760 and 1865, follow a comparable pattern. White attestation was often required for slaves and former slaves in order for them to publish their stories as "written by himself" or "written by herself." Because of that, slave narratives were often preceded by a certificate of authenticity of the kind found in *Slavery in the United States of the Life and Adventures of Charles Ball* (1837):

> We, the undersigned, certify that we have read the book called 'CHARLES BALL'—that we know the black man whose narrative is given in this book, and have heard him relate the principal matters contained in the book concerning himself, long before the book was published.
> "DAVID W. HOLINGS.
> "W. P. ELLIOTT."*[58]

Other narratives open with a note by the author apologizing for the "poor" style of the writing, which incidentally was another way to authenticate the slave authorship of the manuscript.[59] Another type of preamble, such as that found in *Narrative of the Life of Frederick Douglass*, presents respectable white voices expressing sympathy for the author and eagerness for the manuscript to be distributed widely. The voices of Wendell Phillips, lawyer and known abolitionist, and William Lloyd Garrison, cofounder of the antislavery weekly newspaper *The Liberator*, both precede Douglass's narrative. Authenticating or attesting to the voice of a surprisingly literate slave is one goal of white prefaces. Another goal is to prepare readers for the unique experience of reading a voice once thought to be irreversibly silent. The series of letters prefacing *The Interesting Narrative of the Life of Olaudah Equiano* (1794) and *The Narrative of the Life of Frederick Douglass* (1845) build momentum toward the historical moment of the new voice unveiled. Aside from the political (abolitionism) and legal (authentication) purposes, however, prefaces preceding a slave narrative also carry the result of sensationalizing the story, drawing attention to the fact that the story about to be revealed is too crude, horrific, unbelievable to be initially thought to be true. More importantly, introducing the slave narrative with the question of its presumed unreliability makes the black voice come across as somewhat inaudible. The mere mention of its alleged improbability before the narrative has even begun produces interference in the intended communication. The paratextual endorsement of the slave text, though well intentioned, suggests that truth is by default racialized as white property.

There is a clear contradiction between the loudness of the black voice and the muteness of its emission. The formerly silent voice transmits a "loud" topic that cannot go unnoticed, and yet the voice is questioned and hence shut down before it has even been heard—not because the story is untrue, but rather because the story is too true to be heard. In *The Fire Next Time*, James Baldwin speaks of racial injustice within the context of the civil rights movement and writes:

> I have been carried into precinct basements often enough, and I have seen and heard and endured the secrets of desperate white men and women, which they knew were safe with me, because even if I should speak, no one believed me. And they would not believe me precisely because they would know that what I said was true.[60]

When the unthinkable and ineffable ends up being told, not believing or listening to the truth of the voice may be the last resort. But truth is obviously a complex concept with variables. As J. L. Austin has famously shown in *How To Do Things with Words*, language is not only about "true" or "false" statements. Performative utterances, which the author also refers to as "speech acts," are an essential part of language. Betting, promising, swearing, and threatening are all performative utterances that "do something" with a felicitous or infelicitous outcome. Constative utterances, on the other hand, *state* something meant to be true or false. Slave narratives are introduced and marketed as constative utterances with truth as the main concern, thereby obstructing the fact that the black text is also—and even more so—performative. Due to its unprecedented and transgressive nature, the black act of speaking out is experienced as a threat; a threat in the form of a performative utterance. Per Austin, we might say that slave narratives "have on the face of them the look—or at least the grammatical make-up—of 'statements'; but nevertheless they are seen, when more closely inspected, to be, quite plainly, *not* utterances which could be 'true' or 'false.'"[61] Likewise for Baldwin, truth is somewhat irrelevant since the white already knows the statement to be true before it has even been uttered. The real threat lies instead in Baldwin simply speaking, as the black voice always already implies telling on the whites, who thought their secrets were safe. Therefore, the black voice itself is threatening since the mere sound of it indicates a breach of silence and the exposure of the white secret.

Because of his interest in the *pour-autrui* and self-consciousness, Sartre is one of the only philosophers who understood the impact of the creation of the black book in a French context. Few know that although narratives by former slaves of African descent were commonly written in English and published for an intended audience in Britain or northern America in the eighteenth and nineteenth centuries, francophone African and Caribbean writers only started publishing their own black resistance literature in the 1930s with the Négritude movement in Paris, and even slightly sooner with the 1921 publication of *Batouala, véritable roman nègre* (*Batouala: A True*

Black Novel) by Martinican writer René Maran,[62] recipient of
the prestigious Prix Goncourt. In America, by going up north,
slaves became free and benefited from the support of abolitionists encouraging them and helping them to write and publish
their stories. The geographical context of being marooned in
the islands (Saint-Domingue, Martinique, and Guadeloupe)
did not allow for such freedom and support. In other words,
during the slavery era, the geopolitical situation of the colonies,
given their insular environment, could not give birth to the
French black book. Yet in Paris, the epicenter of the French
colonial empire, that would later change. After publication of
one of the earliest slave narratives, the 1760s *Narrative of the
Uncommon Sufferings, and Surprising Deliverance of Briton Hammon, a Negro Man*,[63] it took over a century and a half to make
the French book talk back to the black. The anticolonial literary
movement initiated by Aimé Césaire, Léon-Gontran Damas,
and Léopold Sédar Senghor in Paris introduced French consciousness to the experience of being seen by the Other, being
seen naked, stripped of all fancy apparel that had previously
hidden the dark side of slavery and colonization.[64] "Here are
black men standing, looking at us, and I hope that you—like
me—will feel the shock of being seen. For three thousand years,
the white man has enjoyed the privilege of seeing without being
seen,"[65] Sartre writes in 1947. Sartre reiterates his racial *pour-
autrui* comment in his preface to Frantz Fanon's 1961 essay on
colonization and its aftermath, *Les damnés de la terre* (*The
Wretched of the Earth*):

> Europeans, you must open this book and enter into it. After a few
> steps in the night you will see strangers gathered around a fire;
> come close, and listen, for they are discussing the fate they

will give to your trading posts and to the soldiers who defend them. They will maybe see you, but they will keep talking among themselves, without even lowering their voices. This indifference strikes home.[66]

More than a decade had passed since Sartre's first warning in "Black Orpheus." In this second instance, Sartre makes it sound as if the colonizer had ceased waiting for a returned gaze. The black is no longer looking, busy as he is now talking about "you." Again, the belatedness of the returned gaze is a problem to which Derrida has drawn attention in *The Animal That Therefore I Am*. Derrida emphasizes the question of "Since when?" Since when has this cat been looking at Derrida's naked body unbeknownst to him? Derrida posits that the architectural structure of Western discourse shows a lack of experience when it comes to the perception of being seen. Yet, Derrida himself admits to having only belatedly seen the cat looking at him. His philosophy is inscribed within the retrospective feeling of having been looked at. This belatedness is exactly what Sartre has attempted to pinpoint with the anticolonial gaze. Like a child stealing money from his mother's purse and only after the fact noticing her presence in the room, Sartre suggests that the colonizer has been looked at by the colonized for a long time, so long that the colonizer's reciprocity, long overdue, goes now unnoticed. The scene described here recalls the aforementioned dog scene, also from Sartre, in which people are talking about the dog in his presence without including the dog in the discussion. The unprecedented black voice forces the master or the colonizer into the position of the dog: The white is now being spoken about, forced to listen and yet not looked at. "Ça ne vous regarde pas": It does not concern you and it does not look at you.

SHAME

Shame comes from the intrinsic urge to hide but having nowhere to go, which is what Lisa Guenther calls "ontological
self-encumbrance."[67] Emmanuel Lévinas, in *On Escape*, posits
that "shame arises each time we are unable to make others forget [*faire oublier*] our basic nudity. It is related to everything we
would like to hide and that we cannot bury or cover up."[68] For
that reason, shame is also a question of imbalance since, in contrast to the exposed subject, the beholder of the gaze feels no
reason to hide. The root of shame, as Marc Blanchard also posits in "Neither," lies in "being at a disadvantage."[69] As Blanchard
explains, you are *shameless* if you choose to dance drunk and
naked in the middle of Times Square, but the act becomes
shameful if people fully clothed and sober look at you during
your celebration. At first glance, it could seem outrageous to
argue that the master is at a disadvantage next to the grim conditions of the slave, but Ham's curse leads to an understanding
of the patriarch as the vulnerable one precisely because the
master is the one who is in his own home, fully exposed with
nowhere to hide, while the slave is the houseguest fully clothed
and sober. As we know, the woods are a possible escape for the
slave only, and not for the master who cannot escape his own
home. Every slave is a potential maroon, an escapee taking off
for the woods. Famous maroons such as La Mulâtresse Solitude
in Guadeloupe or François Mackandal in Saint-Domingue have
proven that escape is something that the slave has fully mas-
tered, unlike the master who remains home at all times.[70]

The plantation is a sort of *huis-clos*, like Sartre's *No Exit*, a
play in which the characters are confined to hell, represented
by a Second-Empire drawing room with no exit. The plantation
is a closed space with no way out where the participants are

forced to live with each other in spite of their irreconcilable differences. In his second autobiography, *My Bondage and My Freedom*, ex-slave Frederick Douglass explains the difference between rural plantation life and being a slave in the city. Douglass experienced both, first as a child in Colonel Lloyd's plantation in Maryland and later as a slave at the service of Hugh Auld in Baltimore. In the city, Douglass explains, the slave is "much better fed and clothed, is less dejected in his appearance, and enjoys privileges altogether unknown to the whip-driven slave on the plantation."[71] The reason is that the city slaveholder is not alone; in a condensed urban area, neighbors are like watchdogs. A "desperate slaveholder," Douglass pursues, "will shock the humanity of his non-slave holding neighbors, by the cries of the lacerated slaves."[72] The plantation, on the other hand, is a self-reliant closed space with no external checks and balances. The plantation leaves the master and the slave in an existential face-off initiated by the discomfiture of the unavoidable exposure.

According to Hegel's master-slave dialectic, the independence that the master seems to enjoy in the slave-based economical system turns out to be a fallacy since the master must rely on the labor of the slave for his subsistence, while the slave reaches "real and true independence" by producing his own labor.[73] What Hegel attempts to show is that bondage is not always what it seems to be, which is the case for the slave, who, while working in the Other's house, has the advantage of seeing this Other at his most vulnerable point, in his naked truth. Susan Buck-Morss argues that Hegel's dialectic of lordship and bondage was influenced by Haiti's slave revolution, which took place only a few years before the publication of *Phenomenology of Mind* (1807).[74] The violent 1803 overthrow of the slave regime led to the Republic of Haiti in 1804, the first black republic in the world. Even though it is common to look at Hegel's master-slave dialectic through a Marxist prism, the slave rebellion in Haiti (then Saint-Domingue) best shows what Hegel meant about the vulnerability of the master. The master's Achilles' heel is incidentally the slave having access to the master's house. When the slave strikes, the master has nowhere to go for cover.

More than twenty years after *Phenomenology of Mind*'s publication, the story of Nat Turner's insurrection in Southampton, Virginia, shows with gory detail the vulnerability of the master in his own home. In 1831, Nat Turner, along with a handful of fellow slaves, initiated a killing spree of slave owners, starting with the slaying of his own master "at home." What Turner calls "at home" in *The Confessions of Nat Turner* is his master's house, where his master is sleeping. "It was quickly agreed we should commence at home . . . on that night,"[75] Turner confesses. After the initial blow to Mr. J. Travis, his master, Turner's followers only grow in number through the night and the next morning: up to sixty slaves participate in the insurrection, going from house to house, killing all the white people inhabiting those residences. The night was their strength. Just as one waits for the night to come in order to easily grab sleeping chickens in the coop and kill them, Turner and his acolytes knew when to hit home. François Mackandal is another example. He was a domestic slave in the Normand de Mézy Plantation in Saint-Domingue. Mackandal spent six years plotting his rebellion against slave owners, hoping to get rid of every single one of them. His tactic was to create a network of domestic slaves throughout the island, with a mission to kill their masters by putting poison in their food. Slaves would wait for their masters to invite friends over for dinner in the hope of reaching even more people with their poison. Mackandal was arrested in 1757, but before his arrest he succeeded in making slave owners feel unsafe in their own homes. Berthony Dupont quotes a slave owner saying about the Mackandal terror wave, "We fear going to each other's homes, and we don't know whom to trust, as it is impossible to do away with the service of those wretched."[76] The Mackandal tactic is the perfect Hegelian illustration of the master's vulnerability in a regime of bondage: The master becomes aware of being reliant on the slave for his own subsistence, while also cognizant that this reliance is detrimental to his own survival.

Plantation society was based on what the house slave saw and knew, which she should never have told or used against the master. Ham seeing Noah naked was shameful enough for Noah, but Ham telling of the shameful exposure or making the exposure public further exacerbated the feeling of shame. The slave saw it all since the master had nowhere to hide, then it was a matter of making sure that the slave could not speak.

PERTINENCE

The insidious side of *Sprachlosigeit* resides in its seemingly harmless demeanor and the semblance of unbreakable silence, like the muteness of the animal, which leaves the articulate subject feeling safe to expose the reality of perversion. But, as it were, *Sprachlosigeit*—be it of a human or animal—can communicate as effectively (if not more so) through indirect means. For example, pertinence is to the animal what language is to man. The simple act of the animal's presence makes a statement, like Derrida's cat being in the bathroom. David L. Clark mentions a terrier running around an execution site in a 1941 short film featuring Nazi executions of Jews in Latvia. The presence of the pet, as Clark explains, is the *punctum* of the scene.[77] The true horror of a scene is realized through contrast, when juxtaposed with the mundane, the daily, and the familiar. The familiar presence of the pet brings out the *unheimlich* of the situation, and, in so doing, it is able to convey the horror of what would otherwise exceed the conceivable.[78]

Like the terrier, the slave also has indirect ways of speaking to his or her audience. In *The Trials of Phillis Wheatley*, Henry Louis Gates Jr. examines the case of a slave named Phillis Wheatley, the first person of African descent to publish a book of poems in the English language. In 1772, a year before the publication of her book of poems, Wheatley underwent an oral examination in front of eighteen of the most respected gentlemen in Boston. The purpose of the trial was to determine the authorship of the poems claimed to be Wheatley's. This examination was also indirectly meant to determine whether a black person had the intellectual capacity to produce literature. Wheatley passed the examination with flying colors, which resulted in an attestation of her authorship—"We whose Names are under-written, do assure the World, that the Poems specified in the following Page, were (as we verily believe) written by Phillis, a young Negro Girl."[79] Wheatley paved the way for African American literature, as she was able to prove to white people that blacks were not like monkeys and could incidentally write books.

Yet, as Gates shows in his book, in the twentieth century Wheatley's literature was deemed too white for black critics, and the poet was repeatedly criticized for not taking a public stand against slavery, for wanting to please whites, and for suffering from an Uncle Tom Syndrome. "Too black to be taken seriously by white critics in the eighteenth century, Wheatley was now considered too white to interest black critics in the twentieth."[80] One of Gates's roles in *The Trials of Phillis Wheatley* is to rehabilitate Wheatley by taking her accomplishments for what they are: Wheatley forced a dubious white readership to admit the possibility of black authorship; it was officially the end of the death of the black author. But Wheatley was put on trial, not only because she was a black person producing poems but also because her poems imitated white poetry to perfection. Wheatley did not tell the story of her bondage, as Olaudah Equiano would later do, but chose instead, as a devout Catholic, to speak of religion and to emulate the style of English poet Alexander Pope. But what Wheatley's critics should take into account is that colonial mimicry, which, according to Homi Bhabha is "a subject of a difference that is almost the same, but not quite,"[81] carries an indelible sneer on its face, the sneer of the "not quite," the imperceptible black difference. As early as the 1700s, French missionary Jean-Baptiste Labat had brought up the fact that mocking whites sounded like second nature to blacks. In his diary about his journey to the French West Indies (1693–1705), Labat writes:

> I've already noticed that negroes are vain and glorious, I must add that they are derisive to the extreme, and very few people are as dedicated to know the weaknesses of people, and mostly of the whites, in order to mock them among themselves and constantly ridicule them. . . . I have often been surprised with the weaknesses that they had noticed and the ways that they mocked them, which forced me to learn the language of the Aradas.[82]

The discomfort that Labat felt at witnessing the black talk *about* the white has turned into a white discomfort at witnessing the black talk *like* the white—the same sneer lingering on the black face. But this black sneer is precisely what black critics should be looking for in Wheatley's poetry. Gates reminds us that vernacular comes from the Latin *verna*, "slave born in his master's house."[83] For Gates, vernacularizing consists of adding a black difference to the white text as a way to mark the presence of the slave in the master's house. By trying to make herself at home in the master's literature, the only kind she knows, Wheatley is bound to taint the white book, no matter how white her poems sound. Looking for traces of the taint, of this imperceptible sneer, is something that a freelance writer named Mr. Grigo did, as Gates recounts in his book. Mr. Grigo thinks that he found an anagramic twist in "On Being Brought from Africa to America," a well-known poem in which Wheatley seems to praise slavery for having brought her to Christianity. According to Grigo, if one rearranges all the letters of the poem, the poem becomes a plea, not in favor of slavery, but rather against it. As Gates says, "It is funny to think that the most scorned poem in the tradition, all this time, was a secret, coded love letter to freedom, hiding before our very eyes."[84] Following her predecessor Mackandal's advice, Wheatley may have intentionally left a trail of poison aimed at whites in her poems, or she may not. It is up to the reader to see the sneer on her face.

Because of its state of *différend*, a state in which the black does not have the means (speechlessness) to communicate his or her victimhood, the black voice goes often unsuspected in the white text. This assumed black insignificance allows for a form of bootlegging where the information still comes through, but in a covert way. Toni Morrison, in *Playing in the Dark*, has mentioned the pertinence of black characters in the literature written by white authors. As Morrison explains, those characters reveal a crucial hidden truth about white consciousness and how white authors fathom blackness. "The contemplation of this black presence is central to any understanding of our national literature and should not be permitted to hover at the margins of the literary imagination,"[85] Morrison argues. It is particularly important to contemplate this black presence in a French-speaking context during the slavery era, at a time when the slave had no chance to tell his or her story. In that specific context, black characters were not created by white authors per se but were rather pushing their way through the white text and offering their own kind of contribution to the history of slavery. Because French history does not carry a tradition of slave narration, any silent and knowing presence in a French-speaking context that bears witness to the history of slavery should get critical attention. In eighteenth-century Saint-Domingue, advertisements about runaway slaves featuring biographical and physical information that would aid in the capture of the fugitives are what we could call slave testimonials by proxy. This genre of literature bears witness, through a silent voice, to the atrocity of bondage. These advertisements all sound like *incipits*, the opening of the story of a life about which the reader would like to know more and to understand the events that led to the escape as well as the details of the escape itself. The sample that follows shows the body of the slave used as a book, telling stories of abuse as well as providing a map potentially leading the masters to their chattel slave:

Sacatra, a mixed-race Creole, with no stamp, around 22 years old, bearing white marks on her hands and body, ran away the 19th of this month: we presume that she was led by a White male. Those who will identify her are asked to arrest her and to inform M. Demontis, from Mrs Pondaudin's Plantation, in Gonaïves. There will be a reward.[86]

Pierre-Louis, Griff, stamped on both sides of the chest DUF-FEAU [reversed], 22 to 25 years old, 5 feet and 2 inches, well-built, with a sneaky face scarred with the small pox, said Griff took a big

brown horse, with long hair, stamped on the leg with big letters No 40. The people who will see them are asked to inform
Mr. Boyer, merchant in Archaye, to whom they belong; there
will be a reward.[87]

The second advertisement is particularly interesting given the
analogy that transpires between the slave and the horse. Both
are stamped and presented as living property on the run. Yet, as
the description shows, the slave has a face (a sneaky one at that)
while the horse has none, a way to show that only the slave is
capable of and responsible for the deed. The mention of the face
in this case is not meant to humanize the slave in contrast to the
horse but only to highlight the slave's mischievous nature, as
Labat had already noticed. Much more could be said about, and
speculated over, these advertisements, but suffice it to say that
advertisements about runaway slaves are silent testimonials wor-
thy of attention as they speak of the unsustainability of bondage
through indirect channels of communication.[88]

The slave mocking the master behind his back and this sneer
reaching through Labat writing about it, Wheatley potentially
poisoning her poem between the lines and making it known to
us through her publication that followed the white attestation,
the slave running away on a horse and making it known to us
through the white advertisement, all these examples prove the
omnipresence of a literature of black resistance by white proxy.
Sprachlosigeit therefore does not equate the death of the author
because, no matter the degree of repression and silencing, the
sneer will still linger and tell its own story. Labat undertook to
learn the Arada language in the vain hope of gaining access to
black perception. Derrida, like Labat, has seen the shortcomings of not knowing what the silent animal thinks of you when
looking at you. Not knowing what is on the Other's mind leads

to an impoverished and nearsighted perception of the world, a "What if?" eternal abyss where nothing can take the sneer off the silent face.

In the short story entitled "Axolotl" by Argentinian writer Julio Cortázar,[89] the narrator is obsessed with axolotls and regularly goes to the aquarium at Jardin des Plantes in Paris to stare at this Mexican type of salamander. Transfixed by the odd-looking pink amphibians with no eyelids, the narrator glues his face to the glass while the immobile axolotls look at him. The narrator feels a "muted pain" as he comes to the realization that maybe the axolotls are seeing him. "They were devouring me slowly with their eyes, in a cannibalism of gold." At the end of the story, the reader realizes that, in a twist of magic realism, the beholder of the gaze has become the object of the gaze. The narrator is one of the axolotls looking at "him," this man with his face glued to the glass on the other side of the tank. Even though he is aware now of having the body and muteness of an axolotl, strangely enough, nothing has changed in the narrator's mental skills. He feels, as he says, like a man buried alive. Cortázar's tour de force consists in giving a glimpse of how it would be to look at a man from the eyes of an animal. It would be no different than an eyelidless immobile man trapped in an aquarium and staring at a man staring back at him. This insignificant amphibian thinks and judges just like a man, staring quietly at the man on the other side. Cortázar offers a semblance of an answer to the "What if?" Digging into the Other's perception of oneself only results in the realization of being trapped in the perception of the Other in a specular kind of way. The slave and the cat are not fully silent, as their mere presence in the bathroom or on the plantation is like a mirror projecting an image of the master that he or she would rather not see.

CODA

I felt at times a sense of illegitimacy while writing this book, doubting my authority to speak about the one who will never talk back to me, and being aware that speaking about the animal may lead to the questionable position of speaking *in lieu of* the animal. Whether one is an animal rights activist, zoologist, vegan animal lover, carnivore scholar, or novelist, no one is fully equipped to address the animal. Yet, this question is akin to religion: It leaves no one out. Choosing not to pass judgment on meat eating or God's existence carries as much weight as being a vegetarian or a believer. There is no neutral zone.

South African novelist J. M. Coetzee points to the similarity between religion and the animal question in his 2003 novel, *Elizabeth Costello*. The novel is composed of a series of guest lectures delivered by two fictitious characters: the Australian novelist Elizabeth Costello and her sister, Sister Bridget, who was once a scholar and turned to religion. Costello, who is said to be mostly known for bringing back to life James Joyce's Molly Bloom in one of her novels, irritates her audience by choosing to deliver a talk on animal rights instead of focusing on her expertise as a woman novelist writing about women. Her sister creates a similar stir by lecturing on the role of God and religion in the humanities instead of using her experience to talk about the impact of AIDS on South African children. Abruptly raising the topic of animal consumption or God gets under the audience's skin, because it touches on the question of in-corp-oration (from the French *corps*, "body"), it literally gets "in the body." In both Christianity and the case of the animal, the body of God and the body of the animal become one with the human body through the ingestion of flesh. Jacques Derrida has teased out the transubstantiation element in meat eating in his concept of carno-phallogocentrism. The ingestion of meat reenacts the incorporation of the flesh and the blood of Christ.[1] The transubstantiation image shows how difficult it is to extract oneself from such invested (ingested) topics. By drawing a parallel between the audience's reaction to Costello's address and to that of her sister, Coetzee presents the animal question as, like religion, a personal yet very public issue not to the taste of everyone.

Elizabeth Costello is also an important book when it comes to the question of authority in animal studies. The novel is an off-shoot of Coetzee's 1999 novella entitled *The Lives of Animals*, itself based on a guest lecture about animal rights that Coetzee delivered at Princeton in 1997. Coetzee's lecture at Princeton presents itself as a *mise en abîme* type of storytelling in which Coetzee delivered an address about Elizabeth Costello delivering an address. In both the lecture and the novel, Elizabeth Costello is the author's alter ego. She is an invited guest, like Coetzee, talking about animal rights instead of the novel, just like Coetzee. Through his protagonist, Coetzee is able to acknowledge his own lack of credentials on the animal question. In the novel, Costello is said not to master the topic. "A strange ending to a strange talk," Costello's son, who is in the audience, thinks, "ill-gauged, ill-argued. Not quite her métier, argumentation."[2] And yet, Costello is fully committed to her topic. Coetzee skillfully shows how the need to address the animal question trumps the limitations that one may fear having on that topic.

Costello and Coetzee are like Franz Kafka's protagonist in the short story "A Report to an Academy." The story depicts a former ape (trained to become human) invited to deliver an address to the Academy of Science on his apehood. The former ape turns out to be ill equipped to speak about his former animality. Five years have passed since the guest speaker was an ape, and his now humanness prevents him from speaking the animal truth. "Today," the former ape says, "naturally, I can only sketch from hindsight, and in human words, what I then felt as an ape, and therefore I am sketching it incorrectly, but even if I can no longer attain the old apish truth, my description isn't basically off course, and no doubt about it."[3] Coetzee mentions Kafka's short story in Costello's address to show that, as I would add, "all in all, the author's address may be incorrect but it isn't basically off course." For over a decade, like Coetzee and Costello, I have grappled with the conflict of not feeling fully in my element with the animal question and yet needing to address it. I am now aware that my argumentation may not be the animal truth, but it is "not basically off course." Who are we to talk about the animal? What are our credentials? Those questions also apply to Jacques Derrida, who, in *The Animal That Therefore I Am*, feels the need to tell his audience (also in a formal address as a guest speaker) that "animals are [his] concern,"[4] as if to anticipate the audience's puzzlement at hearing the deconstructionist philosopher talk about the animal. Who is he to talk about the *animot*?[5]

Talking about race and the Holocaust in relation to the animal question also raises issues of legitimacy. In her address,

Costello provocatively uses the dreaded comparison, equating the plague of animals with that of Jews in the Holocaust:

> Denunciation of the camps reverberates so fully with the language of the stockyard and slaughterhouse that it is barely necessary for me to prepare the ground for the comparison I am about to make. The crime of the Third Reich, says the voice of accusation, was to treat people like animals.[6]

A faculty member in the English Department, Abraham Stern, takes offense to the comparison, telling Costello in a written note, "You took over for your own purposes the familiar comparison between the murdered Jews of Europe and slaughtered cattle. The Jews died like cattle, therefore cattle die like Jews, you say. This is a trick with words which I will not accept."[7] Costello made the comparison as a non-Jew, just as Marjorie Spiegel made the comparison with slavery as a non-black, both cases highlighting the impossibility of ever fully inhabiting, incorp-orating, the topic. By having Alice Walker write the foreword to her *Dreaded Comparison*, Spiegel attempts to hide her vulnerability behind the black body. Walker's quote in the foreword, "the animals of the world exist for their own reasons. They were not made for humans any more than black people were made for whites or women for men,"[8] is meant to validate, from a black womanist perspective, Spiegel's comparison, but what it does as well is to bring attention to the questions of authority and legitimacy. Walker may be just as ill equipped as Spiegel to address the comparison.

Who are we to talk about the animal, to talk about the Jew being treated like cattle, or the black like an animal? Walker herself, who received praise for her short story "Am I Blue?" about animal suffering, is today criticized for occasionally eating chickens.[9] Her short story had ended with the following vegetarian message, "as we talked of freedom and justice one day for all, we sat down to steaks. I am eating misery, I thought, as I took the first bite. And spit it out."[10] But, since then, she is no longer a strict vegetarian. Who was she to talk about animal suffering? is not simply a rhetorical question. Indeed, who was she? The adult woman who saw the pain in the horse's eye, the southern girl who enjoyed eating chicken and resumed this habit as an older woman, or the famous black novelist who agreed to write the foreword to Spiegel's sensitive book? Likewise, who am I to talk about the Afro-dog?

ACKNOWLEDGMENTS

When my retired father moved back to Guadeloupe with my mother, after having spent his entire adult life in France, his German shepherd, Faust, had to get familiarized with the new house and the new climate. The dog also had to adjust to a new kind of people who feared him and would not go near him due to the complicated history between dogs and former slaves in the Caribbean. I owe much to Faust, who taught me about the last-longing impact of historical wounds, and to the other dogs in my life (Jean-Paul, Antoine, and François), who have inspired me. I cherish the fact that my parents made me understand, in subtle ways, that my relationship to dogs is inevitably historically charged.

Jarrod Hayes has been a loyal reader of my work over the years, and words cannot express my gratitude for his unwavering support. I would also like to express my gratitude to the fellows at the 2014 Animals & Society Institute and the Animal Studies Program at Wesleyan University (Elan Abrell, Christiane Bailey, Joshua Kercsmar, Anat Pick, Fiona Probyn-Rapsey, and Saskia Stucki) for the rich and productive discussions that gave me a better understanding of the field of animal studies. Lori Gruen and Kari Weil have been instrumental in the completion of this project. I thank them both for their support and for sharing their precious knowledge with me. The book benefited greatly from Kari's reading recommendations, she is my *bonne étoile*. I also thank Margo DeMello for her generous support since our brief encounter at Wesleyan. I am also very grateful to Miriam Tickin for the precious time she invested in this project throughout the years and to Rachel Smith for her attentive reading of the manuscript and her amazing editing skills. I am indebted to the two anonymous readers at Columbia University Press for their helpful comments and encouragements as well as to Ginny Perrin for her meticulous attention to the book in its editing stage and to my editor at Columbia University Press, Wendy Lochner, for her enthusiastic support of the project.

Thank you to my partner in crime in Missoula, Elizabeth Urschel, who followed the ups and downs of the writing process, and to my friends and family (Hiltrud Arens, Astrid Billat, Luc Boisseron, Patrick Dodd, Claudine Cellier, Laura Halperin, Amy and Ashby Kinch, Murray Pierce, Sophie Reyss, and Naomi Shin), who provided moral support along the way. To my dear husband, Ulrich Kamp, and my two boys, Armand and Pierre, thank you for always making me laugh and for your terrible rap songs about "Afro-Dog."

Lastly, I want to thank Frieda Ekotto, who encouraged me to write this book ten years ago and who has never ceased to believe in this project. I am forever grateful for the time she invested in reading many versions of the manuscript and the enthusiasm that she showed at every stage of its completion. This book is partly hers.

NOTES

INTRODUCTION: BLACKNESS WITHOUT ANALOG

1. In 2014, far-right Front National politician Anne-Sophie Leclère was sentenced to nine months in prison for having compared Taubira to a chimpanzee on French television and for having posted a photomontage on Facebook with a picture of a baby monkey purported to be Taubira at eighteen months. In 2015, the Cayenne Court of Appeal canceled the sentence on a technicality.

2. In 2008, a bar owner in Marietta, Georgia, notoriously sold T-shirts featuring the cartoon chimpanzee Curious George peeling a banana, with the caption "Obama in '08."

3. Marjorie Spiegel, *The Dreaded Comparison: Human and Animal Slavery* (1988; repr., New York: Mirror Books, 1996).

4. See the IDEA vs. PETA case online, https://casetext.com/case/insti tute-for-development-of-earth-awareness-v-peta#.U6w_VSRpvCY.

5. Peter Singer, *Animal Liberation: A New Ethics for Our Treatment of Animals* (1975; repr., New York: Avon, 2001). Ryder first used the word "speciesism" in a privately printed leaflet in Oxford. See also Richard D. Ryder's "Speciesism Again: The Original Leaflet," *Critical Society* 2 (Spring 2010): 1–2.

6. Gary L. Francione and Anna Charlton, *Animal Rights: The Abolitionist Approach* (Newark, N.J.: Exempla Press, 2015).

7. Philip Armstrong, "The Postcolonial Animal," *Society and Animals* 10, no. 4 (2002): 413–19.

8. Claire Jean Kim, *Dangerous Crossings: Race, Species, and Nature in a Multicultural Age* (Cambridge: Cambridge University Press, 2015), 285.

9. Kari Weil, *Thinking Animals: Why Animal Studies Now?* (New York: Columbia University Press, 2012).

10. Edward W. Said, *Orientalism* (New York: Vintage Books, 1979), 46.

11. Frantz Fanon, *Les damnés de la terre* (Paris: Gallimard, 1961).

12. V. Y. Mudimbe, *The Idea of Africa* (Bloomington: Indiana University Press, 1994), 30.

13. Stuart Hall, "The West and the Rest: Discourse and Power," in *The Formations of Modernity. Understanding Modern Society: An Introduction*. Book 1, ed. Stuart Hall and Bram Gieben (Oxford and Cambridge: Polity Press in Association with the Open University, 1992): 185–225.

14. Kim, *Dangerous Crossings*, 286.

15. Weil, *Thinking Animals*, 26.

16. Ibid., 25.

17. *Animot* is a neologism composed of the combination of the French *mot* (word) and *animaux* (animals): "The animal is a word, it is an appellation that men have instituted, a name they have given themselves the right and the authority to give to the living other." Jacques Derrida, *The Animal That Therefore I Am* (New York: Fordham University Press, 2008), 23.

18. Salman Rushdie's article "The Empire Writes Back with a Vengeance," *Times* (London), July 3, 1982, enunciated the emerging movement then of postcolonial writing with a cause.

19. For a study of Kanye West's comment with historical retrospection, see Maxwell Strachan, "The Definitive History of 'George Bush Doesn't Care about Black People': The Story behind Kanye West's Famous Remarks," *Huffington Post*, August 28, 2015, http://www.huffingtonpost.com/entry/kanye-west-george-bush-black-people_us_55d67c12e4b020c386de2f5e. The author argues that Kanye West's striking comments were, in hindsight, perceived as pertinent and accurate. Yet most remember the Bush sentence but not the remarks preceding it, remarks about the racially biased coverage of blacks in the media, remarks that the author deems just as important.

20. Saidiya Hartman, *Lose Your Mother: A Journey Along the Atlantic Slave Route* (New York: Farrar, Straus and Giroux, 2007), 133.

21. Michelle Alexander, *The New Jim Crow: Mass Incarceration in the Age of Colorblindness* (New York: New Press, 2010).

22. Ta-Nehisi Coates, *Between the World and Me* (New York: Spiegel and Grau, 2015); Teju Cole, *Known and Strange Things: Essays* (New York: Random House, 2016), 15.

23. "J'arrivais dans le monde, soucieux de faire lever un sens aux choses, mon âme pleine de désir d'être à l'origine du monde, et voir que je me découvrais objet au milieu d'autres objets." ["I came to the world, eager to find meaning in things, my soul full of longing to be at the origins of the world, and I found that I was an object in the midst of other objects."] Frantz Fanon, *Peau noire, masques blancs* (Paris: Éditions du Seuil, 1952), 88.

24. "Le Nègre est, dans l'ordre de la modernité, le seul de tous les humains dont la chair fut faite chose et l'esprit marchandise." Achille Mbembé, *Critique de la raison nègre* (Paris: La Découverte, 2013), 18.

25. "Cet homme-chose, homme-machine, homme-code, homme-flux." Mbembé, *Critique de la raison nègre*, 14.

26. Frank B. Wilderson, *Red, White & Black: Cinema and the Structure of U.S. Antagonisms* (Durham, N.C.: Duke University Press, 2010), 38.

27. "Capital was kick-started by the rape of the African continent." Frank B. Wilderson, "The Prison Slave as Hegemony's (Silent) Scandal," *Social Justice* 30, no. 2 (2003): 22.

28. Wilderson, *Red, White, & Black*, 36.

29. The author also says that 150 Native American tribes have applied to the Bureau of Indian Affairs for sovereign recognition and land retribution, which is for him an example of their historical trace and existence in our civil society.

30. Wilderson, "Prison Slave as Hegemony's (Silent) Scandal," 24.

31. Frank B. Wilderson, "Gramsci's Black Marx: Wither the Slave in Civil Society?," *Social Identities* 9, no. 2 (2003): 233.

32. Ibid.

33. Ibid., 238.

34. Upton Sinclair, *The Jungle* (1906; repr., Charleston, S.C.: Millennium, 2014).

35. Claudia Rankine, *Citizen: An American Lyric* (Minneapolis: Graywolf Press, 2014), 11.

36. W. E. B. Du Bois, *The Souls of Black Folk* (Oxford: Oxford University Press, 2007), 8.

37. Che Gossett, "Blackness, Animality, and the Unsovereign," September 28, 2015, https://www.versobooks.com/blogs/2228-che-gossett -blackness-animality-and-the-unsovereign.

38. Harriet Beecher Stowe, *Uncle Tom's Cabin* (1851; repr., London: Signet Classics, 1966).

39. Sue Donaldson and Will Kymlicka, *Zoopolis: A Political Theory of Animal Rights* (Oxford: Oxford University Press, 2013).

40. Truman Capote, "Music for Chameleons," in *Music for Chameleons* (New York: Random House, 1980).

41. Michel Serres, *The Parasite*, trans. Lawrence R. Schehr (1980; repr., Minneapolis: University of Minnesota Press, 2007).

42. Jean-François Niort, *Le Code Noir: Idées reçues sur un texte symbolique* (Paris: Le Cavalier bleu, 2015).

43. Jean-Paul Sartre, "Black Orpheus," trans. John MacCombie, *Massachusetts Review* 6, no. 1 (Autumn 1964–Winter 1965): 13–52.

44. Democracy Now, "VIDEO: Dakota Access Pipeline Company Attacks Native American Protesters with Dogs and Pepper Spray," September 4, 2016, https://www.democracynow.org/2016/9/4/dakota _access_pipeline_company_attacks_native.

45. Bartolomé de Las Casas, *A Short Account of the Destruction of the Indies*, trans. Nigel Griffin (London: Penguin Books, 1992).

46. Abbe Raynal, *Philosophical and Political History of the Settlements and Trade of the Europeans in the East and West Indies*, vol. 2 (Edinburgh: Bell and Bradfute, 1804), 322.

47. Philippe R. Girard, "War Unleashed: The Use of War Dogs During the Haitian War for Independence," *Napoleonica: La Revue* 3, no. 15 (2012): 80–105.

1. IS THE ANIMAL THE NEW BLACK?

1. See Edward Said, *Orientalism* (New York: Vintage Books, 1979); Edouard Glissant, *Le discours antillais* (Paris: Éditions du Seuil, 1982); Gayatri Chakravorty Spivak, "Can the Subaltern Speak?" In *Marxism and the Interpretation of Culture*, edited by Cary Nelson and Lawrence

Grossberg (London: Macmillan, 1988); Bill Ashcroft, Gareth Griffiths, and Helen Tiffin, *The Empire Writes Back: Theory and Practice in Post-Colonial Literatures* (1989; repr., London: Routledge, 2002); and Jean Bernabé, Patrick Chamoiseau, and Raphaël Confiant, *Eloge de la Créolité* (Paris: Gallimard, 1989). These works built the foundation of what is now commonly referred to as "postcolonial studies."

2. "The 'postcolonial turn' in the social sciences and humanities took place nearly a quarter century ago." Achille Mbembé, "Provincializing France?," trans. Janet Roitman, *Public Culture* 23, no. 1 (2011): 85.

3. Marjorie Spiegel, *The Dreaded Comparison: Human and Animal Slavery* (1988; repr., New York: Mirror Books, 1996), 19.

4. Carol J. Adams, *Neither Man Nor Beast: Feminism and the Defense of Animals* (New York: Continuum, 1994), 91.

5. Aymeric Caron, *Antispéciste* (Paris: Don Quichotte, 2016).

6. "Les animaux que nous élevons ne parlent pas notre langue et nous nous arrangeons pour ne pas entendre ce qu'ils expriment." Caron, *Antispéciste*, 257.

7. "Les antispécistes sont les traducteurs de *L'Amistad*." Ibid.

8. Jeremy Bentham, *Introduction to the Principles of Morals and Legislation* (1789; repr., Oxford: Clarendon Press, 1823).

9. See Tom Regan, *The Case for Animal Rights* (Berkeley: University of California Press, 1983); Gary L. Francione and Anna Charlton, *Animal Rights: The Abolitionist Approach* (Newark, NJ: Exempla Press, 2015).

10. In "Antispécisme ou opportunisme?" (Antispeciesism or opportunism?), French author Jean-Claude Fartoukh shows no mercy for Caron's book, arguing that *Antispéciste* offers an affected type of discourse aimed at being lucratively trendy by mixing racism, sexism, speciesism, and all other sorts of -isms in a hodge-podge of familiar clichés. The rhetoric that consists of using racism as an entryway to address speciesism can indeed come across as formulaic in cases where the question of race never makes it past the entryway. But while there is no reason to doubt that Caron earnestly seeks to establish an intersectional matrix in his critique of speciesism, his book reveals the challenge of such an endeavor. Jean-Claude Fartoukh, *Antispécisme ou opportunisme? Réponses au livre d'Aymeric Caron "Antispéciste"* (self-published, 2016), Kindle, www.les.ecrits.fr.

11. Caron, *Antispéciste*, 10.

12. V. Y. Mudimbe, *The Invention of Africa: Gnosis, Philosophy, and the Order of Knowledge* (Bloomington: Indiana University Press, 1988).

13. Achille Mbembé, *On the Postcolony: Studies on the History of Society and Culture* (Berkeley: University of California Press, 2001), 1.

14. Ibid.

15. Bryan Stevenson, *Just Mercy: A Story of Justice and Redemption* (New York: Spiegel and Grau, 2015), 179.

16. Ibid., 180.

17. Achille Mbembé, "Necropolitics," *Public Culture* 15, no. 1 (Winter 2003): 24.

18. Ibid.

19. Brigid Brophy, "Women: Invisible Cages," in *On The Contrary: Essays by Men and Women*, ed. Martha Rainbolt and Janet Fleetwood (Albany: State University of New York Press, 1984), 215.

20. The police used dogs to control the (predominantly black) crowd during the August 2014 riots that followed the death of Michael Brown in Ferguson, Missouri. After the use of dogs was strongly criticized in a federal investigation on the Ferguson riots, the St. Louis police board banned dogs as crowd control in September 2015.

21. Michelle Alexander, *The New Jim Crow: Mass Incarceration in the Age of Colorblindness* (New York: New Press, 2010).

22. Colin Dayan, *The Law Is a White Dog: How Legal Rituals Make and Unmake Persons* (Princeton, N.J.: Princeton University Press, 2011), xii.

23. Frank B. Wilderson, "Gramsci's Black Marx: Wither the Slave in Civil Society?," *Social Identities* 9, no. 2 (2003): 238.

24. Mumia Abu-Jamal, *Live from Death Row* (New York: Avon Books, 1996), 29.

25. "Felon disenfranchisement laws have been more effective in eliminating black voters in the age of mass incarceration than they were during Jim Crow. Less than two decades after the War on Drugs began, one in seven men nationally had lost the right to vote, and as many as one in four in those states with the highest African American disenfranchisement rate." Alexander, *New Jim Crow*, 193.

26. Ibid., 33.

27. Ibid., 34.

28. Ibid., 58.

29. Bronwen Dickey, *Pit Bull: The Battle over an American Icon* (New York: Borzoi Books, 2016), 199.

30. Ibid., 215.

31. Alexander, *New Jim Crow*, 57.

32. Colin Dayan, "Dead Dogs: Breed Bans, Euthanasia, and Preemptive Justice," *Boston Review* 25, no. 2 (March/April 2010), http://bostonreview.net/dayan-dead-dogs.

33. See, for example, Lawrence D. Bobo and Michael C. Dawson, "Change Has Come: Race, Politics, and the Path to the Obama Presidency," *Du Bois Review: Social Science Research on Race* 6, no. 1 (2009): 1–14; Michael Tesler and David O. Sears, *Obama's Race: The 2008 Election and the Dream of a Post-Racial America* (Chicago: University of Chicago Press, 2010).

34. See Anna Holmes, "America's 'Post-Racial' Fantasy," *New York Times*, June 30, 2015.

35. In 2013, the French Assembly voted in favor of deleting the word "race" from the Penal Code, arguing that the concept of "race" has no place in the French Republic. It is also currently being discussed whether the semantic presence of "race" should be deleted from the French Constitution's first article: "La France est une République indivisible, laïque, démocratique et sociale. Elle assure l'égalité devant la loi de tous les citoyens sans distinction d'origine, de race ou de religion." (France shall be an indivisible, secular, democratic, and social Republic. It shall ensure the equality of all citizens before the law, without distinction of origin, race, or religion. It shall respect all beliefs.)

    Opponents of the proposed amendment argued that the mention of race was added in 1946, after the Nazi debacle, with the very purpose of fighting racism, while proponents believe that the putative existence of "race" reaches back to the scientific fallacy of so-called racial differences that led to fascism in Europe.

36. Mbembé, "Provincializing France?," 93.

37. Jean-François Lyotard, *The Differend: Phrases in Dispute*, trans. Georges Van Den Abbeele (Minneapolis: University of Minnesota Press, 2002), 27.

38. Che Gossett, "Blackness, Animality, and the Unsovereign," September 8, 2015, http://www.versobooks.com/blogs/2228-che-gossett-blackness-animality-and-the-unsovereign.

39. Gosset, "Blackness, Animality, and the Unsovereign."

40. Bentham, *Introduction to the Principles of Morals and Legislation*, 311n1.

41. Ibid.

42. Slavery was first abolished in 1794, reinstated in 1802, and permanently abolished in 1848.

43. Peter Singer examines not only racism but also sexism in his theory of speciesism. The philosopher paved the way for vegan feminism and other types of study tackling discrimination, including homophobia, ableism, and ageism.

44. Peter Singer, *Animal Liberation: A New Ethics for Our Treatment of Animals* (1975; repr., New York: Avon Books, 2001), 7.

45. Ibid.

46. Claire Jean Kim, *Dangerous Crossings: Race, Species, and Nature in a Multicultural Age* (Cambridge: Cambridge University Press, 2015), 26.

47. Wilderson discusses the irremediability of the black condition: "The violence of the Middle Passage and the Slave Estate, technologies of accumulation and fundability, recompose and reenact their horrors on each succeeding generation of Blacks. This violence is both gratuitous (not contingent on transgressions against the hegemony of civil society) and structural (positioning Blacks ontologically outside of Humanity and civil society). Simultaneously, it renders the ontological status of Humanity (life itself) wholly dependent on civil society's repetition compulsion: the frenzied and fragmented machinations through which civil society reenacts gratuitous violence on the Black—that civil society might know itself as the domain of Humans—generation after generation." Frank B. Wilderson, *Red, White & Black: Cinema and the Structure of U.S. Antagonisms* (Durham, N.C.: Duke University Press, 2010), 55.

48. Saidiya Hartman, *Lose Your Mother: A Journey Along the Atlantic Slave Route* (New York: Farrar, Straus and Giroux, 2007), 6.

49. In his famous quote on chattel slavery and animal rights, Bentham justifies the killing of animals for food. "The death they suffer in our hands commonly is, and always may be, speedier, and by that means a less painful one, than that which awaits them on the inevitable course of nature." Bentham, *Introduction to the Principles of Morals*, 311n1.

50. Gary L. Francione and Robert Garner, *The Animal Rights Debate: Abolition or Regulation?* (New York: Columbia University Press, 2010), 22.

51. Gossett, "Blackness, Animality, and the Unsovereign."

52. Toni Morrison, *Playing in the Dark: Whiteness and the Literary Imagination* (Cambridge, Mass.: Harvard University Press, 1992), viii.

53. Ibid., 5.

54. Gary L. Francione, "We're All Michael Vick," August 22, 2007, http://www.abolitionistapproach.com/media/links/p2026/michael-vick.pdf. (Original source: http://www.philly.com/dailynews/opinion/20070822_Were_all_Michael_Vick.html).

55. Claire Jean Kim, "The Wonderful, Horrible Life of Michael Vick," in *Ecofeminism: Feminist Intersections with Other Animals and the Earth*, ed. Carol J. Adams and Lori Gruen (New York: Bloomsbury Academic, 2014), 175–90.

56. Melissa Harris-Perry, "Michael Vick, Racial History and Animal Rights," *The Nation*, December 30, 2010, https://www.thenation.com/article/michael-vick-racial-history-and-animal-rights/.

57. Jim Gorant, *The Lost Dogs: Michael Vick's Dogs and Their Tale of Rescue and Redemption* (Los Angeles: Gotham, 2010), 10.

58. Dickey, *Pit Bull*, 193.

59. Maneesha Deckha, "Disturbing Images: PETA and the Feminist Ethics of Animal Advocacy," *Ethics and the Environment* 3, no. 2 (Fall 2008): 35–76.

60. Deckha argues that emphasizing the connection between gender, race, and animality "is not to devalue the critical work performed by animal advocates or the intensity of the trauma that work can produce. Rather, it is proffered to make animal advocacy more effective while encouraging people who already care a great deal to think of even more forms of marginality if they have already not done so (and, of course, many have)." "Disturbing Images," 50.

61. Maneesha Deckha, "Toward a Postcolonial, Posthumanist Feminist Theory: Centralizing Race and Culture in Feminist Work on Non-human Animals," *Hypatia* 27, no. 3 (Summer 2012): 530.

62. Spiegel, *Dreaded Comparison*, 30.

63. Ibid., 30.

64. Ibid.

65. As mentioned in the introduction, PETA also used the "dreaded" analogy in its 2005 fund-raising exhibit, "Are Animals the New Slaves?" Spiegel's organization, the Institute for the Development of Earth

Awareness (IDEA), filed a complaint against PETA for copyright infringement under the grounds that the negative reception of the exhibit would have a retrospective negative impact on *The Dreaded Comparison*. Both, in similar terms, had addressed the dreaded comparison between (black) slavery and the modern treatment of animals, yet until then only PETA had received negative feedback for its comparative endeavor.

66. Charles Patterson, *Eternal Treblinka: Our Treatment of Animals and the Holocaust* (New York: Lantern Books, 2002), 12.

67. See Peter Singer, "To Defame Religion Is a Human Right," *Guardian*, April 15, 2009, http://www.theguardian.com/commentisfree/belief/2009/apr/15/religion-islam-atheism-defamation.

68. Philip Armstrong, "The Postcolonial Animal," *Society and Animals* 10, no. 4 (2002): 413.

69. Emmanuel Lévinas, "Nom d'un chien ou le droit naturel," *Difficile liberté: Essais sur le judaisme* (Paris: Biblio Essais, 1963): 213–16.

70. Jacques Derrida, *The Animal That Therefore I Am* (New York: Fordham University Press, 2008).

71. Spiegel, *The Dreaded Comparison*, 29.

72. Vicki Hearne, *Animal Happiness: A Moving Exploration of Animals and their Emotions* (New York: Skyhorse Publishing, 2007), 229.

73. In "Demarginalizing the Intersection of Race and Sex," Crenshaw developed a concept first made public by Akasha (Gloria T.) Hell, Patricia Bell-Scott, and Barbara Smith, eds., in *All the Women Are White, All the Blacks Are Men, But Some of Us Are Brave* (New York: Feminist Press, 1982).

74. Kimberlé Crenshaw, "Demarginalizing the Intersection of Race and Sex: A Black Feminist Critique of Antidiscrimination Doctrine, Feminist Theory and Antiracist Politics," *University of Chicago Legal Forum* 1 (1989), Art. 8:166.

75. Ibid., 140.

76. Carol J. Adams, *The Sexual Politics of Meat: A Feminist-Vegetarian Critical Theory* (New York: Continuum, 1990).

77. Jacques Derrida, "Force of Law: The 'Mystical Foundation of Authority.'" In *Acts of Religion*, ed. Gil Anidjar (New York: Routledge, 2010): 228–98.

78. Greta Gaard writes: "An early impetus for the ecofeminist approach was the realization that the posthuman turn in feminist theory liberation of women—the aim of all branches of feminism—cannot be fully expected with the liberation of nature; and conversely, the liberation of nature so ardently desired by environmentalists will not be fully effected without the liberation of women." "Toward a Queer Ecofeminism," *Hypatia* 12, no. 1 (Winter 1997): 115.

79. Carol J. Adams and Lori Gruen, eds., *Ecofeminism: Feminist Intersections with Other Animals and the Earth* (New York: Bloomsbury Academic, 2014), 7.

80. Nella Larsen, *Passing* (Oxford: Penguin Books, 1997), 161.

81. Jennifer C. Nash, "Re-Thinking Intersectionality," *Feminist Review* 89 (2008): 3.

82. Ibid., 7.

83. Ibid., 6.

84. Giorgio Agamben, *The Open: Man and Animal*, trans. Kevin Attel (Stanford, Calif.: Stanford University Press, 2004), 40.

85. See the chapter entitled "Tick" in Agamben, *The Open: Man and Animal*, 45–49.

86. Jakob von Uexküll, "A Stroll Through the Worlds of Animals and Men: A Picture Book of Invisible Worlds," in *Instinctive Behavior: The Development of a Modern Concept*, trans. and ed. Claire H. Schiller (New York: International Universities Press, 1957), 6.

87. Ibid., 48.

88. Ibid.

89. This story is somehow reminiscent of Frantz Fanon who, in *Peau noire, masques blancs* (*Black Skin, White Masks*) (Paris: Éditions du Seuil, 1952), uses the anecdote of a man from Martinique who spent some time in France and feigns to forget the use of a tool when he is back on his native island. The amnesia regarding the tool symbolizes the black man's desire to believe that he now thinks like a French man.

90. Uexküll, "A Stroll Through the Worlds of Animals and Men," 48.

91. Paul Ricoeur, *Freud and Philosophy: An Essay on Interpretation* (New Haven: Yale University Press, 1970).

92. Eve Kosofsky Sedgwick, "Paranoid Reading and Reparative Reading; or You're So Paranoid, You Probably Think This Introduction

Is About You," in *Novel Gazing: Queer Readings in Fiction*, ed. Eve Kosofsky Sedgwick (Durham, N.C.: Duke University Press, 1997), 1–37.

93. A. Breeze Harper, "Race as a 'Feeble Matter' in Veganism: Interrogating Whiteness, Geopolitical Privilege, and Consumption Philosophy of 'Cruelty-Free' Products," *Journal of Critical Animal Studies* 8, no. 3 (2010): 5–27.

94. Mel Y. Chen, *Animacies: Biopolitics, Racial Mattering, and Queer Affect* (Durham, N.C.: Duke University Press, 2012), 14, 94.

95. Chen here responds to Shoshana Felman, who sees Austin's joke as innocent and a manifestation for black humor. See Felman's *The Scandal of the Speaking Body: Don Juan with J. L. Austin, or Seduction in Two Languages* (Stanford, Calif.: Stanford University Press, 1993).

96. Chen, *Animacies*, 96.

97. Ibid.

98. Pattrice Jones, "Afterword: Liberation as Connection and the Decolonization of Desire," in *Sistah Vegan: Black Female Vegans Speak on Food, Identity, Health and Society*, ed. A. Breeze Harper (New York: Lantern Books, 2010), 196.

99. Adama Maweja, "The Fulfilment of the Movement," in *Sistah Vegan: Black Female Vegans Speak on Food, Identity, Health and Society*, ed. A. Breeze Harper (New York: Lantern Books, 2010), 125.

100. A. Breeze Harper, "The Birth of the Sistah Vegan Project," in *Sistah Vegan: Black Female Vegans Speak on Food, Identity, Health and Society*, ed. A. Breeze Harper (New York: Lantern Books, 2010), xv.

101. Tashee Meadows, "Because They Matter," in *Sistah Vegan: Black Female Vegans Speak on Food, Identity, Health and Society*, ed. A. Breeze Harper (New York: Lantern Books, 2010), 151.

102. See Alice Walker's preface to Spiegel, *The Dreaded Comparison*, and her short story "Am I Blue?," in *Crossroads: Creative Writing Exercises in Four Genres*, ed. Diane Thiel, 207–10 (Albuquerque, N.M.: Pearson Education Press, 1986).

103. Jones, "Afterword," 187.

104. Harper, "Birth of the Sistah Vegan Project," 35.

105. Ibid.

106. Ibid., xiv.

107. Ibid.

108. Breeze's Vegan Sistah project offers a vegan praxis to the Black Lives Matter movement, at the same time that it seeks to challenge "Neoliberal Whiteness While Building Anti-Racist Solidarity Amid Vegan of Color and Allies (Before, After, & Beyond Ferguson)." See http://www.sistahvegan.com/upcoming-sistah-vegan-conference-2015/.

109. Lori Gruen, "Samuel Dubose, Cecil the Lion, and the Ethics of Avowal," *Al Jazeera America*, July 31, 2005, http://america.aljazeera.com/opinions/2015/7/samuel-dubose-cecil-the-lion-and-the-ethics-of-avowal.html.

110. "His [Colonel Lloyd's] horses were of the finest form and noblest blood. His carriage-house contained three splendid coaches, three or four gigs, besides dearborns and barouches of the most fashionable style. This establishment was under the care of two slaves—old Barney and young Barney—father and son. To attend to this establishment was their sole work. But it was by no means an easy employment; for in nothing was Colonel Lloyd more particular than in the management of his horses. The slightest inattention to these was unpardonable, and was visited upon those, under whose care they were placed, with the severest punishment; no excuse could shield them, if the colonel only suspected any want of attention to his horses—a supposition which he frequently indulged, and one which, of course, made the office of old and young Barney a very trying one. They never knew when they were safe from punishment" (Frederick Douglass, *Narrative of the Life of Frederick Douglass: An American Slave. Written by Himself*, ed. Benjamin Quarles [Cambridge, Mass.: Belknap Press of Harvard University Press, 1960], 17).

111. Brophy, "Women: Invisible Cages," 215.

112. Yasmin Nair, "Racism and the American Pit Bull," *Current Affairs*, September 19, 2016, https://www.currentaffairs.org/2016/08/racism-and-the-american-pit-bull.

113. Kim, *Dangerous Crossings*, 201.

114. Douglass, *Narrative of the Life of Frederick Douglass*, 74.

115. Adams, *Sexual Politics of Meat*, 168.

116. Teri J. Gordon, "Synesthetic Rhythms: African American Music and Dance Through Parisian Eyes," *The Scholar and Feminist Online: Josephine Baker: A Century in the Spotlight* 6, nos. 1–2 (Fall 2007–Spring 2008), http://sfonline.barnard.edu/baker/print_gordon.htm.

117. For more detail on the meaning of "interpellation" or "hailing" in an Althusser context, see "Ideology and Ideological State Apparatuses," in which the author defines interpellation as an ideological subjection from the authority of a hegemonic power: "I shall then suggest that ideology 'acts' or 'functions' in such a way that it 'recruits' subjects among the individuals into subjects (it transforms them all) by that very precise operation which I have called interpellation or hailing, and which can be imagined along the lines of the most commonplace everyday police (or other) hailing: 'Hey, you there!'" Louis Althusser, "Ideology and Ideological State Apparatuses (Notes Towards an Investigation)," in *Lenin and Philosophy and Other Essays* (New York: Monthly Review Press, 1971), 174.

118. See Tabitha Soren's interview with Tupac Shakur, https://www .youtube.com/watch?v=ljSCZyv97FY.

2. BLACKS AND DOGS IN THE AMERICAS

1. Transcript of *Malcolm X: Make It Plain, American Experience*, season 6, episode 5, directed by Orlando Bagwell, aired January 26, 1994, http:// www.pbs.org/wgbh/amex/malcolmx/filmmore/pt.html; also quoted in Colin Dayan, *With Dogs at the Edge of Life* (New York: Columbia University Press, 2016), 8.

2. Colin Dayan, *The Law Is a White Dog: How Legal Rituals Make and Unmake Persons* (Princeton, N.J.: Princeton University Press, 2011).

3. As Dayan, and also Bronwen Dickey in *Pit Bull: The Battle over an American Icon* (New York: Borzoi Books, 2016) and Vicki Hearne in *Bandit: Dossier of a Dangerous Dog* (Pleasantville, N.Y.: Akadine Press, 1991) have shown, when it comes to the pit bull, the *scienter* rule applies to the so-called pit bull breed rather than the individual animal. Bans and regulations against pit bulls over the past few decades in America have indicated that the pit bull owner is held responsible for the deemed dangerous pit bull regardless of whether the said dog has shown any signs of being potentially dangerous.

4. "It is a particular sensation, this double-consciousness, this sense of always looking at one's self through the eyes of others, of measuring one's soul by the tape of a world that looks on in amused contempt and pity. One ever feels his twoness,—an American, a Negro; two souls,

two thoughts, two unreconciled strivings; two warring ideals in one dark body, whose dogged strength alone keeps it from being torn asunder." W. E. B. Du Bois, *The Souls of Black Folk* (1903; repr., Chapel Hill: University of North Carolina Press, 2013), 8–9.

5. *Investigation of the Ferguson Police Department*, U.S. Department of Justice, Civil Rights Division, March 4, 2015, https://www.justice.gov /sites/default/files/opa/press-releases/attachments/2015/03/04/fergu son_police_department_report.pdf, 31.

6. See, among other outlets, Arturo Garcia, "Virginia Republican Quickly Scrubs Facebook Joke about Police Dogs Eating Baltimore Protestors," *Raw Story*, May 5, 2015, http://www.rawstory.com/2015 /05/virginia-republican-quickly-scrubs-facebook-joke-about-police -dogs-eating-baltimore-protesters/.

7. Donna Haraway, *The Companion Species Manifesto: Dogs, People, and Significant Otherness* (Chicago: Prickly Paradigm Press, 2003), 1.

8. Bill Wasik and Monica Murphy, *Rabid: A Cultural History of the World's Most Diabolical Virus* (New York: Penguin Books, 2013), 206.

9. Ibid., 65.

10. Gilles Deleuze and Félix Guattari, *A Thousand Plateaus: Capitalism and Schizophrenia*, trans. Brian Massumi (New York: Continuum, 1987), 234.

11. Deleuze and Guattari's becoming animal partially differs from Haraway's, given that her becoming does not refer to the individuated animal but to a molecular (pack) transformation. But like Haraway, the "contagion," the "virus," and the "symbiosis" in the process of becoming animal that Deleuze and Guattari mention also appears to be nonviolent, intentional, and kind. In Deleuze and Guattari, a human "fascination for the pack, for multiplicity" is what fuels the becoming. Deleuze and Guattari, *A Thousand Plateaus*, 89.

12. Haraway, *Companion Species Manifesto*, 32.

13. Harlan Weaver, "'Becoming in Kind:' Race, Class, Gender and Nation in Cultures of Dog Rescues and Dogfighting," *American Quarterly* 65, no. 2 (September 2013): 689.

14. Lori Gruen, *Entangled Empathy: An Alternative Ethic for Our Relationships with Animals* (New York: Lantern Books, 2015), 27.

15. Weaver, "'Becoming in Kind,'" 2.

16. Bill Wasik and Monica Murphy, *Rabid: A Cultural History of the World's Most Diabolical Virus* (New York: Penguin Books, 2013).

17. See Dayan's *With Dogs at the Edge of Life* for more on the canine profiling of pit bulls in modern America, including the 2012 *Tracey v.
Solesky* case in Maryland that ruled pit bulls an "inherently dangerous" breed and the 2009 ban on pit bulls (and other breeds deemed
dangerous) by the New York City Housing Authority.

18. Dayan, *With Dogs at the Edge of Life*, 6.

19. Ibid., 5.

20. Hearne, *Bandit*, 15.

21. Susan McHugh, *Dog* (London: Reaktion Books, 2004), 61.

22. Claire Jean Kim, "The Wonderful, Horrible Life of Michael Vick," in
Ecofeminism: Feminist Intersections with Other Animals and the Earth,
ed. Carol J. Adams and Lori Gruen (New York: Bloomsbury Academic, 2014), 187.

23. For a historical linkage between black men and beasts in relation to
Michael Vick, see also Claire Jean Kim, "Slaying the Beast: Reflections on Race, Culture, and Species" *Kalfou* (Spring 2010): 57–74.

24. Wasik and Murphy, *Rabid*, 11.

25. Ibid., 108.

26. Kim, "The Wonderful, Horrible Life of Michael Vick," 177.

27. Ibid.

28. Jim Gorant, *The Lost Dogs: Michael Vick's Dogs and Their Tale of Rescue
and Redemption* (Los Angeles: Gotham, 2010), 10.

29. Carla Freccero, "Figural Historiography: Dogs, Humans, and Cynanthropic Becomings," in *Comparatively Queer*, ed. Jarrod Hayes, Margaret Higonnet, and William J. Spurlin (New York: Palgrave, 2010),
60–61.

30. Marion Schwartz, *A History of Dogs in the Early Americas* (New Haven:
Yale University Press, 1997), 76.

31. Patrick Chamoiseau, *L'esclave vieil homme et le molosse* (Paris: Gallimard, 1997).

32. Jacques Derrida, *The Animal That Therefore I Am* (New York: Fordham University Press, 2008), 308.

33. Dayan, *The Law Is a White Dog*.

34. Paul Youngquist, "The Cujo Effect," in *Gorgeous Beasts: Animal Bodies
in Historical Perspective* (University Park: Penn State University Press,
2012), 52–79.

35. Youngquist, "Cujo Effect," 64.

36. Dayan, *The Law Is a White Dog*, 246.
37. *Sentell v. New Orleans & Carrollton*, R. Co. 16 U.S. 698 (1897), https://supreme.justia.com/cases/federal/us/166/698/case.html, retrieved September 27, 2016.
38. "When [free men of color] arrived at the gate of a city, they were required to alight from their horse; they were disqualified for sitting at a white man's table, for frequenting the same school, for occupying the same place at church, for having the same name, for being interred in the same cemetery, for receiving the succession of his property." John Relly Beard, *The Life of Toussaint L'Ouverture, The Negro Patriot of Hayti* (London: Ingram, Cooke, and Co., 1853), 37, in Documenting the American South, University Library, University of North Carolina at Chapel Hill, http://docsouth.unc.edu/neh/beardj/menu.html.
39. See the biography of Jimmy Winkfield by Ed Hotaling, *Wink: The Incredible Life and Epic Journey of Jimmy Winkfield* (Columbus, Ohio: McGraw-Hill, 2005).
40. Carol J. Adams, *The Sexual Politics of Meat: A Feminist-Vegetarian Critical Theory* (New York: Continuum, 1990), 27; and Jacques Derrida, "'Eating Well,' or the Calculation of the Subject: An Interview with Derrida," in *Who Comes After the Subject?*, ed. E. Cadava, O. Connor, and J. L. Nancy (New York: Routledge, 1991): 96–119.
41. See Sara E. Johnson, "'You Should Give Them Blacks to Eat:' Waging Inter-American Wars of Torture and Terror," *American Quarterly* 61, no. 1 (March 2009): 65–92, for a detailed description of tactics of terror using bloodhounds, not only in Saint-Domingue during the Haitian Revolution (1791–1803) but also in Jamaica during the Second Maroon War (1795–1796) and in Territorial Florida during the Second Seminole War (1835–1842).
42. Madison Smart Bell, *Toussaint Louverture: A Biography* (New York: Pantheon Books, 2007), 252.
43. Ibid.
44. In "War Unleashed: The Use of War Dogs During the Haitian War for Independence," *Napoleonica: La Revue* 3, no. 15 (2012): 80–105, the most exhaustive and well-researched account of the use of dogs during the Leclerc/Rochambeau expedition in Saint-Domingue, Philippe R. Girard explains that public opinion deems Rochambeau responsible for the idea of using dogs against the blacks.

45. "Ces animaux, qui, par leur taille et leur grosseur, ressemblaient à des loups, étaient couverts de bandelettes de soie; ils avaient la tête chargée de plumes aux couleurs les plus éclatantes." Thomas Madiou, *Histoire d'Haiti*, vol. 2, *1814–84* (Port-au-Prince, Haiti: Courtois, 1847), 411.

46. Marcus Rainsford, *An Historical Account of the Black Empire of Hayti* (London: Albion Press, 1805), 426–27.

47. "Les bourreaux lancent les chiens dans le cirque, aux applaudissement des spectateurs. Ces animaux flairent l'infortuné; mais ils reculent; les bourreaux les excitant en vain. Alors le général Boyer, qui était assis près de Rochambeau, se précipite dans l'arène, et perce d'un coup de sabre le ventre de l'infortuné. A la vue du sang qui jaillit, il est saisi d'un délire de vérocité et traine lui-même un des dogues contre la victime. Aussitôt tous les chiens s'élancent sur le patient dont les cris déchirants redoublent les applaudissements; ils dévorent les entrailles, et n'abandonnent leur proie qu'après s'être assouvis de chair palpitante." Madiou, *Histoire d'Haiti*, 412.

48. Girard, "War Unleashed," 34.

49. Ibid.

50. Ibid., 35.

51. Bell, *Toussaint Louverture*, 249.

52. Johnson, "'You Should Give Them Blacks to Eat,'" 68.

53. Sigmund Freud, *Totem and Taboo: Resemblances Between the Mental Lives of Savages and the Neurotics* (New York: Moffat, Yard and Company, 1918).

54. Since the Conquest, the idea that the whites, after much time spent in the Indies, will become indistinguishable from the natives and the blacks, has been persistent. Ralph Bauer and José Antonio Mazzotti write that historian Juan López de Velasco was the first to use the term "Criollo" for Spaniards who were born in the Indies and who, according to Velasco, "turn out like the natives even though they are not mixed with them [by] declining to the disposition of the land." Ralph Bauer and José Antonio Mazzotti, eds., *Creole Subjects in the Colonial Americas: Empires, Texts, Identities* (Chapel Hill: University of North Carolina Press, 2009), 4.

55. Freud, *Totem and Taboo*, 224.

56. Olaudah Equiano, *The Life of Olaudah Equiano*, in *The Classic Slave Narratives*, ed. Henry Louis Gates (New York: Signet Classics, 2002), 64.

57. Adams, *The Sexual Politics of Meat*, 31.

58. About the European fantasy of the cannibal Other, see the introduction by Peter Hulme, "The Cannibal Scene," in *Cannibalism and the Colonial World*, ed. Francis Barker, Peter Hulme, and Margaret Iversen (Cambridge: Cambridge University Press, 1998), 1–38.

59. Julia Kristeva, *Powers of Horror* (New York: Columbia University Press, 1982), 4.

60. Youngquist, "Cujo Effect," 65.

61. Rainsford, *Historical Account of the Black Empire of Hayti*, 312.

62. Solomon Northup, *Twelve Years a Slave* (New York: Dover Thrift, 1970), 246.

63. Ibid., 241.

64. Rainsford, *Historical Account of the Black Empire of Hayti*, 426.

65. Romain Gary, *Chien Blanc* (Paris: Gallimard, 1972), 13.

66. Ibid., 19–20.

67. The serial killer was initially thought to be white, since serial killers were generally known to be white males. However, Wayne Williams, the man the police eventually arrested for this killing spree, was African American.

68. See Dayan, *With Dogs at the Edge of Life*.

69. Pierre Boulle, *La planète des singes* (Paris: Julliard, 1963).

70. See interview with Mundruczó, "Morelia 2014 Interview: White Dog Director Kornél Mundruczó, http://screenanarchy.com/2014/10/morelia-2014-interview-white-god.html, accessed March 4, 2016.

71. J. M. Coetzee, *Disgrace* (New York: Penguin Books, 1999), 142.

72. Claude Lévi-Strauss, *Le totémisme aujourd'hui* (Paris: Presses Universitaires de France, 1962).

73. Haraway, *Companion Species Manifesto*, 5.

74. Derrida, *The Animal That Therefore I Am*, 374.

75. "Performance offers more to animal knowledge than any other cultural form: its reliance on physicality, materiality, and embodiment makes it especially useful for venturing into areas where language is absent." Una Chaudhuri and Holly Hughes, eds., *Animal Acts: Performing Species Today* (Ann Arbor: University of Michigan Press, 2014), 10.

76. "Il me sembla que de cette morsure je mourrais car elle ne me lâchait plus, elle s'enfonçait, elle était pénétrante elle plantait toutes ses dents dans mon cœur. Les dents duraient. En sanglotant nous entrâmes dans l'éternité folle. Le chien ne pouvait plus me lâcher. . . . Nous ne bougions plus attelés à la douleur, effarés. La Terre renversée sur le côté." Hélène Cixous, "Stigmates," *Lectora* 7 (2001): 200.

77. Martin Heidegger, *The Fundamental Concepts of Metaphysics: World, Finitude, Solitude* (Bloomington: Indiana University Press, 1995).

78. J. M. Coetzee, *Diary of a Bad Year* (New York: Penguin Books, 2008), 63.

79. James Baldwin, "Going to Meet the Man," in *Going to Meet the Man: Stories* (New York: Vintage International, 1995), 1751.

80. Baldwin, "Going to Meet the Man," 1760.

81. Ibid., 1769.

82. Frederick Douglass, "Reception Speech: At Finsbury Chapel, Moorfields, England, May 12, 1846," in *My Bondage and My Freedom* (New York: Penguin Books, 2003), 304.

83. Bartolomé de Las Casas, *A Short Account of the Destruction of the Indies*, trans. Nigel Griffin (London: Penguin Books, 1992), 74.

84. Michel-Rolph Trouillot, *Silencing the Past: Power and the Production of History* (Boston: Beacon Press, 1997), 25.

85. Karen Delise, *The Pit Bull Placebo: The Media, Myths and Politics of Canine Aggression* (Koropi, Greece: Anubis Publishing, 2007), 9–10.

86. Harriet Beecher Stowe, *Uncle Tom's Cabin* (1851; repr., New York: Penguin Books, 1966), 85.

87. Ibid., 83.

88. Anne M. Wagner, "Warhol Paints History, or Race in America," in *Representations* 55 (Summer 1996): 104.

89. Ibid., 112.

90. Fredric Jameson, *Postmodernism or, The Cultural Logic of Late Capitalism* (New York: Verso, 1991).

91. Jean-Claude Baker, *Josephine: The Hungry Heart* (New York: Cooper Square Press, 2001), 118.

92. Weaver, "'Becoming in Kind,'" 694.

3. THE COMMENSAL DOG IN A CREOLE CONTEXT

1. *Animot* is a neologism used by Jacques Derrida in *The Animal That Therefore I Am* (New York: Fordham University Press, 2008). It is a combination of the French words *animal* and *mot* (word). By emphasizing the "animal word" (*animot*), Derrida presents the "animal" as a mere signifier created by human logos, rather than a set signified.

2. Abdelfattah Kilito, "Dog Words," in *Displacements: Cultural Identities in Question*, ed. Angelika Bammer (Bloomington: Indiana University Press, 1994), xxii.

3. Ibid., xxiii.

4. Ibid.

5. Ibid., xxvii.

6. Aimé Césaire, "Des Crocs," in *Ferrements* (Paris: Seuil, 1960).

7. The poem in the original French:

> Va-t-en chien des nuits va-t-en
> Inattendu et majeur à mes tempes
> Tu tiens entre tes crocs saignante
> Une chair qu'il m'est par trop facile de
> Reconnaître

> (AIMÉ CÉSAIRE, "VA-T-EN CHIEN DES NUITS," IN
> *FERREMENTS* [PARIS: SEUIL, 1960], 198)

8. Frantz Fanon, *Peau noire, masques blancs* (Paris: Éditions du Seuil, 1952), 91.

9. W. E. B. Du Bois, *The Souls of Black Folk* (Oxford: Oxford University Press, 2007), 8.

10. Patrick Chamoiseau, *L'esclave vieil homme et le molosse* (Paris: Gallimard, 1997), 94.

11. Gilles Deleuze and Félix Guattari, *A Thousand Plateaus: Capitalism and Schizophrenia*, trans. Brian Massumi (New York: Continuum, 1987), 273.

12. Ibid., 271, 273.

13. "Fugitive beings are pure relations of speeds and slownesses." Ibid., 271.

14. Ibid., 22.

15. Nomadism is an essential part of Deleuze and Guattari's theory in *A Thousand Plateaus*. See chapter 12, "1227: Treatise on Nomadology— The War Machine," 351–423.

16. See Edouard Glissant's *Poétique de la relation* (Paris: Gallimard, 1990) and *Introduction à une Poétique du Divers* (Paris: Gallimard, 1996)

17. See also Patrick Chamoiseau's *Solibo Magnifique* (Paris: Gallimard, 1988), a novel in which embedded narrative structure and diglossia reminiscent of William Faulker's *As I Lay Dying* (1930) takes on the mangrove metaphor.

18. Maryse Condé, *Traversée de la Mangrove* (Paris: Mercure de France, 1989).

19. "You can never get rid of ants because they form an animal rhizome whenever segmentary lines explode into a line of flight, but the line of flight is part of the rhizome." Deleuze and Guattari, *A Thousand Plateaus*, 9.

20. See also Bénédicte Boisseron, "A Creole Line of Escape: The Story of a Becoming-Dog," *Sites* 10, no. 2 (2006): 205–16.

21. Maryse Condé, in *La civilisation bossale: Réflexion sur la littérature orale de la Guadeloupe et de la Martinique* (Paris: L'Harmattan, 1978), gives a detailed description of the *bossale*.

22. "On ne sait pas, en effet, si l'indifférenciation issue de l'opposition entre les traits *humains* (Blancs) *vs non-humain* (animaux, végétaux) est dans un rapport d'antériorité, de simultanéité, ou de postériorité avec l'indifférenciation issue de l'opposition entre les traits *Blancs versus Noirs*." Jean Bernabé, "De la négritude à la créolité: Éléments pour une approche comparée," *Etudes Françaises* 28, no. 2/3 (Fall 1992–Winter 1993): 25.

23. See Gilles Deleuze and Félix Guattari, *Kafka: Pour une littérature mineure* (Paris: Les Éditions de Minuit, 1975).

24. "In any cases, if I am (following) *after* it, the animal therefore comes after me, earlier than me (*früher* is Kant's word regarding the animal, and Kant will be one of our witnesses to come). The animal is therefore before me, there next to me, there in front of me—I who am (following) after it. And also, therefore, since it is before me, it is behind me." Derrida, *Animal That Therefore I Am*, 10.

25. The equivalent of *va-t-en* (to address humans) in Creole is *foukan.* *Mach* is used to drive away dogs, while *chi* is to shoo chickens.

26. See the poem by Charles Baudelaire, "Le serpent qui danse," in *Les Fleurs du mal* (1857; repr., Paris: Poche, 1972).

27. "Haïti où la Négritude se mit debout pour la première fois et dit qu'elle croyait à son humanité." Aimé Césaire, *Cahier d'un retour au pays natal* (Paris: Présence Africaine, 2000), 65.

28. Jean-Paul Sartre, *Being and Nothingness* (New York: Washington Square Press, 1956).

29. On racial passing and Anatole Broyard, see the chapter entitled "Anatole Broyard: Racial Betrayal and the Art of Being Creole," in Bénédicte Boisseron's *Creole Renegades: Rhetoric of Betrayal and Guilt in the Caribbean Diaspora* (Gainesville: Florida University Press, 2014).

30. "When a person died, the spirit, stolen by the oungan, awakened from what had seemed sure death into a new existence in canine disguise." Colin Dayan, *The Law Is a White Dog: How Legal Rituals Make and Unmake Persons* (Princeton, N.J.: Princeton University Press, 2011), 209.

31. Sue Donaldson and Will Kymlicka, *Zoopolis: A Political Theory of Animal Rights* (Oxford: Oxford University Press, 2013), 212.

32. Colin Jerolmack, "How Pigeons Became Rats: The Cultural-Spatial Logic of Problem Animals," *Social Problems* 55, no. 1 (February 2008): 71–94.

33. Donna Haraway, *The Companion Species Manifesto: Dogs, People, and Significant Otherness* (Chicago: Prickly Paradigm Press, 2003), 38.

34. Jerolmack, "How Pigeons Became Rats," 8.

35. William Ian Miller, *Humiliation: And Other Essays on Honor, Social Discomfort, and Violence* (Ithaca, N.Y.: Cornell University Press, 1995), 21.

36. Eliza Ruiz-Izaguirre, "Village Dogs in Coastal Mexico: The Street as a Place to Belong," *Society and Animals* (forthcoming).

37. Truman Capote, "Music for Chameleons," *Music for Chameleons* (New York: Random House, 1980), 131.

38. Ibid., 126.

39. Ibid., 127.

40. Edouard Glissant, *Le discours antillais* (Paris: Éditions du Seuil, 1982), 40.

41. See, in particular, Patrick Chamoiseau's *Chronique des sept misères* (Paris: Gallimard, 1988) and Raphaël Confiant's *Le nègre et l'Amiral Robert* (Paris: Bernard Grasset, 1988).

42. Chamoiseau, *Chronique des sept misères*, 46.

43. See Raphaël Confiant's tribute to *jardins créoles* in his novel *La dissidence* (Paris: Éditions Écriture, 2002), which is the third installment of his trilogy about the production of sugar in the Caribbean.

44. Octave Mannoni, *Prospero and Caliban: The Psychology of Colonization* (Ann Arbor: University of Michigan Press, 1990), 106–7.

45. Ibid., 47.

46. Marcel Mauss, *The Gift: Forms and Functions of Exchange in Archaic Societies*, trans. Ian Cunnisoon (London: Cohen and West, 1966), 35.

47. Michel Serres, *The Parasite*, trans. Lawrence R. Schehr (Baltimore: Johns Hopkins University Press, 2007), 22.

48. Ibid.

49. Ibid.

50. Ibid., 22–23.

51. Cary Wolfe, *Animal Rites: American Culture, the Discourse of Species* (Chicago: University of Chicago Press, 2003), 8.

52. Serres, *The Parasite*, 24.

53. Ibid., 24.

54. Wolfe, *Animal Rites*, 7.

55. Serres, *The Parasite*, 169.

56. Raymond Coppinger and Lorna Coppinger, *What Is a Dog?* (Chicago: University of Chicago Press, 2016), 91.

57. *Encyclopaedia Britannica*, http://www.britannica.com/science/commensalism, last retrieved May 26, 2016.

58. Giorgio Agamben, *The Open: Man and Animal*, trans. Kevin Attel (Stanford, Calif.: Stanford University Press, 2004), 40.

59. Du Bois, *The Souls of Black Folk*, 8.

60. See Louis Althusser, "Ideology and Ideological State Apparatuses (Notes Towards an Investigation)," in *Lenin and Philosophy and Other Essays*, 127–86 (New York: Monthly Review Press, 1971).

61. Frans de Waal, *Are We Smart Enough to Know How Smart Animals Are?* (New York: Norton, 2016), quoted in Joshua Rothman, "The Metamorphosis: What Is It Like to Be an Animal?," *New Yorker*, May 30, 2016, 73.

62. Mannoni, *Prospero and Caliban*, 47.

63. Frantz Fanon, *The Wretched of the Earth*, trans. Richard Philcox (New York: Grove Press, 2004), 37.

64. See chapter 1 for more on this conundrum in Jean-François Lyotard's *The Differend: Phrases in Dispute* (Minneapolis: University of Minnesota Press, 2002).

65. Aimé Césaire, *A Tempest*, trans. Richard Miller (New York: Theater Communications Group, 1992).

66. Mannoni, *Prospero and Caliban*, 109.

67. Dominique Lestel, *Apologie du carnivore* (Paris: Fayard, 2011) has been translated by Gary Steiner as *Eat This Book: A Carnivore's Manifesto* (New York: Columbia University Press, 2016).

68. "Il importe donc de renverser l'exigence éthique végétarienne en montrant que c'est plutôt le fait de manger de la viande qui est un devoir éthique. Appelons cela *l'impératif carnivore*." Lestel, *Apologie du carnivore*, 15.

69. Serres, *The Parasite*, 82.

70. Patrick Chamoiseau, *L'empreinte à Crusoé* (Paris: Gallimard, 2012), 23.

71. "La vie d'un homme n'a de sens que s'il la vit sous l'exigence la plus élevée possible; n'être ni un animal, ni un de ces sauvages qui infestent le monde." Ibid., 22.

72. Ibid., 46.

73. "Mes imaginations autour des cannibales se faisaient bien plus abominables quand elles se déployaient sans la mesure d'un peu de conscience." Ibid.

74. "Je vivais en dehors—-et sans doute même: en dehors—, je mangeais dehors, œuvrais dehors, dormais dehors, rêvais dehors, pissais et déféquais dehors; je fuyais les retraites, demeurais exposé au plus vif." Ibid., 89.

75. See Jean Bernabé, Patrick Chamoiseau, and Raphaël Confiant, *Eloge de la Créolité* [In praise of Creoleness] (Paris: Gallimard, 1989).

76. "Les murs menacent tout le monde, de l'un et l'autre côté de leur obscurité. C'est la relation à l'Autre (à tout L'Autre, dans ses présences animales, végétales, environnementales, culturelles et humaines) qui nous indique la partie la plus haute, la plus honorable, la plus enrichissante de nous-mêmes." Edouard Glissant and Patrick Chamoiseau,

Quand les murs tombent: L'identité nationale hors-la-loi? (Paris: Galaade, 2007), 12.

77. Glissant, *Le discours antillais*, 187.

78. Haraway, *Companion Species Manifesto*, 23.

79. Ibid., 15.

80. Alan Graham, "Historical Phytogeography of the Greater Antilles," *Brittonia* 55, no. 4 (September–December 2003): 357–83.

81. Victor Segalen, *Essay on Exoticism: An Aesthetics of Diversity*, trans. Yaël Rachel Schlic (Durham, N.C.: Duke University Press, 2002).

82. "On m'eût fort étonné en disant qu'une espèce animale ou végétale pouvait avoir le même aspect des deux côtés du globe. Chaque animal, chaque arbre, chaque brin d'herbe, devait être radicalement différent, afficher au premier coup d'œil sa nature tropicale." Claude Lévi-Strauss, *Tristes tropiques* (Paris: Plon, 1955), 50.

83. Ibid., 44.

4. DOG OWNERSHIP IN THE DIASPORA

1. "Les animaux sont des êtres vivants doués de sensibilité. Sous réserve des lois qui les protègent, les animaux sont soumis au régime des biens." (Animals are living and sentient beings. Unless there are special laws protecting them, animals are submitted to the legal regime of property.) French Civil Code, Article 515–14 (2015), https://www.legifrance.gouv.fr/affichCode.do;jsessionid=8FDFA8AE567C57EBF5D80ECF462329BC.tpdila09v_1?idSectionTA=LEGISCTA000006090204&cidTexte=LEGITEXT000006070721&dateTexte=20161123, retrieved November 23, 2016.

2. "Sont meubles par leur nature, les corps qui peuvent se transporter d'un lieu à un autre." French Civil Code, Article 528 (1804), https://www.legifrance.gouv.fr/affichCode.do;jsessionid=3FDF632BF7E5DAF060961F9129127FB8.tplgfr32s_1?idSectionTA=LEGISCTA000006136242&cidTexte=LEGITEXT000006070721&dateTexte=18040204, retrieved February 5, 2018.

3. "Sont meubles par leur nature les animaux *et les corps* qui peuvent se transporter d'un lieu à un autre." French Civil Code, Article 528 (1999), https://www.legifrance.gouv.fr/affichCodeArticle.do?idArticle=LEGIARTI000006428711&cidTexte=LEGITEXT000006070721&dateTexte=20140424, retrieved February 5, 2018 (emphasis mine).

4. When presenting the message to the media, Hutin argued, one must resort to "une vulgarisation journalistique du message pour qu'il soit appréhendé par le plus grand nombre" (journalistic vulgarization of the message so that it is understood by most). Quoted in Thierry Auffret Der Kemp, Jean-Marc Neumann, and Jean-Claude Nouët, "Vérités sur le régime juridique de l'animal en France et les actions de la LFDA en faveur de son évolution," *Droit Animal, éthique, science, Revue trimestrielle de la Fondation LFDA* 80 (January 2014): 7.

5. Gregory R. Smulewicz-Zucker, "The Problem with Commodifying Animals," in *Strangers to Nature: Animal Lives and Human Ethics*, ed. Gregory R. Smulewicz-Zucker (Plymouth, Mass.: Lexington Books, 2012), 165.

6. See "Les animaux reconnus comme 'êtres sensibles,' un pas 'totalement symbolique,'" *Le Monde*, April 16, 2014.

7. "Tout animal étant un être sensible doit être placé par son propriétaire dans des conditions compatibles avec les impératifs biologiques de son espèce." Code Rural et de la pêche maritime, Article L214–1, https://www.legifrance.gouv.fr/affichCode.do;jsessionid=19752E8FEE683 A4C3880D07E58098AAD.tpdilao9v_1?idSectionTA=LEGISCTA 000022200247&cidTexte=LEGITEXT000006071367&date Texte=20161129, retrieved November 28, 2015 (emphasis mine).

8. Gary L. Francione and Anna Charlton, *Animal Rights: The Abolitionist Approach* (UK: Exempla Press, 2015).

9. "Le code civil considère encore les animaux comme des 'biens meubles,' au même titre qu'une *armoire* ou une *chaise* (LFDA's emphasis) . . . il est donc incompréhensible que le code civil continue de les considérer comme des 'choses.'" Der Kemp, Neumann, and Nouët, "Vérités sur le régime juridique de l'animal en France," 6.

10. The Code Noir also extended to French Guyana in 1704, Mascareignes in 1723, and Île de France (Maurice) and Bourbon (La Réunion) in 1724. The Louisiana Code Noir was a revised version of the original one.

11. *Le Code noir et autres textes de lois sur l'esclavage* (Saint-Maur-des-Fossés: Éditions Sépia, 2006). The 1724 version of the Code Noir, revised for Louisiana, also includes article 44.

12. "All Negroes and Indians,. . . mulattoes or mustizoes who now are, or shall hereafter be, in this Province, and all their issue and offspring,

born and to be born, shall be, and they are hereby declared to be, and remain forever hereafter, absolute slaves, and shall follow the condition of the mother, and shall be deemed, held, taken, reputed and adjudged in law, to be chattels personal, in the hands of their owners and possessors, and their executors, administrators, and assigns, to all intents, constructions and purposes whatsoever." Article 1, 1740 Slave Code of South Carolina, in *Duhaime's Law Dictionary*, http://www.duhaime.org/LawMuseum/LawArticle-1494/1740-Slave-Code-of-South-Carolina.aspx, retrieved December 1, 2016.

13. See *Duhaime's Law Dictionary* for the complete definition of "chattel": "Moveable items of property which are neither land nor permanently attached to land or a building, either directly or vicariously through attachment to real property." Ibid.

14. See Jean-François Niort, "Le problème de l'humanité de l'esclave dans le *Code Noir* de 1685 et la législation postérieure: pour un approche nouvelle," *Cahiers aixois d'histoire des droits de l'outre-mer français (PUAM)*, no. 4 (2008): 4n19.

15. See Taubira's speech, http://afrikhepri.org/discours-de-christiane-taubira-delannon/, retrieved November 15, 2016.

16. Gary L. Francione and Anna Charlton, "The Case Against Animals," *Aeon*, September 8, 2016, https://aeon.co/essays/why-keeping-a-pet-is-fundamentally-unethical.

17. Francione and Charlton, *Animal Rights*, 11 (emphasis in original).

18. Wesley J. Smith, "Animal Rights Means No Dogs and Cats," *National Review*, September 9, 2016, http://www.nationalreview.com/corner/439893/animal-rights-means-no-dogs-and-cats.

19. Ibid.

20. "Il serait en effet utopique qu'ils [animals] ne puissent pas continuer à pouvoir être appropriés." Van Der Kemp, Neumann, and Nouët, "Vérités sur le régime juridique de l'animal," 6.

21. Ibid.

22. The author says he discovered the Code Noir at a later stage in his philosophical initiation. He writes, "Enfin, je suis tombé sur le monstre" (And finally, I came across the monster). Louis Sala-Molins, *Le Code Noir ou le calvaire de Canaan* (Paris: Presses Universitaires de France, 1987), 74.

23. "Le fond le plus profound de l'horreur . . . , le pire raffinement dans la méchanceté, la plus glaciale technicité dans le commerce de la chair humaine et du génodice." Ibid., 76.

24. Ibid., 20.

25. "L'esclave n'est pas une personne, il n'est pas un animal, il est un bien meuble, une de ces choses stipulables et transmissibles, comme une somme d'argent ou comme toutes "autres choses mobiliaires." Ibid., 71.

26. See Sue Peabody, *"There Are No Slaves in France": The Political Culture of Race and Slavery in the Ancien Regime* (Oxford: Oxford University Press, 1996).

27. See also historian Marcel Dorigny's preface to Niort's *Le Code Noir*, which weighs in on the use of the word "monstrous" by Sala-Molins. Jean-François Niort, *Le Code Noir: Idées recues sur un texte symbolique* (Paris: Le Cavalier Bleu, 2015).

28. "Contradictoire et d'incohérent avec lui-même parce que reconnaissant simultanément l'humanité de l'esclave et sa 'chosification' ou ('réification') juridique." Niort, *Le Code Noir*, 39.

29. "Les hommes naissent et demeurent libres et égaux en droits," Déclaration des droits de l'homme et du citoyen de 1789, https://www.legifrance.gouv.fr/Droit-francais/Constitution/Declaration-des-Droits-de-l-Homme-et-du-Citoyen-de-1789, retrieved December 5, 2016.

30. See, for example, Guadeloupean journalist Jean-Pierre Anselme's blog, https://blogs.mediapart.fr/jean-pierre-anselme, and also Danik Zandronis, Guadeloupean blogger for Carib Creole News (CNN), who has launched what has been called a "Creole Fatwa" against Jean-François Niort: https://www.valeursactuelles.com/les-ayatollahs-de-lesclavagisme-53017.

31. Raymond Coppinger and Lorna Coppinger, *What Is a Dog?* (Chicago: University of Chicago Press, 2016), 42.

32. "Many who write about these categories assume that the family dog is at least a pet dog while the village/neighborhood dogs are strays, street dogs. . . . The experts assumed they had been pets but were now abandoned." Ibid., 144.

33. Teju Cole, *Open City* (New York: Random House, 2012).

34. Paul Gilroy, *The Black Atlantic* (Cambridge, Mass.: Harvard University Press, 1993).

35. Saidiya Hartman, *Lose Your Mother: A Journey Along the Atlantic Slave Route* (New York: Farrar, Straus and Giroux, 2007), 3.

36. Frank B. Wilderson, "The Prison Slave as Hegemony's (Silent) Scandal," *Social Justice* 30, no. 2 (2003): 25.

37. In the 1897 case *Sentell v. New Orleans and Carrollton Railroad Company*, Justice Henry Brown was assigned the task of determining whether Sentell, the owner of a valuable Newfoundland bitch, should be compensated for the accidental killing of his dog by the driver of an electric car. In the well-known 1896 *Plessy v. Ferguson* case, Justice Brown had to decide whether being prohibited from and arrested for sitting in a whites-only railroad car constituted an infringement of a black person's constitutional rights.

    See also chapter 2, "Afro-Dog: Blacks and Dogs in the Americas," for a discussion on these two legal cases as addressed in Colin Dayan's *The Law Is a White Dog: How Legal Rituals Make and Unmake Persons* (Princeton, N.J.: Princeton University Press, 2011).

38. *Sentell v. New Orleans & Carrollton R. Co. 166 U.S. 698* (1897), retrieved January 4, 2017, https://supreme.justia.com/cases/federal/us/166/698 /case.html.

39. "L'esclave noir existe juridiquement s'il désobéit, et le corps social veille à cruellement sanctionner cette existence-là. En revanche, il ne *mérite* pas juridiquement, s'il obéit au bon plaisir du maître ou du corps social en son entier." Sala-Molins, *Le Code Noir*, 66.

40. "C'est la marque d'une faute qui les désigne, un germe de méchanceté." Ibid., 30.

41. Francione and Charlton, *Animal Rights*, 24.

42. Gilles Deleuze and Félix Guattari, *A Thousand Plateaus: Capitalism and Schizophrenia*, trans. Brian Massumi (New York: Continuum, 1987), 233.

43. See Mark Binelli, "City of Strays: Detroit's Epidemic of 50,000 Abandoned Dogs," *Rolling Stone*, March 20, 2012; Chris Christoff, "Abandoned Dogs Roam Detroit in Packs as Humans Dwindle," *Bloomberg*, August 20, 2013.

44. Three thousand stray dogs is a rough estimate from the World Animal Awareness Society (http://michiganradio.org/post/msu-researchers

-want-figure-out-how-many-stray-dogs-are-really-roaming-detroit), but the organization, through the American Strays Project, is currently conducting research to identity an accurate number for the stray dog population in Detroit. See https://www.wa2s.org/american-strays .html.

45. Alessandra Stanley, "Killers Who Just Won't Lighten Up," *New York Times*, August 8, 2013.

46. James Baldwin, *The Fire Next Time* (New York: Dial Press, 1963), 9.

47. Ta-Nehisi Coates, *Between the World and Me* (New York: Spiegel and Grau, 2015), 9.

48. At twenty-five years old, Baldwin experienced the French prison system after being arrested for receiving stolen goods. Unbeknownst to him, Baldwin had been in possession of a stolen bed sheet from a French hotel.

49. James Baldwin, "Equal in Paris," in *Collected Essays* (New York: Library of America, 2001), 106.

50. Ibid., 25.

51. Ibid., 38.

52. Ta-Nehisi Coates, "I Might Be Charlie Hebdo," *Atlantic*, January 14, 2015.

53. Jennifer Schuessler, "Ta-Nehisi Coates Asks: Who's French? Who's American?," *New York Times*, October 17, 2016.

54. See the 1985 film *Le thé au harem d'Archimède* (Tea in the harem) by Mehdi Charef, based on Charef's 1983 book (*Le thé au harem d'Archi Ahmed*), for a depiction of the Maghrebians' condition of *zonard* in the French housing projects.

55. Azouz Begag, *Les chiens aussi* (Paris: Poche, 2004), 61.

56. Ibid., 89.

57. "Terminée l'obligation de porter des cartes de résidence sur nous, plus de contrôle d'identité, plus de laisse, de collier, de muselière." Ibid., 94.

58. Hartman, *Lose Your Mother*.

59. Baldwin, *Fire Next Time*, 73.

60. Charles Patterson's *Eternal Treblinka: Our Treatment of Animals and the Holocaust* (New York: Lantern Books, 2002) is similar to Marjorie Spiegel's *The Dreaded Comparison: Human and Animal Slavery* (1988; repr., New York: Mirror Books, 1996) in its way of comparing the

mistreatment of animals with that of not the black here but the Jew during the Holocaust.

61. Richard Wagner, *Heldentum und Christentum: Aus den Ausführungen zu Religion und Kunst* (Stuttgart: Verlag Urachhaus, 1937).

62. Wagner was himself influenced by Arthur de Gobineau's scientific theory of racial taxonomy in *Essai sur l'inégalité des races humaines* [Essay on the inequality of the human races] (Paris: Librairie de Firmin-Didot, 1884). In addition to preserving the purity of the Aryan race, Wagner advocated for a vegetarian diet to reverse the effect of interspecies blood contamination.

63. Boria Sax, *Animals in the Third Reich: Pets, Scapegoats, and the Holocaust* (New York: Continuum, 2002), 144.

64. Hans Fantel, "I Once Admired Hitler," *New York Times*, April 30, 1995.

65. The German Animal Protection Association (*Tierschutzverein*) was in charge of euthanizing dogs owned by Jewish Germans.

66. This interspecies common fate recalls a scene in Asher Kravitz's novel *The Jewish Dog*, in which the Jewish protagonist walks to his usual coffee shop with his dog and tells his dog, "I have wonderful news for you. No more waiting outside alone." The protagonist then proceeds to read to his dog the new sign posted on the coffee shop's entrance door: "'No entrance for dogs and Jews.'" Asher Kravitz, *The Jewish Dog*, trans. Michal Kessler (2007; repr., New York: Penlight Publications, 2015), 56.

67. Cixous's "Stigmates" is also mentioned in chapter 2, in the context of what I call counter-*Sprachlosigkeit*, "counter-speechlessness."

68. "Est-ce que je suis juif, pensait-il? Mais qu'est-ce que ça veut dire juif, souffrait-il de ne pas savoir." Hélène Cixous, "Stigmates," *Lectora* 7 (2001 [1995]): 199.

69. "Pour lui—c'était incontestable—nous fumes des hommes." Emmanuel Lévinas, "Nom d'un chien ou le droit naturel," in *Difficile liberté: Essais sur le Judaisme* (Paris: Biblio Essais, 1963), 216.

70. Kravitz, *Jewish Dog*, 16.

71. Ibid., 228.

72. "Blondi cannot climb ladders. And why should she? She's a German shepherd, not a circus clown. How times change; Hitler is no longer a simple soldier, but the Fürher. He needs a dog that represents something. A dog that proudly represents his race." Jonathan Crown,

Sirius: A Novel About a Little Dog Who Almost Changed History (New York: Scribner, 2016), 180.

73. John Campbell, "'My Constant Companion': Slaves and Their Dogs in the Antebellum South," in *Working Toward Freedom: Slave Society and Domestic Economy in the American South*, ed. Larry E. Hudson (Rochester, N.Y.: University of Rochester Press, 1994), 56.

74. Ibid.

75. "C'était incontestable—nous fumes des hommes." Lévinas, "Nom d'un chien ou le droit natural," 216.

76. Bronwen Dickey, *Pit Bull: The Battle over an American Icon* (New York: Borzoi Books, 2016), 218.

77. "In South Carolina, an anti-dog law passed in 1859. The litany of complaints and criticisms is so impressive as to suggest that, for slave-holders the slave/slave-dog combination was one of the most disruptive aspects of plantation life. No less an authority than James Henry Hammond, prominent slaveholder and U.S. senator, clearly believed as much, declaring in 1858 that "a man should not let his negroes have dogs [—] between [to] give him [*sic*] a gun or Sword." Campbell, "'My Constant Companion,'" 63.

78. Ibid., 67.

79. Keys, an animal trainer, tells the narrator what "white dog" means: "C'est un chien blanc. Il vient du Sud. On appelle là-bas 'chiens blancs' les toutous spécialement dressés pour aider la police contre les Noirs." ["It's a white dog. It comes from the South. Over there, we call 'white dogs' the doggies trained to help the police against Blacks."] Romain Gary, *Chien Blanc* (Paris: Gallimard, 1970), 25.

80. See Karen Delise, *The Pit Bull Placebo: The Media, Myths, and Politics of Canine Aggression* (Koropi, Greece: Anubis Publishing, 2007); Colin Dayan, "Dead Dogs: Breed Bans, Euthanasia, and Preemptive Justice," *Boston Review* 25, no. 2 (March/April 2010), http://bostonreview.net /dayan-dead-dogs; Claire Jean Kim, *Dangerous Crossings: Race, Species, and Nature in a Multicultural Age* (Cambridge: Cambridge University Press, 2015); Dickey, *Pit Bull*.

81. Erin C. Tarver, "The Dangerous Individual('s) Dog: Race, Criminal-ity and the 'Pit Bull,'" *Culture, Theory and Critique* (2014): 281.

82. "One study of every *New York Times* article published between 1987 and 2000 on pit bull owners, for example, found that they consistently

portrayed such individuals as thuggish and unsympathetic (Cohen and Richardson 2002)." Ibid., 282.

83. Claire Jean Kim, *Dangerous Crossings: Race, Species, and Nature in a Multicultural Age* (Cambridge: Cambridge University Press, 2015).

84. Michelle Alexander, *The New Jim Crow: Mass Incarceration in the Age of Colorblindness* (New York: New Press, 2010).

85. See Leon Gast's 1996 documentary about the Rumble in the Jungle, *When We Were Kings*.

86. Charles Ball, *Fifty Years in Chains, or, The Life of an American Slave* (New York: H. Dayton, 1859), in Documenting the American South, University Library, University of North Carolina at Chapel Hill, http://docsouth.unc.edu/fpn/ball/menu.html.

87. "When I approached him [his dog], he licked my hands, and then rising on his hind feet and placing his fore paws on my breast, he uttered a long howl, which thrilled through my heart, as if he had said, 'My master, do not leave me behind you.'" Ibid., 310.

88. "How Jack pitied her! . . . He resolved to do what he could to protect her from Mary and his mother. He bought her a dog, which became a great favorite with both." Harriet E. Wilson, *Our Nig* (New York: Vintage Books, 2011), 37.

89. John Berger, *About Looking* (1980; repr., New York: Vintage, 1991), 6.

5. THE NAKED TRUTH ABOUT CATS AND BLACKS

1. John Berger, *About Looking* (1980; repr., New York: Vintage, 1991), 6.

2. Jacques Derrida, "The Animal That Therefore I Am (More to Follow)," *Critical Inquiry* 28, no. 2 (Winter 2002): 369–418.

3. Martin Heidegger, *The Fundamental Concepts of Metaphysics: World, Finitude, Solitude* (Bloomington: Indiana University Press, 1995).

4. Berger, *About Looking*, 16.

5. Ibid., 6.

6. Vinciane Despret, *Que diraient les animaux si on leur posait les bonnes questions?* [What would animals say if we would ask them the right questions?] (Paris: La Découverte, 2012).

7. David M. Goldenberg, *Curse of Ham: Race and Slavery in Early Judaism, Christianity and Islam* (Princeton, N.J.: Princeton University Press, 2006), 142.

8. Olaudah Equiano, a former slave from Africa, published one of the first slave narratives, *The Interesting Narrative of the Life of Olaudah Equiano* (1789), available in *The Classic Slave Narratives*, ed. Henry Louis Gates Jr. (New York: Signet Classics, 2002). The autobiography exposes the untold horrors of slavery in America. Fredrick Douglass is the author of the now canonical autobiography *Narrative of the Life of Frederick Douglass, an American Slave* (1845; repr., Cambridge, Mass.: Belknap Press of Harvard University Press, 1960). He later published another autobiographical narrative, *My Bondage and My Freedom* (1855; repr., New York: Penguin Classics, 2003).

9. Robert Bernasconi and David Wood, eds., *Provocation of Levinas: Rethinking the Other* (London: Routledge, 1988), 170.

10. Ibid., 86.

11. Jacques Derrida, *The Animal That Therefore I Am* (New York: Fordham University Press, 2008).

12. Frantz Fanon, *Peau noire, masques blancs* (Paris: Éditions du Seuil, 1952).

13. Jean-Paul Sartre, *Being and Nothingness*, trans. Hazel E. Barnes (1943; repr., New York: Washington Square Press, 1956).

14. According to Jennifer Knust, many scholars see a sexual dimension in the curse of Ham because in Leviticus also "inappropriate sexual contact is repeatedly described as 'uncovering nakedness' (Lev. 18:6–18), and, in one passage, seeing nakedness is also linked to illicit, incestuous sex (Lev. 20:17)." Jennifer Knust, "Who's Afraid of Canaan's Curse? Genesis 9:18–29 and the Challenge of Reparative Reading," *Biblical Interpretation* 22 (2014): 21. Seeing Noah's nakedness would, in that context, be a euphemism for Ham's sexual deviance, potentially of an incestuous nature with his mother.

15. Knust writes that the mere act of seeing someone naked could have been enough for eternal damnation. "In an ancient Israelite context," Knust explains, "the very act of gazing on Noah's nakedness could have been bad enough to merit an eternally binding curse since, according to the logic of ancient shaming, gazing subverted Noah's patriarchal authority, violated his honor, and humiliated everyone involved." Knust, "Who's Afraid of Canaan's Curse?," 395.

16. Bernasconi and Wood, "Provocation of Levinas," 169.

17. Ibid., 170.

18. Berger, *About Looking*, 16.

19. Derrida, *Animal That Therefore I Am*, 4. David Wills, the translator, uses the expression "stark naked" to translate Derrida's use of *à poil*. In an endnote, Wills explains the meaning of *à poil* as follows: "a common expression for 'naked,' literally meaning 'down to one's (animal) hair.'" Ibid., 162n5.

20. "Maman, regarde le nègre, j'ai peur!" Fanon, *Peau noire, masques blancs*, 90.

21. "Je me découvrais objet au milieu d'autres objets." Ibid., 88.

22. Bernasconi and Wood, *Provocation of Levinas*, 170.

23. Dany Laferrière, *La chair du maître* (Paris: Lanctot, 1997).

24. Bernasconi and Wood, *Provocation of Levinas*, 169.

25. "Regarde, il est beau ce nègre." Fanon, *Peau noire, masques blancs*, 92.

26. "Le beau nègre vous emmerde, madame!" Ibid.

27. "La honte lui orna le visage." Ibid.

28. Charles Darwin, *The Expressions of the Emotions in Man and Animals*, ed. Francis Darwin (London: John Murray, Albemable Street, 1890), 328.

29. Ibid., 229.

30. Ibid., 334.

31. Ibid., 345.

32. Derrida, *Animal That Therefore I Am*, 11.

33. Ibid., 90.

34. Ibid., 132.

35. Ibid., 133.

36. Martin Heidegger, *The Fundamental Concepts of Metaphysics: World, Finitude, Solitude,* trans. William McNeill and Nicholas Walker (Bloomington: Indiana University Press, 1995).

37. Jean-Paul Sartre, *The Family Idiot: Gustave Faulbert 1821–1827*, vol. 1, trans. Carol Cosman (Chicago: University of Chicago Press, 1981), 137.

38. Florence Burgat, "Facing the Animal in Sartre and Levinas," in *"Animots*: Postanimality in French Thought," ed. Matthew Senior, David L. Clark, and Carla Freccero, *Yale French Studies*, no. 127 (2015): 177.

39. Heidegger, *Fundamental Concepts of Metaphysics*, 210.

40. Gayatri Chakravoty Spivak, "Can the Subaltern Speak?," *Marxism and the Interpretation of Culture*, ed. Cary Nelson and Lawrence Grossberg (London: Macmillan, 1988).

41. "Ils attendent le pire, ils n'attendent pas l'inconcevable." Charlotte
    Delbo, *Auschwitz et après: Aucun de nous ne reviendra* (Paris: Les Édi-
    tions de Minuit, 1970), 11.

42. Jean-François Lyotard, *The Differend: Phrases in Dispute*, trans. Georges
    Van Den Abbeele (Minneapolis: University of Minnesota Press, 2002).

43. Roland Barthes, "The Death of the Author," in *Image, Music, Text*,
    trans. Stephen Heath (New York: Hill and Wang, 1978), 142–48.

44. Equiano, *Life of Olaudah Equiano*, 66.

45. See the transcript of Henry Louis Gates Jr.'s appearance with Jamelle
    Bouie and Rebecca Onion, "Who Should Tell the Story of Slavery?,"
    Slate Academy: The History of American Slavery, July 24, 2015, http://
    www.slate.com/articles/life/the_history_of_american_slavery/2015
    /07/history_of_american_slavery_transcript_henry_louis_gates_on
    _slave_narratives.html.

46. James Albert Ukawsaw Gronniosaw, *A Narrative of the Most Remark-
    able Particulars in the Life of James Albert Ukawsaw Gronniosaw, an Afri-
    can Prince, as Related by Himself*, ed. Walter Shirley, 10, in Documenting
    the American South, University Library, University of North Carolina
    at Chapel Hill (2001), http://docsouth.unc.edu/neh/gronniosaw/gron
    nios.html.

47. Salman Rushdie, "The Empire Writes Back with a Vengeance," *Times*
    (London), July 3, 1982, 7–8.

48. John Jea, *The Life, History, and Unparalleled Sufferings of John Jea, the
    African Preacher. Compiled and Written by Himself*, 10, in Documenting
    the American South. University Library, University of North Caro-
    lina at Chapel Hill (2001), http://docsouth.unc.edu/neh/jeajohn/jea
    john.html.

49. Ibid., 33.

50. Ibid.

51. Octave Mannoni, *Clefs pour l'imaginaire* (Paris: Seuil, 1985).

52. Equiano, *Life of Olaudah Equiano*, 62.

53. Solomon Northup, *Twelve Years a Slave* (New York: Dover Thrift,
    1970), 109.

54. Patsey, a beautiful and proud female slave, a "splendid animal," as
    Northup describes her at the beginning, fell victim to a "licentious
    master and a jealous mistress" whose lust and hate ended up beating
    the spirit, pride, and beauty out of her. Ibid., 188, 189.

55. See Doris Garraway, *The Libertine Colony: Creolization in the Early French Caribbean* (Durham, N.C.: Duke University Press, 2005).

56. Ibid., 26.

57. Joan Dayan, *Haiti, History, and the Gods* (Berkeley: University of California Press, 1995).

58. Charles Ball, *Slavery in the United States: A Narrative of the Life and Adventures of Charles Ball* (New York: John S. Taylor, 1937).

59. As an example of that, *The Narrative of Lunsford Lane, Formerly of Raleigh, N.C.* (1842) contains the following lines in the preambulatory note entitled "To The Public":

> While in the South I succeeded by stealth in learning to read and write a little, and since I have been in the North I have learned more. But I need not say that I have been obliged to employ the services of a friend, in bringing this Narrative into shape for the public eye. And it should perhaps be said on the part of the writer, that it has been hastily compiled, with little regard to style, only to express the ideas accurately and in a manner to be understood.

> LUNSFORD LANE,
> Boston, July 4, 1842.

> (LUNSFORD LANE, *THE NARRATIVE OF LUNSFORD LANE, FORMERLY OF RALEIGH, N.C.* [BOSTON: J. G. TORREY, PRINTER, 1842], IV, IN DOCUMENTING THE AMERICAN SOUTH, UNIVERSITY LIBRARY, UNIVERSITY OF NORTH CAROLINA AT CHAPEL HILL, HTTP://DOCSOUTH.UNC.EDU /NEH/LANELUNSFORD/LANE.HTML.)

60. James Baldwin, *The Fire Next Time* (New York: Dial Press, 1963), 53–54.

61. J. L. Austin, *How to Do Things with Words* (Oxford: Oxford University Press, 1962), 12.

62. René Maran, *Batouala: Véritable roman nègre* (Paris: Albin Michel, 1921).

63. Briton Hammon, *A Narrative of the Uncommon Sufferings, and Surprising Deliverance of Briton Hammon, a Negro Man* (Boston: Green and Russel, 1760).

64. Aimé Césaire, *Cahier d'un retour au pays natal* (Paris: Présence Africaine, 2000); Léon-Gontran Damas, *Pigments* (Paris: Guy Lévis Mano, 1937); Léopold Sédar Senghor, *Anthologie de la nouvelle poésie nègre et malgache de langue française* (Paris: Presses Universitaires de France, 1948).

65. Jean-Paul Sartre, "Black Orpheus," trans. John MacCombie, *Massachusetts Review* 6, no. 1 (Autumn 1964–Winter 1965): 13.

66. "Européens, ouvrez ce livre, entrez-y. Après quelques pas dans la nuit vous verrez des étrangers réunis autour d'un feu, approchez, écoutez: ils discutent du sort qu'ils réservent à vos comptoirs, aux mercenaires qui les défendent. Ils vous verront peut-être, mais ils continueront de parler entre eux, sans même baisser la voix. Cette indifférence frappe au cœur." Jean-Paul Sartre, preface to *Les damnés de la terre*, by Frantz Fanon (Paris: Gallimard, 1961), 43.

67. Guenther defines this ontological self-encumbrance as the "irremissibility of having-to-be, and the impossibility of escaping to an 'otherwise than being.'" Lisa Guenther, "Shame and the Temporality of Social Life," *Continental Philosophy Review* 44, no. 1, (March 2011): 29.

68. Emmanuel Lévinas, *On Escape: De l'évasion*, trans. Bettina Bergo (Stanford, Calif.: Stanford University Press, 2003), 64.

69. Marc Blanchard, "Neither," *L'Esprit Créateur* 39, no. 4 (Winter 1999): 26.

70. François Mackandal was the Maroon leader of a slave revolt in Saint-Domingue in the 1800s. La Mulâtresse Solitude is a historical figure who joined a Maroon community in Guadeloupe and fought against the reinstatement of slavery by Napoléon Bonaparte in 1802.

71. Frederick Douglass, *My Bondage and My Freedom* (New York: Penguin Classics, 2003), 110.

72. Ibid.

73. G. W. F. Hegel, *The Phenomenology of Mind*, trans. J. B. Baillie (1807; repr., New York: Dover Publications, 2003), 110.

74. Susan Buck-Morss, "Hegel and Haiti," *Critical Inquiry* 26, no. 4 (Summer 2000): 821–65.

75. Nat Turner, *The Confessions of Nat Turner, the Leader of the Late Insurrection in Southampton, VA* (Baltimore: Lucas and Deaver, 1831), 12, in Documenting the American South, University Library, University of North Carolina at Chapel Hill (2001), http://docsouth.unc.edu/neh/turner/turner.html.

76. "Nous tremblons d'aller les uns chez les autres, et nous ne savons à qui nous fier, étant impossible de se passer du service de ces misérables." Berthony Dupont, *Jean-Jacques Dessalines: Itinéraire d'un révolutionnaire* (Paris: L'Harmattan, 2006), 48.

77. In Roland Barthes's *La chambre Claire (Camera Lucida)*, *punctum* denotes the defining detail of the picture, as opposed to *studium*, which refers to the cultural interpretation of the picture. Roland Barthes, *La chambre claire: Note sur la photographie* (Paris: Collection cahiers du cinéma/Gallimard, 1980).

78. David L. Clark, "What Remains to Be Seen: Animal, Atrocity, Witness," *Yale French Studies*, no. 127 (2015): 143–71.

79. Henry Louis Gates Jr., *The Trials of Phillis Wheatley: America's First Black Poet and Her Encounters with the Founding Fathers* (New York: Basic Civitas Books, 2010), 30.

80. Ibid., 82.

81. Homi Bhabha, *The Location of Culture* (London: Routledge Classics, 1994), 122.

82. "J'ai déjà remarqué que les nègres sont vains et glorieux; je dois ajouter qu'ils sont railleurs à l'excès, et que peu de gens s'appliquent avec plus de succès qu'eux à connaître les défauts des personnes, et surtout des blancs, pour s'en moquer entre eux et en faire des railleries continuelles. . . . J'ai souvent été surpris des défauts qu'ils avaient remarqués, et de la manière dont ils s'en moquaient, ce qui m'obligea à apprendre la langue des Aradas." Jean-Baptiste Labat, *Voyage aux îles: Chronique aventureuse des Caraïbes* (Paris: Phébus Libretto, 1993), 232–33.

83. Henry Louis Gates Jr., *The Signifying Monkey: A Theory of African-American Literary Criticism* (Oxford: Oxford University Press, 1988), 6.

84. Gates, *Trials of Phillis Wheatley*, 89.

85. Toni Morrison, *Playing in the Dark: Whiteness and the Literary Imagination* (Cambridge, Mass.: Harvard University Press, 1992), 5.

86. "Sacatra, Griffone créole, sans étampe, âgée d'environ 22 ans, ayant des marques blanches aux mains & sur le corps, est partie marone le 19 de ce mois: on présume qu'elle a été entraîné par un Blanc. Ceux qui la reconnaîtront, sont priés de la faire arrêter & d'en donner avis à M. Demontis, public prosecutor de l'habitation de Mde Pongaudin, aux Gonaïves. Il y aura récompense." *Affiches américaines*, August 13, 1783, issue no. 33, page 456, advertisement #1, in Marronnage in Saint-Domingue (Haïti), http://www.marronnage.info/en/lire.php?id=11358&type=annon, retrieved February 7, 2018.

87. "Pierre-Louis, Griff, étampé sur les seins DUFFEAU [renversé], âgé de 22 ans à 25 ans, taille de 5 pieds 2 pouces, bien fait, ayant la figure sournoise & marquée de petite-vérole; ledit Griff a enlevé un grand Cheval sous poil alezan, à grande crinière, étampé sur une cuisse en grosses lettres Nro 40. Les personnes qui en auront connaissance sont priés d'en donner avis à M. Boyer, Négociant à l'Archahaye, à qui ils appartiennent; il y aura bonne récompense." *Affiches américaines*, January 22, 1785, issue no. 4, page 37, advertisement #3.

88. The following advertisement, less succinct than the two others, provides information on the circumstance of the flight, as it indicates that the slave had been sent out on a mission and hence given the opportunity to escape:

> A Mulatto, named Pierre & François, using both names in his marooning, short and fair complexion, *perruquier* [hairdresser], having gone to France, & having sold merchandise in the Ances district, claiming to be free, left as a maroon last October 1, holding a letter that was not handed over to M. Durocher, residing in Fond. Those who will identify him are asked to inform Mrs. Lacroix, Formon (esperluette) Kacques, merchant in Cayes, or M. Sarrazin, merchant in Port-au-Prince.
>
> (*AFFICHES AMÉRICAINES*, JANUARY 1, 1785)

The advertisement also suggests a breach of trust, a trust that the slave had probably gained by keeping his feelings to himself. Pierre François was presumably all the more trustworthy given that he coiffed the whites, which gave him direct access to their intimate quarters inside the house, possibly even inside the bedroom or the boudoir. When the master learns that the trusted slave has fled, the master retrospectively sees, as with Derrida's cat, that the slave had been observing her, preying on her, potentially despising her *all along* in the boudoir. The advertisement also indicates that Pierre François abhorred his bondage to the extent that, as a mulatto house slave holding the somewhat privileged occupation of *perruquier*, he chose life on the run with the risk of bodily harm upon capture over bondage.

89. Julio Cortàzar, "Axolotl," in *Hopscotch: Blow-up and Other Stories* (New York: Random House, 1967), 580.

CODA

1. Jacques Derrida explains in an interview, "Eating is, after all, the great mystery of Christianity, the transubstantiation occurs in the act of incorporation itself: bread and wine become the flesh and blood of Christ. But it is not simply God's body that is incorporated via a mystical eating—it is also his words." Daniel Birnbaum and Anders Olsson, "An Interview with Jacques Derrida on the Limits of Digestion," *Journal #02* (January 2009), http://www.e-flux.com/journal/02/68495 /an-interview-with-jacques-derrida-on-the-limits-of-digestion/.

2. J. M. Coetzee, *Elizabeth Costello* (New York: Penguin Books, 2003), 80.

3. Franz Kafka, "A Report to an Academy," in *The Metamorphosis and Other Stories*, trans. Stanley Appelbaum (Mineola, N.Y.: Dover Thrift, 2008), 81–88.

4. Jacques Derrida, *The Animal That Therefore I Am* (New York: Fordham University Press, 2008), 103.

5. See Bénédicte Boisseron, "After Jacques Derrida (More to Follow): From a-Cat-emic to Caliban," *Yale French Studies*, no. 127 (2015): 95–109, for a more detailed study of the guest speaker's feeling of inadequacy in regard to the animal question.

6. Coetzee, *Elizabeth Costello*, 65.

7. Ibid., 95.

8. Marjorie Spiegel, *The Dreaded Comparison: Human and Animal Slavery* (1988; repr., New York: Mirror Books, 1996), 14.

9. See the Vegan Feminist Agitator blog, "On Alice Walker and History as Destiny," *The Vegan Street Blog*, March 19, 2014, http://veganfemi nistagitator.blogspot.com/2014/03/on-alice-walker-and-history-as -destiny.html, for criticism on Walker eating chicken.

10. Alice Walker, "Am I Blue?," *Crossroads: Creative Writing Exercises in Four Genres*, ed. Diane Thiel (Albuquerque, N.M.: Pearson Education Press, 1986), 141.

BIBLIOGRAPHY

Abu-Jamal, Mumia. *Live from Death Row*. New York: Avon Books, 1996.

Adams, Carol J. *Neither Man Nor Beast: Feminism and the Defense of Animals*. New York: Continuum, 1994.

——. *The Sexual Politics of Meat: A Feminist-Vegetarian Critical Theory*. New York: Continuum, 1990.

Adams, Carol J., and Lori Gruen, eds. *Ecofeminism: Feminist Intersections with Other Animals and the Earth*. New York: Bloomsbury Academic, 2014.

Agamben, Giorgio. *The Open: Man and Animal*. Translated by Kevin Attel. Stanford, Calif.: Stanford University Press, 2004.

Alexander, Michelle. *The New Jim Crow: Mass Incarceration in the Age of Colorblindness*. New York: New Press, 2010.

Althusser, Louis. "Ideology and Ideological State Apparatuses (Notes Towards an Investigation)." In *Lenin and Philosophy and Other Essays*, 127–86. New York: Monthly Review Press, 1971.

Armstrong, Philip. "The Postcolonial Animal." *Society and Animals* 10, no. 4 (2002): 413–19.

Ashcroft, Bill, Gareth Griffiths, and Helen Tiffin. *The Empire Writes Back: Theory and Practice in Post-Colonial Literatures*. 1989. Reprint, London: Routledge, 2002.

Austin, J. L. *How to Do Things with Words*. Oxford: Oxford University Press, 1962.

Baker, Jean-Claude. *Josephine: The Hungry Heart*. New York: Cooper Square Press, 2001.

Baldwin, James. "Equal in Paris." In *Collected Essays*, 101–16. New York: Library of America, 2001.

——. *The Fire Next Time*. New York: Dial Press, 1963.

——. "Going to Meet the Man." In *Going to Meet the Man: Stories*. New York: Vintage International, 1995.

Ball, Charles. *Fifty Years in Chains, or, The Life of an American Slave*. New York: H. Dayton, 1859. In Documenting the American South, University Library, University of North Carolina at Chapel Hill. http://doc south.unc.edu/fpn/ball/menu.html.

——. *Slavery in the United States: A Narrative of the Life and Adventures of Charles Ball*. New York: John S. Taylor, 1937. In Documenting the American South, University Library, University of North Carolina at Chapel Hill. http://docsouth.unc.edu/neh/ballslavery/menu.html.

Barthes, Roland. *La chambre claire: Note sur la photographie*. Paris: Collection cahiers du cinéma/Gallimard, 1980.

——. "The Death of the Author." In *Image, Music, Text*. Translated by Stephen Heath, 142–48. New York: Hill and Wang, 1978.

Baudelaire, Charles. *Les Fleurs du mal*. 1857. Reprint, Paris: Poche, 1972.

Bauer, Ralph, and José Antonio Mazzotti, eds. *Creole Subjects in the Colonial Americas: Empires, Texts, Identities*. Chapel Hill: University of North Carolina Press, 2009.

Beard, John Relly. *The Life of Toussaint L'Ouverture, The Negro Patriot of Hayti*. London: Ingram, Cooke, and Co., 1853. In Documenting the American South, University Library, University of North Carolina at Chapel Hill. http://docsouth.unc.edu/neh/beardj/menu.html.

Begag, Azouz. *Les chiens aussi*. Paris: Poche, 2004.

Bell, Madison Smart. *Toussaint Louverture: A Biography*. New York: Pantheon Books, 2007.

Bentham, Jeremy. *Introduction to the Principles of Morals and Legislation*. 1789. Reprint, Oxford: Clarendon Press, 1823.

Berger, John. *About Looking*. 1980. Reprint, New York: Vintage, 1991.

Bernabé, Jean. "De la négritude à la créolité: Éléments pour une approche comparée." *Etudes Françaises* 28, no. 2/3 (Fall 1992–Winter 1993): 23–38.

Bernabé, Jean, Patrick Chamoiseau, and Raphaël Confiant. *Eloge de la Créolité*. Paris: Gallimard, 1989.

Bernasconi, Robert, and David Wood, eds. *Provocation of Levinas: Rethinking the Other*. London: Routledge, 1988.

Bhabha, Homi. *The Location of Culture*. London: Routledge Classics, 1994.

Binelli, Mark. "City of Strays: Detroit's Epidemic of 50,000 Abandoned Dogs." *Rolling Stone*, March 20, 2012.

Birnbaum, Daniel, and Anders Olsson. "An Interview with Jacques Derrida on the Limits of Digestion." *Journal #02* (January 2009). http://www.e-flux.com/journal/02/68495/an-interview-with-jacques-derrida-on-the-limits-of-digestion/.

Blanchard, Marc. "Neither." *L'Esprit Créateur* 39, no. 4 (Winter 1999): 26–38.

Bobo, Lawrence D., and Michael C. Dawson. "Change Has Come: Race, Politics, and the Path to the Obama Presidency." *Du Bois Review: Social Science Research on Race* 6, no. 1 (2009): 1–14.

Boisseron, Bénédicte. "After Jacques Derrida (More to Follow): From A-cat-emic to Caliban." *Yale French Studies*, no. 127 (2015): 95–109.

——. "A Creole Line of Escape: The Story of a Becoming-Dog." *Sites* 10, no. 2 (2006): 205–16.

——. *Creole Renegades: Rhetoric of Betrayal and Guilt in the Caribbean Diaspora*. Gainesville: University Press of Florida, 2014.

Boulle, Pierre. *La planète des singes*. Paris: Julliard, 1963.

Brophy, Brigid. "Women: Invisible Cages." In *On The Contrary: Essays by Men and Women*, edited by Martha Rainbolt and Janet Fleetwood, 215–20. Albany: State University of New York Press, 1984.

Buck-Morss, Susan. "Hegel and Haiti." *Critical Inquiry* 26, no. 4 (Summer 2000): 821–65.

Burgat, Florence. "Facing the Animal in Sartre and Levinas." In *"Animots*: Postanimality in French Thought*," edited by Matthew Senior, David L. Clark, and Carla Freccero. *Yale French Studies*, no. 127 (2015): 172–89.

Campbell, John. "'My Constant Companion:' Slaves and Their Dogs in the Antebellum South." In *Working Toward Freedom: Slave Society and Domestic Economy in the American South*, edited by Larry E. Hudson, 53–76. Rochester, N.Y.: University of Rochester Press, 1994.

Capote, Truman. "Music for Chameleons." In *Music for Chameleons*. New York: Random House, 1980.

Caron, Aymeric. *Antispéciste*. Paris: Don Quichotte, 2016.

Césaire, Aimé. *Cahier d'un retour au pays natal*. Paris: Présence Africaine, 2000.

——. "Des crocs." In *Ferrements*. Paris: Seuil, 1960.

——. *A Tempest*. Translated by Richard Miller. New York: Theater Communications Group, 1992.

——. "Va-t-en chien des nuits." In *Ferrements*. Paris: Seuil, 1960.

Chamoiseau, Patrick. *Chronique des sept misères*. Paris: Gallimard, 1988.

——. *L'empreinte à Crusoé*. Paris: Gallimard, 2012.

——. *L'esclave vieil homme et le molosse*. Paris: Gallimard, 1997.

——. *Solibo Magnifique*. Paris: Gallimard, 1988.

Charef, Mehdi. *Le thé au harem d'Archi Ahmed*. Paris: Mercure de France, 1988.

Chaudhuri, Una, and Holly Hughes, eds. *Animal Acts: Performing Species Today*. Ann Arbor: University of Michigan Press, 2014.

Chen, Mel Y. *Animacies: Biopolitics, Racial Mattering, and Queer Affect*. Durham, N.C.: Duke University Press, 2012.

Christoff, Chris. "Abandoned Dogs Roam Detroit in Packs as Humans Dwindle." *Bloomberg*, August 20, 2013.

Cixous, Hélène. "Stigmates." *Lectora* 7 (2001): 195–202.

Clark, David L. "What Remains to Be Seen: Animal, Atrocity, Witness." *Yale French Studies*, no. 127 (2015): 143–71.

Coates, Ta-Nehisi. *Between the World and Me*. New York: Spiegel and Grau, 2015.

Coetzee, J. M. *Diary of a Bad Year*. New York: Penguin Books, 2008.

——. *Disgrace*. New York: Penguin Books, 1999.

——. *Elizabeth Costello*. New York: Penguin Books, 2003.

Cole, Teju. *Known and Strange Things: Essays*. New York: Random House, 2016.

——. *Open City*. New York: Random House, 2012.

Condé, Maryse. *La civilisation bossale: Réflexion sur la littérature orale de la Guadeloupe et de la Martinique*. Paris: L'Harmattan, 1978.

——. *Traversée de la Mangrove*. Paris: Mercure de France, 1989.

Confiant, Raphaël. *La dissidence*. Paris: Éditions Écriture, 2002.

——. *Le nègre et l'Amiral Robert*. Paris: Bernard Grasset, 1988.

Coppinger, Raymond, and Lorna Coppinger. *What Is a Dog?* Chicago: University of Chicago Press, 2016.

Cortàzar, Julio. "Axolotl." In *Hopscotch; Blow-up and Other Stories*. New York: Random House, 1967.

Crenshaw, Kimberlé. 1989. "Demarginalizing the Intersection of Race and Sex: A Black Feminist Critique of Antidiscrimination Doctrine, Feminist Theory and Antiracist Politics." *University of Chicago Legal Forum* 1, Art. 8: 139–67.

Crown, Jonathan. *Sirius: A Novel About a Little Dog Who Almost Changed History*. New York: Scribner, 2016.

Damas, Léon-Gontran. *Pigment*. Paris: Guy Lévis Mano, 1937.

Darwin, Charles. *The Expressions of the Emotions in Man and Animals*. Edited by Francis Darwin. London: John Murray, Albemarle Street, 1890.

Dayan, Colin. "Dead Dogs: Breed Bans, Euthanasia, and Preemptive Justice." *Boston Review* 25, no. 2 (March/April 2010), http://bostonreview .net/dayan-dead-dogs.

——. *The Law Is a White Dog: How Legal Rituals Make and Unmake Persons*. Princeton, N.J.: Princeton University Press, 2011.

——. *With Dogs at the Edge of Life*. New York: Columbia University Press, 2016.

Dayan, Joan. *Haiti, History, and the Gods*. Berkeley: University of California Press, 1995.

Deckha, Maneesha. "Disturbing Images: PETA and the Feminist Ethics of Animal Advocacy." *Ethics and the Environment* 3, no. 2 (Fall 2008): 35–76.

——. "Toward a Postcolonial, Posthumanist Feminist Theory: Centralizing Race and Culture in Feminist Work on Nonhuman Animals." *Hypatia* 27, no. 3 (Summer 2012): 527–45.

Delbo, Charlotte. *Auschwitz et après: Aucun de nous ne reviendra*. Paris: Les Éditions de Minuit, 1970.

Deleuze, Gilles, and Félix Guattari. *Kafka: Pour une littérature mineure*. Paris: Les Éditions de Minuit, 1975.

——. *A Thousand Plateaus: Capitalism and Schizophrenia*. Translated by Brian Massumi. New York: Continuum, 1987.

Delise, Karen. *The Pit Bull Placebo: The Media, Myths, and Politics of Canine Aggression*. Koropi, Greece: Anubis Publishing, 2007.

Der Kemp, Thierry Auffret, Jean-Marc Neumann, and Jean-Claude Nouët. "Vérités sur le régime juridique de l'animal en France et les actions de la LFDA en faveur de son évolution." *Droit Animal, éthique, science, Revue trimestrielle de la Fondation LFDA* 80 (January 2014): 4–8.

Derrida, Jacques. *The Animal That Therefore I Am*. New York: Fordham University Press, 2008.

——. "The Animal That Therefore I Am (More to Follow)." Translated by David Wills. *Critical Inquiry* 28, no. 2 (Winter 2002): 369–418.

——. "'Eating Well,' or the Calculation of the Subject: An Interview with Derrida." In *Who Comes After the Subject?* Edited by E. Cadava, O. Connor, and J. L. Nancy, 96–119. New York: Routledge, 1991.

Despret, Vinciane. *Que diraient les animaux si on leur posait les bonnes questions?* Paris: La Découverte, 2012.

Dickey, Bronwen. *Pit Bull: The Battle over an American Icon*. New York: Borzoi Books, 2016.

Donaldson, Sue, and Will Kymlicka. *Zoopolis: A Political Theory of Animal Rights*. Oxford: Oxford University Press, 2013.

Douglass, Frederick. *My Bondage and My Freedom*. 1855. Reprint, New York: Penguin Classics, 2003.

——. *Narrative of the Life of Frederick Douglass: An American Slave. Written by Himself.* Edited by Benjamin Quarles. 1845. Reprint, Cambridge, Mass.: Belknap Press of Harvard University Press, 1960.

Du Bois, W. E. B. *The Souls of Black Folk*. 1903. Reprint, Chapel Hill: University of North Carolina Press, 2013.

Dupont, Berthony. *Jean-Jacques Dessalines: Itinéraire d'un révolutionnaire*. Paris: L'Harmattan, 2006.

Equiano, Olaudah. *The Life of Olaudah Equiano*. In *The Classic Slave Narratives*, edited by Henry Louis Gates Jr. New York: Signet Classics, 2002.

Fanon, Frantz. *Les damnés de la terre*. Paris: Gallimard, 1961.

——. *Peau noire, masques blancs*. Paris: Éditions du Seuil, 1952.

——. *The Wretched of the Earth*. Translated by Richard Philcox. New York: Grove Press, 2004.

Fantel, Hans. "I Once Admired Hitler." *New York Times*, April 30, 1995.

Fartoukh, Jean-Claude. *Antispécisme ou opportunisme? Réponses au livre d'Aymeric Caron "Antispéciste."* Self-published, 2016. Kindle. www.les -ecrits.fr.

Felman, Shoshana. *The Scandal of the Speaking Body: Don Juan with J. L. Austin, or Seduction in Two Languages*. Stanford, Calif.: Stanford University Press, 1993.

Francione, Gary L. "We're All Michael Vick." August 22, 2007. http:// www.abolitionistapproach.com/media/links/p2026/michael-vick.pdf.

Francione, Gary L., and Anna Charlton. *Animal Rights: The Abolitionist Approach*. Newark, N.J.: Exempla Press, 2015.

——. "The Case Against Animals." *Aeon*, September 8, 2016. https://aeon.co/essays/why-keeping-a-pet-is-fundamentally-unethical.

Francione, Gary L., and Robert Garner. *The Animal Rights Debate: Abolition or Regulation?* New York: Columbia University Press, 2010.

Freccero, Carla. "Figural Historiography: Dogs, Humans, and Cynanthropic Becomings." In *Comparatively Queer*, edited by Jarrod Hayes, Margaret Higonnet, and William J. Spurlin, 45–67. New York: Palgrave, 2010.

Freud, Sigmund. *Totem and Taboo: Resemblances Between the Mental Lives of Savages and the Neurotics*. New York: Moffat, Yard and Company, 1918.

Gaard, Greta. "Toward a Queer Ecofeminism." *Hypatia* 12, no. 1 (Winter 1997): 114–37.

Garraway, Doris. *The Libertine Colony: Creolization in the Early French Caribbean*. Durham, N.C.: Duke University Press, 2005.

Gates, Henry Louis, Jr. *The Signifying Monkey: A Theory of African-American Literary Criticism*. Oxford: Oxford University Press, 1988.

——. *The Trials of Phillis Wheatley: America's First Black Poet and Her Encounters with the Founding Fathers*. New York: Basic Civitas Books, 2010.

Gary, Romain. *Chien Blanc*. Paris: Gallimard, 1972.

Gilroy, Paul. *The Black Atlantic*. Cambridge, Mass.: Harvard University Press, 1993.

Girard, Philippe R. "War Unleashed: The Use of War Dogs During the Haitian War for Independence." *Napoleonica: La Revue* 3, no. 15 (2012): 80–105.

Glissant, Edouard. *Le discours antillais*. Paris: Éditions du Seuil, 1982.

——. *Introduction à une Poétique du Divers*. Paris: Gallimard, 1996.

——. *Poétique de la relation*. Paris: Gallimard, 1990.

Glissant, Edouard, and Patrick Chamoiseau, *Quand les murs tombent: L'identité nationale hors-la-loi?* Paris: Galaade, 2007.

Gobineau, Arthur. *Essai sur l'inégalité des races humaines*. Paris: Librairie de Firmin-Didot, 1884.

Goldenberg, David M. *Curse of Ham: Race and Slavery in Early Judaism, Christianity and Islam*. Princeton, N.J.: Princeton University Press, 2006.

Gorant, Jim. *The Lost Dogs: Michael Vick's Dogs and Their Tale of Rescue and Redemption.* Los Angeles: Gotham, 2010.

Gordon, Teri J. "Synesthetic Rhythms: African American Music and Dance Through Parisian Eyes." *The Scholar and Feminist Online: Josephine Baker: A Century in the Spotlight,* Double Issue 6, nos. 1–2 (Fall 2007–Spring 2008). http://sfonline.barnard.edu/baker/print_gordon.htm.

Gossett, Che. "Blackness, Animality, and the Unsovereign." September 28, 2015. https://www.versobooks.com/blogs/2228-che-gossett-blackness-animality-and-the-unsovereign.

Graham, Alan. "Historical Phytogeography of the Greater Antilles." *Brittonia* 55, no. 4 (September–December 2003): 357–83.

Gronniosaw, James Albert Ukawsaw. *A Narrative of the Most Remarkable Particulars in the Life of James Albert Ukawsaw Gronniosaw, an African Prince, as Related by Himself.* Edited by Walter Shirley. 2001. In Documenting the American South, University Library, University of North Carolina at Chapel Hill. http://docsouth.unc.edu/neh/gronniosaw/gronnios.html.

Gruen, Lori. *Entangled Empathy: An Alternative Ethic for Our Relationships with Animals.* New York: Lantern Books, 2015.

——. "Samuel Dubose, Cecil the Lion, and the Ethics of Avowal." *Al Jazeera,* July 31, 2015. http://america.aljazeera.com/opinions/2015/7/samuel-dubose-cecil-the-lion-and-the-ethics-of-avowal.html.

Guenther, Lisa. "Shame and the Temporality of Social Life." *Continental Philosophy Review* 44, no. 1 (March 2011): 23–39.

Hall, Stuart. "The West and the Rest: Discourse and Power." In *The Formations of Modernity. Understanding Modern Society: An Introduction.* Book 1, edited by Stuart Hall and Bram Gieben, 185–225. Oxford and Cambridge: Polity Press in Association with the Open University, 1992.

Hammon, Briton. *A Narrative of the Uncommon Sufferings, and Surprising Deliverance of Briton Hammon, a Negro Man,* Boston: Green and Russel, 1760. In Documenting the American South, University Library, University of North Carolina at Chapel Hill. http://docsouth.unc.edu/neh/hammon/menu.html.

Haraway, Donna. *The Companion Species Manifesto: Dogs, People, and Significant Otherness.* Chicago: Prickly Paradigm Press, 2003.

Harper, A. Breeze. "Race as a 'Feeble Matter' in Veganism: Interrogating Whiteness, Geopolitical Privilege, and Consumption Philosophy of 'Cruelty-Free' Products." *Journal of Critical Animal Studies* 8, no. 3 (2010): 5–27.

———, ed. *Sistah Vegan: Black Female Vegans Speak on Food, Identity, Health and Society.* New York: Lantern Books, 2010.

Harris-Perry, Melissa. "Michael Vick, Racial History and Animal Rights." *The Nation*, December 30, 2010. https://www.thenation.com/article /michael-vick-racial-history-and-animal-rights/.

Hartman, Saidiya. *Lose Your Mother: A Journey Along the Atlantic Slave Route.* New York: Farrar, Straus and Giroux, 2007.

Hearne, Vicki. *Animal Happiness: A Moving Exploration of Animals and their Emotions.* New York: Skyhorse Publishing, 2007.

———. *Bandit: Dossier of a Dangerous Dog.* Pleasantville, N.Y.: Akadine Press, 1991.

Hegel, G. W. F. *The Phenomenology of Mind.* Translated by J. B. Baillie. 1807. Reprint, New York: Dover Publications, 2003.

Heidegger, Martin. *The Fundamental Concepts of Metaphysics: World, Finitude, Solitude.* Translated by William McNeill and Nicholas Walker. Bloomington: Indiana University Press, 1995.

Hell, Akasha (Gloria T.), Patricia Bell-Scott, and Barbara Smith, eds. *All the Women Are White, All the Blacks Are Men, But Some of Us Are Brave.* New York: Feminist Press, 1982.

Holmes, Anna. "America's 'Post-Racial' Fantasy." *New York Times*, June 30, 2015.

Hotaling, Ed. *Wink: The Incredible Life and Epic Journey of Jimmy Winkfield.* Columbus, Ohio: McGraw-Hill, 2005.

Hulme, Peter. "The Cannibal Scene." In *Cannibalism and the Colonial World.* Edited by Francis Barker, Peter Hulme, and Margaret Iversen, 1–38. Cambridge: Cambridge University Press, 1998.

Jameson, Fredric. *Postmodernism or, The Cultural Logic of Late Capitalism.* New York: Verso, 1991.

Jea, John. *The Life, History, and Unparalleled Sufferings of John Jea, the African Preacher. Compiled and Written by Himself.* 2001. In Documenting the American South, University Library, University of North Carolina at Chapel Hill. http://docsouth.unc.edu/neh/jeajohn/jeajohn.html.

Jerolmack, Colin. "How Pigeons Became Rats: The Cultural-Spatial Logic of Problem Animals." *Social Problems* 55, no. 1 (February 2008): 72–94.

Johnson, Sara E. "'You Should Give Them Blacks to Eat:' Waging Inter-American Wars of Torture and Terror." *American Quarterly* 61, no. 1 (March 2009): 65–92.

Jones, Pattrice. "Afterword: Liberation as Connection and the Decolonization of Desire." In *Sistah Vegan: Black Female Vegans Speak on Food, Identity, Health and Society*, edited by A. Breeze Harper, 187–201. New York: Lantern Books, 2010.

Kafka, Franz. "A Report to an Academy." In *The Metamorphosis and Other Stories*, translated by Stanley Appelbaum, 81–88. Mineola, N.Y.: Dover Thrift, 2008.

Kilito, Abdelfattah. "Dog Words." In *Displacements: Cultural Identities in Question*, edited by Angelika Bammer, xxi–xxxi. Bloomington: Indiana University Press, 1994.

Kim, Claire Jean. *Dangerous Crossings: Race, Species, and Nature in a Multicultural Age*. Cambridge: Cambridge University Press, 2015.

——. "Slaying the Beast: Reflections on Race, Culture, and Species." *Kalfou* (Spring 2010): 57–74.

——. "The Wonderful, Horrible Life of Michael Vick." In *Ecofeminism: Feminist Intersections with Other Animals and the Earth*, edited by Carol J. Adams and Lori Gruen, 175–90. New York: Bloomsbury Academic, 2014.

Knust, Jennifer. "Who's Afraid of Canaan's Curse? Genesis 9:18–29 and the Challenge of Reparative Reading." *Biblical Interpretation* 22 (2014): 388–413.

Kosofsky Sedgwick, Eve. "Paranoid Reading and Reparative Reading; or You're so Paranoid, You Probably Think This Introduction Is About You." In *Novel Gazing: Queer Readings in Fiction*, edited by Eve Kosofsky Sedgwick, 1–37. Durham, N.C.: Duke University Press, 1997.

Kravitz, Asher. *The Jewish Dog*. Translated by Michal Kessler. 2007. Reprint, New York: Penlight Publications, 2015.

Kristeva, Julia. *Powers of Horror*. New York: Columbia University Press, 1982.

Labat, Jean-Baptiste. *Voyage aux îles: Chronique aventureuse des Caraïbes.* Paris: Phébus Libretto, 1993.

Laferrière, Dany. *La chair du maître.* Paris: Lanctôt, 1997.

Lane, Lunsford. *The Narrative of Lunsford Lane, Formerly of Raleigh, N.C.* Boston: J. G. Torrey, 1842. In Documenting the American South, University Library, University of North Carolina at Chapel Hill. http://docsouth.unc.edu/neh/lanelunsford/lane.html.

Larsen, Nella. *Passing.* Oxford: Penguin Books, 1997.

Las Casas, Bartolomé de. *A Short Account of the Destruction of the Indies.* Translated by Nigel Griffin. London: Penguin Books, 1992.

Le Code noir et autres textes de lois sur l'esclavage. Saint-Maur-des-Fossés: Éditions Sépia, 2006.

Lestel, Dominique. *Apologie du carnivore.* Paris: Fayard, 2011.

Lévinas, Emmanuel. "Nom d'un chien ou le droit naturel." In *Difficile liberté: Essais sur le judaisme,* 213–16. Paris: Biblio Essais, 1963.

——. *On Escape: De l'évasion.* Translated by Bettina Bergo. Stanford, Calif.: Stanford University Press, 2003.

Lévi-Strauss, Claude. *Le totémisme aujourd'hui.* Paris: Presses Universitaires de France, 1962.

——. *Tristes tropiques.* Paris: Plon, 1955.

Lyotard, Jean-François. *The Differend: Phrases in Dispute.* Translated by Georges Van Den Abbeele. Minneapolis: University of Minnesota Press, 2002.

Madiou, Thomas. *Histoire d'Haiti.* Vol. 2, *1814–84.* Port-au-Prince, Haiti: Courtois, 1847.

Mannoni, Octave. *Clefs pour l'imaginaire.* Paris: Seuil, 1985.

——. *Prospero and Caliban: The Psychology of Colonization.* Ann Arbor: University of Michigan Press, 1990.

Maran, René. *Batouala: véritable roman nègre.* Paris: Albin Michel, 1921.

Marronnage in Saint-Domingue (Haïti). http://www.marronnage.info/en/lire.php?id=11358&type=annon.

Mauss, Marcel. *The Gift: Forms and Functions of Exchange in Archaic Societies.* Translated by Ian Cunnisoon. London: Cohen and West, 1966.

Maweja, Adama. "The Fulfilment of the Movement." In *Sistah Vegan: Black Female Vegans Speak on Food, Identity, Health and Society,* edited by A. Breeze Harper, 123–38. New York: Lantern Books, 2010.

Mbembé, Achille. *Critique de la raison nègre.* Paris: La Découverte, 2013.
——. "Necropolitics." *Public Culture* 15, no. 1 (Winter 2003): 11–40.
——. *On the Postcolony: Studies on the History of Society and Culture.* Berkeley: University of California Press, 2001.
——. "Provincializing France?" Translated by Janet Roitman. *Public Culture* 23, no. 1 (2011): 85–119.
McHugh, Susan. *Dog.* London: Reaktion Books, 2004.
Meadows, Tashee. "Because They Matter." In *Sistah Vegan: Black Female Vegans Speak on Food, Identity, Health and Society,* edited by A. Breeze Harper, 150–54. New York: Lantern Books, 2010.
Miller, William Ian. *Humiliation: And Other Essays on Honor, Social Discomfort, and Violence.* Ithaca, N.Y.: Cornell University Press, 1995.
Morrison, Toni. *Playing in the Dark: Whiteness and the Literary Imagination.* Cambridge, Mass.: Harvard University Press, 1992.
Mudimbe, V. Y. *The Idea of Africa.* Bloomington: Indiana University Press, 1994.
——. *The Invention of Africa: Gnosis, Philosophy, and the Order of Knowledge.* Bloomington: Indiana University Press, 1988.
Nair, Yasmin. "Racism and the American Pit Bull." *Current Affairs,* September 19, 2017. https://www.currentaffairs.org/2016/08/racism-and-the-american-pit-bull.
Nash, Jennifer C. "Re-Thinking Intersectionality." *Feminist Review* 89 (2008): 1–15.
Niort, Jean-François. *Le Code Noir: Idées reçues sur un texte symbolique.* Paris: Le Cavalier bleu, 2015.
——. "Le problème de l'humanité de l'esclave dans le *Code Noir* de 1685 et la législation postérieure: pour un approche nouvelle." *Cahiers aixois d'histoire des droits de l'outre-mer français (PUAM),* no. 4 (2008): 1–29.
Northup, Solomon. *Twelve Years a Slave.* New York: Dover Thrift, 1970.
Patterson, Charles. *Eternal Treblinka: Our Treatment of Animals and the Holocaust.* New York: Lantern Books, 2002.
Peabody, Sue. *"There Are No Slaves in France": The Political Culture of Race and Slavery in the Ancien Regime.* Oxford: Oxford University Press, 1996.
Rainsford, Marcus. *An Historical Account of the Black Empire of Hayti.* London: Albion Press, 1805.
Rankine, Claudia. *Citizen: An American Lyric.* Minneapolis: Graywolf Press, 2014.

Raynal, Abbe. *Philosophical and Political History of the Settlements and Trade of the Europeans in the East and West Indies.* Vol. 2. Edinburgh: Bell and Bradfute, 1804.

Regan, Tom. *The Case for Animal Rights.* Berkeley: University of California Press, 1983.Ricoeur, Paul. *Freud and Philosophy: An Essay on Interpretation.* New Haven: Yale University Press, 1970.

Rothman, Joshua. "The Metamorphosis: What Is It Like to Be an Animal?" *New Yorker,* May 30, 2016, 70–74.

Ruiz-Izaguirre, Eliza. "Village Dogs in Coastal Mexico: The Street As a Place to Belong." *Society and Animals* (forthcoming).

Rushdie, Salman. "The Empire Writes Back with a Vengeance." *Times* (London), July 3, 1982.

Ryder, Richard D. "Speciesism Again: The Original Leaflet." *Critical Society* 2 (Spring 2010): 1–2.

Said, Edward W. *Orientalism.* New York: Vintage Books, 1979.

Sala-Molins, Louis. *Le Code Noir ou le calvaire de Canaan.* Paris: Presses Universitaires de France, 1987.

Sartre, Jean-Paul. *Being and Nothingness.* Translated by Hazel E. Barnes. 1943. Reprint, New York: Washington Square Press, 1956.

——. "Black Orpheus." Translated by John MacCombie. *Massachusetts Review* 6, no. 1 (Autumn 1964–Winter 1965): 13–52.

——. *The Family Idiot: Gustave Faulbert.* Vol. 1, *1821–1827.* Translated by Carol Cosman. Chicago: University of Chicago Press, 1981.

Sax, Boria. *Animals in the Third Reich: Pets, Scapegoats, and the Holocaust.* New York: Continuum, 2002.

Schuessler, Jennifer. "Ta-Nehisi Coates Asks: Who's French? Who's American?" *New York Times,* October 17, 2016.

Schwartz, Marion. *A History of Dogs in the Early Americas.* New Haven: Yale University Press, 1997.

Segalen, Victor. *Essay on Exoticism: An Aesthetics of Diversity.* Translated by Yaël Rachel Schlic. Durham, N.C.: Duke University Press, 2002.

Senghor, Léopold Sédar. *Anthologie de la nouvelle poésie nègre et malgache de langue française.* Paris: Presses Universitaires de France, 1948.

Serres, Michel. *The Parasite.* Translated by Lawrence R. Schehr. 1980. Reprint, Minneapolis: University of Minnesota Press, 2007.

Sinclair, Upton. *The Jungle.* 1906. Reprint, Charleston, S.C.: Millennium, 2014.

Singer, Peter. *Animal Liberation: A New Ethics for Our Treatment of Animals.* 1975. Reprint, New York: Avon Books, 2001.

——. "To Defame Religion Is a Human Right." *Guardian*, April 15, 2009. http://www.theguardian.com/commentisfree/belief/2009/apr/15/reli gion-islam-atheism-defamation.

Smith, Wesley J. "Animal Rights Means No Dogs and Cats." *National Review*, September 9, 2016.

Smulewicz-Zucker, Gregory R. "The Problem with Commodifying Animals." In *Strangers to Nature: Animal Lives and Human Ethics*, edited by Gregory R. Smulewicz-Zucker, 157–74. Plymouth, Mass.: Lexington Books, 2012.

Spiegel, Marjorie. *The Dreaded Comparison: Human and Animal Slavery.* 1988. Reprint, New York: Mirror Books, 1996.

Spivak, Gayatri Chakravoty. "Can the Subaltern Speak?" In *Marxism and the Interpretation of Culture*, edited by Cary Nelson and Lawrence Grossberg, 271–313. London: Macmillan, 1988.

Stanley, Alessandra. "Killers Who Just Won't Lighten Up." *New York Times*, August 8, 2013.

Steiner, Gary. *Eat This Book: A Carnivore's Manifesto*. New York: Columbia University Press, 2016.

Stevenson, Bryan. *Just Mercy: A Story of Justice and Redemption*. New York: Spiegel and Grau, 2015.

Stowe, Harriet Beecher. *Uncle Tom's Cabin*. 1851. Reprint, New York: Penguin Books, 1966.

Tarver, Erin C. "The Dangerous Individual('s) Dog: Race, Criminality and the 'Pit Bull.'" *Culture, Theory and Critique* 55, no. 3 (2014): 273–85.

Tesler, Michael, and David O. Sears. *Obama's Race: The 2008 Election and the Dream of a Post-Racial America*. Chicago: University of Chicago Press, 2010.

Trouillot, Michel-Rolph. *Silencing the Past: Power and the Production of History*. Boston: Beacon Press, 1997.

Turner, Nat. *The Confessions of Nat Turner, the Leader of the Late Insurrection in Southampton, VA*. Baltimore: Lucas and Deaver, 1831. In Documenting the American South, University Library, University of North Carolina at Chapel Hill. http://docsouth.unc.edu/neh/turner/turner.html.

Uexküll, Jakob. "A Stroll Through the Worlds of Animals and Men: A Picture Book of Invisible Worlds." In *Instinctive Behavior: The Development of a Modern Concept*, translated and edited by Claire H. Schiller, 5–80. New York: International Universities Press, 1957.

Wagner, Anne M. "Warhol Paints History, or Race in America." *Representations* 55 (Summer 1996): 98–119.

Wagner, Richard. *Heldentum und Christentum: aus den Ausführungen zu Religion und Kunst*. 1881. Reprint, Stuttgart: Verlag Urachhaus, 1937.

Walker, Alice. "Am I Blue?" In *Crossroads: Creative Writing Exercises in Four Genres*, edited by Diane Thiel, 207–10. Albuquerque, N.M.: Pearson Education Press, 1986.

Wasik, Bill, and Monica Murphy. *Rabid: A Cultural History of the World's Most Diabolical Virus*. New York: Penguin Books, 2013.

Weaver, Harlan. "'Becoming in Kind:' Race, Class, Gender and Nation in Cultures of Dog Rescues and Dogfighting." *American Quarterly* 65, no. 2 (September 2013): 689–709.

Weil, Kari. *Thinking Animals: Why Animal Studies Now?* New York: Columbia University Press, 2012.

Wilderson, Frank B. "Gramsci's Black Marx: Wither the Slave in Civil Society?" *Social Identities* 9, no. 2 (2003): 225–40.

——. "The Prison Slave as Hegemony's (Silent) Scandal." *Social Justice* 30, no. 2 (2003): 18–27.

——. *Red, White & Black: Cinema and the Structure of U.S. Antagonisms*. Durham, N.C.: Duke University Press, 2010.

Wilson, Harriet E. *Our Nig*. New York: Vintage Books, 2011.

Wolfe, Cary. *Animal Rites: American Culture, the Discourse of Species*. Chicago: University of Chicago Press, 2003.

Youngquist, Paul. "The Cujo Effect." In *Gorgeous Beasts: Animal Bodies in Historical Perspective*, edited by Joan B. Landes, Paula Young Lee, and Paul Youngquist, 52–79. University Park: Penn State University Press, 2012.

INDEX

animal ownership (*cont.*)
  animals, in France, 121–25, 128,
  228nn1–3, 229n7; minorities'
  right to pet ownership, xxiv,
  145–50. *See also* animals; dogs
Animal Rights Debate, The
  (Francione), 16–18. *See also*
  Francione, Gary
animal rights discourse: abolitionist
  and civil rights movements
  invoked by, x–xi, xxi, 1–2, 3–4,
  13, 16–17, 19–20; abolitionist vs.
  welfarist position, 16–17; animal
  voices absent from, xiv, 4;
  Bentham and, 13–15, 16–17,
  210n49 (*see also* Bentham,
  Jeremy); Deckha on the
  connection between gender,
  race, and animality, 19, 211n60;
  emphasizing the real animal in,
  68–69; French debate over
  animal sentience and legal
  status, 121–25, 128, 145; Holocaust
  analogy, 198; liminal animals
  not discussed, 92–93; and the
  Michael Vick case, 17–18, 152–53;
  race-animal analogy used, x–xi,
  xv–xvi; slavery analogy used,
  x–xi, 1, 3–6, 19–21, 127, 211–12n65
  (*see also* slavery). *See also*
  abolitionist approach; animals;
  animal studies; speciesism
*Animal Rights: The Abolitionist
  Approach* (Francione and
  Charlton), 127–28, 136–37. *See
  also* Francione, Gary
Animal Rites (Wolfe), 103

animals: the animal question, in
  Coetzee's work, 195–98; the
  animal question, in philosophy,
  166–72, 197 (*see also* Derrida,
  Jacques); "becoming against,"
  48–49, 76; blushing not seen in,
  165; capacity for thought or
  "pretending pretense," 168–69,
  171; commensal animals, xxiii,
  92 (*see also* commensalism);
  commodification/reification of,
  2, 123; as companions, 154–55,
  157; creolization of, xxii (*see also*
  Creoleness: Creole dogs);
  Derrida on following after,
  88–89, 224n24; domestication
  of, 113, 136–37, 170–71;
  emphasizing the real animal in
  animal discourse, 68–69;
  essentialization of, 22;
  examining black and animal
  defiance, 36; exotic animals,
  34–35; focus on suffering of, 14,
  22; human-animal (species)
  fluidity, 91, 92; human-animal
  "becoming," 39–41, 84–86,
  217n11; human-animal divide,
  81–83, 89, 111, 167–68; humanity
  built/defined by, 66–67;
  interspecies performance
  (animal acts), 68, 221n75; killing
  for food, 210n49; La Fontaine's
  serpent fable, 100–104; language
  and animality, 82; legal status
  of, in France, 121–25, 128, 145,
  228nn1–3, 229n7; as lessees,
  100–104; Lévinas on the animal

face, 159–60, 161–62; liminal animals, xxiii, 93, 95–96, 105–6; multitudinous worlds of (*Umwelt* theory), 26–27, 107; "nonhuman" as term for, 108; as observers (animal gaze), 157–58, 162–63, 166–67, 170–72, 192–93 (*see also* Derrida, Jacques); and pertinence, 187–88; proliferation phobia, 137–38, 141, 142; sacrificial killing of, 59–60; sentience of, 38, 68, 70, 121–22, 123–24, 229n7; silence/ speechlessness of, xiv, 4, 157–58, 164, 168, 173, 187, 192–93 (see also *Sprachlosigeit*); slaughter of, 144–45; slavery analogy, x–xi, xiii, xv–xvi, xviii, xxi, 1, 3–6, 14–16, 31, 211–12n65; species fluidity, 111; value of black vs. animal lives, xiii–xv, xviii–xix, 31–32, 34, 204n19; Wilderson's cows analogy, xviii; women and, 8, 35; "zone of proximity," 85. *See also* animal ownership; animal rights discourse; animal studies; black-animal comparison; pets; speciesism; *and specific types of animal*
Animals in the Third Reich (Sax), 145
animal studies, x–xi, xii–xiii, xxi–xxii, xxv, 1–2, 23–25. *See also* animal rights discourse; intersectionality
Animal That Therefore I Am, The (Derrida). *See* Derrida, Jacques

animot (Derridean concept), xiv, 22, 26, 68, 81, 169, 204n17, 223n1. *See also* Derrida, Jacques
anthropocentrism, 103, 104
anticolonial gaze, 182–83
Antispéciste (*Antispeciesism*) (Caron), 2–6, 207nn6, 10
ants, 224n19
apes, 32–33, 82–83, 197. *See also* monkeys
à poil, as term, 160, 162, 238n19. *See also* nakedness
Armstrong, Philip, xi, 21
Atlanta serial murders, 65, 221n67
attack dogs. *See* dogs; pit bulls; police dogs
Auschwitz et après (*Auschwitz and After*) (Delbo), 173, 239n41
Austin, J. L., 28, 68, 181–82, 214n95
"Axolotl" (Cortázar), 193

Baartman, Saartjie, 35
Baker, Jean-Claude, 79, 80
Baker, Josephine, 35, 36, 79
Baldwin, James: on black and Jewish land ownership, 144, 148; dog owned, 79; *The Fire Next Time*, 139–40, 143, 144, 180, 181; "Going to Meet the Man," 72–73; imprisonment of, 180, 233n48; influence of, xvi; on institutionalized violence in France, 140–41
Ball, Charles, 154, 236n87
Baltimore riots (2015), 39. *See also* Black Lives Matter

Charlton, Anna, 127–28, 136–37.
See also Francione, Gary
chattel, as term, 49, 125, 230n13.
See also meuble; slavery
Chaudhuri, Una, 68, 69, 221n75
Chen, Mel Y., 28–29, 214n95
Chien Blanc (White Dog) (Gary),
63–65, 69, 148, 150, 235n79.
See also White Dog (1982 film)
Chirac, Jacques, 125–26
Cincinnati Zoo, 32–33
Citizen (Rankine), xix–xx
Civil Code (France), 121–24,
228nn1–3
civil rights movement, police dogs
and, xxii, xxv, 7–8, 51, 65; and
Baldwin's "Going to Meet the
Man," 72, 73; in Warhol's Race
Riot, 76–77, 78
Cixous, Hélène, 69–70, 146–47,
222n76, 234nn67–68
Clark, David L., 187–88
Clay, Thomas Savage, 149
Clinton, Bill, and the Clinton
administration, 10–11
Coates, Ta-Nehisi, xvi, 139–40,
141–42
Code Noir (French slave code,
1685): durability of legacy,
xvi–xvii; French colonies under,
15, 130, 229n10; in Louisiana,
125, 135–36, 229n10; Niort on,
xxiii–xxiv, 129–32, 231n28; not
applicable in France, 130;
Sala-Molins on, 129, 230n22,
231nn23, 25; slave as meuble

under, xvi, 49, 125–26, 128–29
(see also meuble). See also France
Le Code Noir (Niort), xxiv, 129–32,
231n28
Le Code Noir ou le calvaire de
Canaan (The Black Code or
Canaan's ordeal) (Sala-Molins),
129, 230n22, 231nn23, 25
Coetzee, J. M., 66–67, 71, 195–98
Cole, Teju, xvi, 133
colonialism and colonization:
Africa seen as epistemological
Other, 5; the black book in the
French colonial context, 181–83;
Caliban as metaphor for the
colonized, 98, 111, 112 (see also
Mannoni, Octave); cannibalism
and colonization, 60–61, 112;
colonial mimicry, 189–90,
242n82; colonial mistrust of the
Other, 112, 114; commensalism
as poetics of postcolonial
resistance, xxiii; dogs used
against indigenous peoples,
73–74; Fanon on violence and
decolonization, 104, 109; French
colonies, 90 (see also Algeria;
the Caribbean; and specific
colonies); human suffering
under, 21; and the intersection
of race and animality, 108; and
the killing of black men,
women, animals by white men,
32, 34; large, fierce dogs
imported, 48; Mannoni on the
relationship of colonizer and

colonialism and colonization (*cont.*)
colonized, 98–100; Mbembé on
the brutality of colonization, 7;
police dogs in colonial Africa,
154; post-colonial turn, in social
sciences and humanities, 1,
207nn1–2; and the racial denial
of personhood, 7; Serres on the
relationship of colonizer and
colonized, 100–104; subaltern
studies and colonial "us" vs.
"them" rhetoric, xii–xiii;
veganism as decolonization,
29–31. *See also* Native
Americans; slavery
"color blindness" and racial
consciousness, 11–13, 209n35
Columbus, Christopher, 48, 60, 112
commensalism: as antidote to
potlatch economy, 104;
commensal dogs, xxiii, 89, 92,
94–95, 105–6 (*see also* village
dogs); in Creole culture, 95–98,
106–7; defined and about, xxiii,
92–95, 106; Martinique's
relationship to France in terms
of, 107–10
Companion Species Manifesto, The
(Haraway), 39–40, 41–42, 93,
116. *See also* Haraway, Donna
Condé, Maryse, 87
Confessions of Nat Turner, The
(Turner), 186
Confiant, Raphaël, 97, 115
Connor, Bull, xxv, 72, 73, 78
contracts, 104. *See also* gift-giving

Coppinger, Raymond and Lorna,
105–6, 118, 132–33
Cortázar, Julio, 193
Crawford, John, 139
Crenshaw, Kimberlé, 23
Creoleness: animal consciousness
within Creole ideology, 115–16;
commensalism and Creole
culture, xxiii, 95–98, 106–7
(*see also* commensalism); "créole"
as term, 87–88; Creole dogs,
xxii–xxiii, 87, 94–95, 98, 106,
107; creolization of animals
generally, xxii; philosophy
developed by Martinican
writers, 115–16 (*see also specific
writers*); rhizome metaphor
for Creole culture, 86–87, 115.
See also the Caribbean; race:
race fluidity; *and specific islands*
creolization: Glissant's creolization
of the concept of chaos, 86–87;
white fear of, 59, 220n54
Critique de la raison nègre (*Critique
of Black Reason*) (Mbembé),
xvi–xvii. *See also* Mbembé,
Achille
Crown, Jonathan, 147–48, 234–35n72
Cudjoe (Jamaican rebel leader), 50
"Cudjoe Effect," 50–51, 80
Cugoano (author of a slave
narrative), 175
Cujo (1983 film), 50
Cujo Effect, The (Youngquist), 50.
See also Youngquist, Paul
Curious George, ix, 46, 203n2

Sentell v. New Orleans); as proxy for white fantasy of cannibalism, 56–60, 71–73; and rabies, 39–40, 42–43, 44; Sartre on, 169–70, 183; and slaves, 48–51, 62–63, 73, 74–76, 79, 83–84, 87–89, 148–50; stray dogs, 132–33, 137–39, 231n32, 232–33n44; vicious/ dangerous dogs, black men associated with, xxii, 42–47, 50, 151–52 (*see also* pit bulls); village dogs, 82, 85–86, 94–95, 105–6, 118, 132–33, 231n32 (*see also* dogs: commensal dogs); "white dogs," 63–65, 150–51, 235n79 [see also *Chien blanc* (Gary); *White Dog* (1982 film)]. *See also* pets; pit bulls; police dogs

"Dog Words" (Kilito), 82, 83, 85–86

domestication, of animals, 113, 136–37, 170–71. *See also* animals; dogs; pets

Donaldson, Sue, xxiii, 92–93, 105

Donovan, Josephine, 29

double-consciousness, Du Bois on, xxi, 38, 84, 107, 216–17n4

Douglass, Frederick: as author of slave narrative, 159, 174, 237n8; on being ranked with animals, 34, 36; on the difference between rural and urban slaves' life, 185; on horses being valued over slaves, 32, 52, 215n110; on the role of dogs on plantations, 73; white preface to *Narrative* of, 179

Drake, James, 78

Dreaded Comparison: Human and Animal Slavery, The (Spiegel), x, 1–2, 3–4, 19–20, 22, 31, 198, 199. *See also* Spiegel, Marjorie

Du Bois, W. E. B., xxi, 38, 84, 107, 216–17n4

DuBose, Samuel, 32, 34

Dupont, Berthony, 187, 242n76

Duval, Jeanne (Baudelaire's mistress), 89, 97

ecofeminism, 24, 29, 213n78. *See also* feminism

Ecofeminism (Adams and Gruen), 24

"edibility" of blacks, 53–54, 55–60, 71–72, 73

Elizabeth Costello (Coetzee), 195–98

L'empreinte à Crusoé (Crusoe's footprint) (Chamoiseau), 113–15, 118–19, 227nn71, 73–74

en dehors ("from the outside"), 114, 115–16, 118–19

Equiano, Olaudah, 60, 159, 174–75, 237n8

L'esclave vieil homme et le molosse (*The Old Slave Man and the Mastiff*) (Chamoiseau), 49, 84–86, 87, 115

Essay on Exoticism (Segalen), 117

Eternal Treblinka: Our Treatment of Animals and the Holocaust (Patterson), 20–21, 233–34n60

ethics of avowal, 34

Expressions of the Emotions in Man and Animals, The (Darwin), 165–66

domestication urged, 126–28, 136–37; blackness largely ignored in the argument of, 17–18; property status of animals contested, xi, 17, 124, 153. *See also* abolitionist approach; veganism

Freccero, Carla, 47–48

freedom: colonized peoples and, 97–99; as feral claim, 51

freedom of movement, 10, 51–53, 79–80, 134–36, 219n38

freeloading, 94

French Arabs, 140–43

French Guyana, 90, 126, 229n10. *See also* the Caribbean

French Universalism, 14–15

Freud, Sigmund, 59

Fuller, Sam, 65, 67, 150–51

Gaard, Greta, 213n78

Garner, Eric, 80, 139

Garraway, Doris, 178

Gary, Romain, 63–65, 69, 148, 150, 235n79. See also *White Dog* (1982 film)

Gates, Henry Louis, Jr., 175, 188–90

Germany. *See* Nazi Germany

Gift, The (Mauss), 100

gift-giving, 100–104

Gilroy, Paul, 133

Girard, Philippe R., xxvi, 57–58, 219n44

Glissant, Edouard, 86–87, 97, 115–16, 227n76

"Going to Meet the Man" (Baldwin), 72–73. *See also* Baldwin, James

Goldenberg, David M., 159

Goldsworthy, Andrew, 116

Gorant, Jim, 18, 46–47

Gordon, Terri J., 35

Gossett, Che, xxi, 13, 17, 18

Graham, Alan, 117

gratitude, ingratitude, and indebtedness, 99–104

Gray, Freddie, 39

Gronniosaw, James, 175, 176

Gruen, Lori, 24, 29, 31–32, 41

Guadeloupe, 83, 90, 92, 125, 182, 241n70. *See also* the Caribbean; Condé, Maryse; Niort, Jean-François; La Mulâtresse Solitude

Guattari, Félix: on animal proliferation, 137; on human-animal becoming, 40, 217n11; on the "line of escape," 88, 224n19; "rhizome" of, 86–87, 224n19; on the zone of proximity, 85

Guénif-Souilamas, Nacira, 141–42

Guenther, Lisa, 184, 241n67

Haiti: Césaire on, 90, 225n27; feral dogs in, 83; revolution and republic of, 110, 185–86 (*see also* Saint-Domingue); voodoo tradition of canine metamorphosis, 92

Hall, Stuart, xiii

Haller, Albrecht von, 44

Ham, curse of. *See* curse of Ham

Hammond, James Henry, 235n77

Harambe (gorilla), 32–33

on the teleological nature of abolition, 13; in Haraway's and Weaver' s works, 41–42; of Holocaust victims and animals, 20–21; and the human relation to nature, 102–4; importance of in any system of oppression, 1; Mrs. Williams and the police dog as parable of, 6–8; speciesism and, 24, 102–3; as theoretical tool, xxi–xxii, 25, 35–36; *Umwelt* theory and the intersectional approach, 25–29; Vick case and the intersectionality of race and animals in America, 45–46; women and animals seen as similarly positioned, 34–35

interspecies alliances, xx

interspecies performance, 68, 221n75

Introduction to the Principles of Morals and Legislation, An (Bentham), 4, 6, 13–15, 127

Invention of Africa, The (Mudimbe), 5. *See also* Mudimbe, V. Y.

Jacobs, Harriet, 175

Jamaica, 50

Jameson, Fredric, 78–79

Jea, John, 175–77

Jerolmack, Colin, 93–94

"Le jeu le plus dangereux" (Chamayou), 60

Jewish Dog, The (Kravitz), 147–48, 234n66

Jews: in Algeria, 69–70, 146–47; comparisons between African Americans and, 144, 233–34n60; and dog ownership, 145–48; Holocaust, xvii, 20–21, 146, 147, 173, 198; *kishta* (Hebrew-Yiddish word for "shoo"), 81; in the Third Reich, 144–48

Jim Crow, new, 9–12, 208n25. *See also* felony disenfranchisement; mass incarceration

Johnson, Sara E., 58

Jones, Pattrice, 29, 30

Jungle, The (Sinclair), xviii

justice system (U.S.): blacks restrained/killed by police power, 80, 136 (*see also* Brown, Michael; police dogs); Kim on race and, 45; mass incarceration and felony disenfranchisement, 9–11, 140, 208n25; police dogs in the courtroom, 6–8; tough-on-crime laws, 10–11, 152. *See also* civil rights riots and police dog attacks; Ferguson, Missouri; police power of the state; *and specific cases and individuals*

Just Mercy (Stevenson), 6–7. *See also* Stevenson, Bryan

Kafka, Franz, 197

Kheel, Marti, 29

Kilito, Abdelfattah, 82, 83, 85–86

Kim, Claire Jean: on the ethics of avowal, 34; on the Michael Vick case, 18, 45, 152; on the race-animal analogy, xi–xii, xiii, xiv, 16; on the racialization of pit bulls, 44

animal subjugation compared
to, x–xi, xiii, xv–xvi, xxi, 1, 3–6,
14–16, 19–21, 31, 127, 211–12n65;
Bentham's opposition to, 14, 17;
and blackness today, 132–34;
captured Africans and the
Middle Passage, 60, 133; in the
Caribbean vs. America, 182; in
Chamoiseau's *L'empreinte à
Crusoé*, 119; claiming/
challenging humanity, 90–91;
curse of Ham and, 136, 158–59,
160–61, 173, 176, 177 (*see also*
curse of Ham); dehumanization
vs. de-personhood, xxiv; dogs
and slaves, xxii, xxiv, 48–51,
62–63, 73, 74–76, 79, 83–84,
87–89, 148–50 (*see also* dogs);
durability of legacy, xvi–xvii, 10,
16, 210n47, 132–34; "edibility" of
slaves, 53–54 (*see also* "edibility");
English and American slave
laws, 125, 132, 229–30n12; and
escape, 184, 191–92, 243nn86–87,
243–44n88; France's abolition
of, 14–15; French slave code (*see*
Code Noir); fungibility of
slaves, xv, 129; Hegel's master-
slave dialectic, 185–86; horses
and slaves, 32, 52–53, 192,
215n110; mutilation of slaves,
53–54; rural vs. urban slave life,
185; Saint-Domingue slave
rebellion, xxvi, 3, 54–63, 83, 112,
219n44; silence and voice of
slaves, 173–82 (*see also* silence);

slave as *meuble* (moveable
property), xvi, 49, 125–26,
128–29, 136 (see also *meuble*);
value of black vs. animal lives,
32; vulnerability of the master,
184, 185–87, 243–44n88; whites
and the black/slave gaze, xxiv,
160–61, 162–63
*Slavery in the United States of the
Life and Adventures of Charles
Ball* (Ball), 179
Smith, Wesley J., 127–28
Smulewicz-Zucker, Gregory R., 123
Society for the Prevention of
Cruelty to Animals (SPCA), 4,
42–43
South Carolina, 125, 132, 229–30n12,
235n77
SPCA, 4, 42–43
species fluidity, 91, 92, 111. *See also*
Caliban
speciesism: Caron on, 2–6, 207n6;
connections between other
-isms and, 102–3; connections
between racism and, x–xii, xix;
Fartoukh's critique of Caron,
207n10; and intersectionality,
24, 102–3; popularization of
term/concept, 2–3, 15; Spiegel
on, 20; as term, x, xv–xvi, 2,
203n5. *See also* animals
Spiegel, Marjorie: dispute over
The Dreaded Comparison, x,
211–12n65; Harper's response to,
31; slavery analogy employed by,
1–2, 3–4, 19–20, 198; unique pain

Spiegel, Marjorie (*cont.*)
   of black experiences dismissed
   by, 22; Walker's preface to *The
   Dreaded Comparison*, 198, 199
Spivak, Gayatri Chakravorty, 172
Sprachlosigeit (silence/
   speechlessness), 157–58, 170–71,
   173, 187, 192–93. *See also* silence
Standing Rock protest, xxv, xxvi
Stevenson, Bryan, 6–7, 9, 16
"Stigmates" (Cixous), 69–70,
   146–47, 222n76, 234nn67–68
Stowe, Harriet Beecher, xxii, 75, 77
Strachan, Maxwell, 204n19
stray dogs, 132–33, 137–39, 231n32,
   232–33n44; Algerian immigrants
   as, 143; blacks as, 132–36
"Stroll Through the Worlds of
   Animals and Men, A" (Uexküll),
   26. *See also* Uexküll, Jakob von
suffering, Bentham's focus on, 14,
   22. *See also* Bentham, Jeremy
symbiotic relationships, 106.
   See also commensalism

Tainos, 48
Tarver, Erin C., 151–53, 235–36n82
Taubira, Christiane, ix, 126, 203n1
Tempest, A (Césaire), 110
Tempest, The (Shakespeare), 110.
   See also Caliban
"They Fight a Fire That Won't Go
   Out" (photo essay; Moore),
   76–77, 78
Thousand Plateaus, A (Deleuze and
   Guattari), 86–87, 137. *See also*
   Deleuze, Gilles; Guattari, Félix

Tierschutzgesetz (Third Reich animal
   welfare laws), 144–45, 234n65
Tortuga (Tortue Island), 57–58
Totem and Taboo (Freud), 59
transubstantiation, 196
Traversée de la mangrove (*Crossing
   the Mangrove*) (Condé), 87
Trials of Phillis Wheatley, The
   (Gates), 188–90
Tristes tropiques (Lévi-Strauss),
   117–18, 228n82
Trouillot, Michel-Rolph, 74, 86
Turner, Nat, 186
Twelve Years a Slave (Northup), 62,
   177–78, 239n54

Uexküll, Jakob von, 25–29
Umwelt theory, 25–29, 107
Uncle Tom's Cabin (Stowe), xxii, 75,
   77, 78
United States: "color blindness"
   and racial consciousness in,
   11–12; disposability of black lives
   in, xiii–xiv, xv, xvi, 16 (*see also*
   Black Lives Matter); durability
   of slavery's legacy in, xvi–xvii,
   10, 16, 210n47, 132–34 (*see also*
   slavery). *See also* justice system
   (U.S.); police dogs; *and specific
   states, cities, events, legal cases,
   and individuals*
United States v. The Amistad (1841),
   3–4, 5. See also *Amistad* case

"Va-t-en chien des nuits" (Go away,
   night dog) (Césaire), 83–84, 89,
   223n7

CPSIA information can be obtained
at www.ICGtesting.com
Printed in the USA
LVHW040148240719
624987LV00003B/4/P